What People Are Saying about *Do I Have to Give Up Me to Be Loved by God?* . . .

"*Do I Have to Give Up Me to Be Loved by God?* is a treasure chest full of gifts which provide the essential tools for achieving inner peace, joy and fulfillment. A glorious book!"

—**John Gray**
author, *Men Are from Mars, Women Are from Venus*

"Margaret Paul is an insightful and profound teacher. She skillfully helps us explore, heal and deepen our relationship with God."

—**Barbara De Angelis, Ph.D.**
author, *Secrets About Life Every Woman Should Know*

"Margaret Paul has written a powerful book that explores one of the most significant relationships of all—our relationship with God. She creatively teaches us the value of stepping into a new spiritual paradigm—into love and trust of self, others and God."

—**Jack Canfield**
motivational speaker, trainer
coauthor, *Chicken Soup for the Soul* series

"Margaret's latest book is a powerful, effective method for learning to love ourselves at the deepest spiritual level so that we can love others fully."

—**Gay Hendricks, Ph.D.**, and **Kathlyn Hendricks, Ph.D.**
authors, *Conscious Loving* and *The Conscious Heart*

Do I Have to Give Up Me to Be Loved by God?

Do I Have to Give Up Me to Be Loved by God?

MARGARET PAUL, PH.D.

Health Communications, Inc.
Deerfield Beach, Florida

www.bcibooks.com

Poem on page 334 reprinted by permission of Erika Chopich. ©1999 Erika Chopich.

Faith *reprinted by permission of Patrick Overton.* ©1999 Patrick Overton.

Library of Congress Cataloging-in-Publication Data

Paul, Margaret.
   Do I have to give up me to be loved by God? / Margaret Paul.
     p.   cm.
   Includes bibliographical references (p.   ).
   1. Spiritual life.   2. Self-realization—Religious aspects.   I. Title
BL624.P38 1999   99-43082
291.4'4—dc21   CIP

©1999 Margaret Paul

ISBN 1-55874-697-8

Publisher: Health Communications, Inc.
               3201 S.W. 15th Street
               Deerfield Beach, FL 33442-8190

Cover design by Andrea Perrine Brower
Inside book design by Lawna Patterson Oldfield

Dedicated

to

my Teachers in the spiritual realm who
love and guide me every moment;

to

Dr. Erika J. Chopich,
whose devotion to her spiritual path is truly
an inspiration to all the lives she touches.

Contents

Section III: Putting God into Action

Acknowledgments

Many years ago, when I was studying very hard to learn to be a good psychotherapist, I read two books that changed my life regarding my understanding of healing. The first one was *The Search for Authenticity* by Dr. James F. T. Bugental. In this book, Jim, whom I subsequently came to know, described two distinct paths in life: the Path of Dread and the Path of Courage. His paths are directly responsible for my work evolving into the Earthly Path of Fear and the Spiritual Path of Love and Courage. I am grateful to Jim for being one of my mentors.

The second book, equally life-changing, was *Affirmation and Reality* by Dr. William Ofman. After reading his book, I studied with Bill, avidly absorbing his unique humanistic-existential philosophy. I am very grateful to him for teaching me about our all having "good reasons" for our feelings and behavior, and for the difference he has made in my life.

The third and most profound mentor in my life has been my best friend, co-writer and co-creator of the Inner Bonding process, Dr. Erika J. Chopich. Erika's devotion to being a spiritually connected loving human being is a guiding light in my life. She has helped to birth all the work presented in this book. Erika, thank you for being you. You are a blessing to this planet.

I feel very blessed to have family who support and embrace my path. Thanks to Mom, Dad, Eric, Karol, Josh, Sheryl, Mikko and Bob. I love you all dearly. I am deeply grateful to Bob for meeting me all over the country to co-lead my Inner Bonding intensives, and for his help in evolving Inner Bonding.

Many thanks to my dear friends and certified Inner Bonding facilitators Nancy Weston and Sharon Pearson for their devotion to learning, healing, loving and caring. Their presence on the planet fills my heart with gratitude. And thanks to Charlie Bloom for being my friend and for joining us on this profound journey.

My appreciation also goes to Drs. David and Rebecca Grudermeyer for their wonderful work and their expansion on the concept of willingness. Their book, *Sensible Self-Help*, is a great contribution.

Many thanks to Maria Angel for the Inner Bonding logo, which depicts the adult linked to the child, surrounded by Spirit. It also uses an image of the globe to symbolize the message, "When you heal yourself, you heal the world," and wings to symbolize the message, "Inner Bonding gives you wings to fly." I am also grateful to Kristi Whitfield for the current form of the Life Paths chart in this book.

Thanks to Don Eaton, who, after reading *Do I Have to Give Up Me to Be Loved by You?* suggested the title of this book many years ago. Don is a nationally acclaimed singer-songwriter and an inspiring teacher. He is the founder of a wonderful nonprofit corporation, Small Change, devoted to feeding hungry bodies and souls. To contact Don for conferences, concerts, or to help Small Change, call 503-645-6418.

I am very grateful to certified Inner Bonding facilitator Jan Conley for her love, dedication and support in my office, as well as her devotion to Inner Bonding.

Many thanks to my agent, Jane Jordan Browne, for never losing faith in me and for finding the right publisher for this book. Thanks to my brilliant editor, Margot Silk Forrest. She is truly a pleasure to work with.

Finally, I am deeply grateful to everyone who has come to my Inner Bonding workshops and intensives, and all my clients who practice Inner Bonding. Thank you for your stories, the personal details of which I have changed for this book. You have brought me immeasurable joy through your devotion to your spiritual path.

Foreword

I think it's safe to say that each of us has at least one issue we are passionate about and struggle with, issues that rob us of our peace, our joy and our ability to experience love. With that in mind, would you think me crazy if I said there was a single process that could solve all the issues with which we as human beings struggle?

I have such a strong belief in human potential that for years I have been compelled to study and promote public education on issues such as holistic health (the interconnectedness of our body, mind and spirit), as well as many of the practices encompassed in our way of life. The same is true with alternative healing modalities, the difficulties our society has with racial and religious issues, domestic violence, child abuse and the abuse of our Mother Earth and the animal kingdom. I have spent a lot of time and energy exploring the heart-wrenching "whys" and the potential solutions. Through my films, public appearances and even a couple of books, I've had opportunities to share what I was learning along the way.

Over the years, I began noticing a common denominator in all these problems and came to the conclusion that there is only *one* issue: humankind's lack of experience in feeling our Divine self and our innate connection with the Divine. All other issues stem from this.

The farther I have gone on my personal journey, exploring my own prejudices, fears, sense of inadequacies, fears, unacknowledged griefs . . . oh, did I mention fears? . . . the more firmly I believe this to be so.

This *one* issue, then, begs the same exploration of the "whys" and potential solutions. Within the pages of this enlightened yet practical book, we are offered a lucid look at the "whys" and taught a most loving process as a potential solution.

This process will take you on a life-changing journey down a path full of awakenings, tears, compassion, reunion, joy and peace. This path, in reference to our divinity, is one seldom even thought about, much less explored.

I am eternally grateful to this five-foot-two, sparkly-eyed spiritual warrior some of us call the Samurai for all the courageous work she's done on herself and the exceptional gift she has to help others realize that peace, love and security are an inside job. In fact they are our sovereign rights.

Lindsay Wagner
actress, author, humanitarian

Introduction

Until very, very recently, the idea of having a direct, personal relationship with God, complete with *two-way communication*, was assumed to be fanciful at best—and blasphemous at worst. Now, we are discovering that it is possible not only to pray to God, but to *converse* with God; and not only to converse with God, but to have a *friendship* with God. This revelation carries implications as far-reaching as any discovery in the history of the human race—and much more than most.

Still, there are questions. Chief among them: Is it true? Does God so love us that the hand of true friendship is genuinely held out to us, and always has been? And, if such a friendship is really possible, if we really can receive this much love from God, what does it take to experience that? And, equally important, what does God want out of all of this? What does He expect of us? What does She demand?

Most of us have been raised to think that God's requirements in this regard are pretty stringent; that the bar is high. We have to behave in a certain way, we have to come to God in a certain way, and we have to believe in a certain way, in order for God to keep His greatest promise: the promise of His love. These awesome requirements, some have felt, may make it necessary for us to give up many of the good things in life, much of the joy of our experience, and, indeed, a great deal of who we really are, and how we define ourselves. Others say, no it is not like that. We have to give up nothing. God wants no more from us than we want and need and demand of someone whom we call friend. So, we are in a quandary. Who to believe? What to accept? How to know?

Now comes wonderful Margaret Paul, to look at these questions as we would look at them, and to give them answers that we can understand. *Do I have to give up me to be loved by God?* That is the key question, and I couldn't have put it more succinctly. Nor could I have answered it more profoundly than it has been answered between these covers.

In the *Conversations with God* trilogy, and its follow-up book, *Friendship with God*, we are told over and over again that the purpose of life is to recreate yourself anew in the next grandest version of the greatest vision ever you held about Who You Are. Here, in the treasure that you now hold in your hands, is a method for recreating yourself as a powerful, spiritually connected, loving adult self, capable of taking personal responsibility for your own feelings and behavior. This will feel imminently more possible when you realize that you can develop a deep connection with your own spiritual guidance; that God will assist you in healing the fears and false beliefs held within the wounded aspect of yourself, enabling you to remember and use your loving and creative essence. This book offers you a process through which you may do that. It also contains a powerful method for healing relationship and family conflict, as well as for healing self-destructive and addictive behavior.

I am very excited about this material. It takes the truths found in *Conversations with God* and others of the newest wisdom literature, and renders them functional in every day life. Anything that takes a huge wisdom and turns it into a practical tool is a treasure, indeed. It is one thing to behold the wisdom, and quite another to be able to use it. As Margaret, herself, puts it in this book, "I have . . . met people who have opened themselves to God with their whole hearts, but they still do not know how to personally experience God." This text shows you how. And that is a priceless gift.

Throughout most of my young life I felt unworthy. Unworthy to have the career I wanted, unworthy to have the romantic partners I desired, and certainly unworthy to have a friendship with God. It took me over half a century, and what I thought to be a major miracle, to turn that around. Now I find the major miracle—my conversation with God—was not major at all. It is being experienced by people—some consciously, and some unconsciously. God is talking with us all the time, and all we have to do is learn to listen, and then to work with what we hear in a life-changing way.

Margaret Paul has for over a dozen years been working with, and teaching to others, a process which allows people to do just that. She has been astonished at how rapidly that process creates deep and profound changes that allow people to behave more lovingly with themselves and others. Now, everything you could want to know about that process, and the eternal truths that underlie it, has been placed in a book. This book. This marvelous gift that has come to be placed before your eyes.

Make no mistake. It was not placed there by accident, by happenstance, or by coincidence. At some level you must have asked for some answers, some greater clarity, some additional guidance, some more assistance as you walk life's path. At some level, you must have drawn this material to you. I am glad that you did. It will lighten your heart, renew your mind, and rejuvenate your soul. It will, in short, be a book you will cherish forever.

Neale Donald Walsch

author, *Conversations with God* and *Friendship with God*

SECTION I

Living Without God

This section explores the fears we have about opening up to God and how we got these fears. We take a close look at our need for control over God and the Resistance Syndrome that blocks our direct experience of God.

The material in this section, as well as in the rest of the book, has come from my personal experience with God. It is *my* truth, not *the* truth. Whatever does not feel true to you, toss aside and, using the Six-Step Process you will learn in Section II, discover your own truth.

ONE

Crying Alone in the Night

Shelly is stuck in the downside of life. An attractive, slightly overweight first-time client, Shelly, forty-six, sits across from me clutching the arms of her chair. The anxiety quivering from her body seems to be more a reaction to her sad life than to my questions. Choking back tears, Shelly pours out her story, a story similar to those I hear every day. She tells me how alone she feels in her life. She tells me of her struggles with food, TV and shopping addictions. She says they are the only ways she knows to handle the unbearable feelings of loneliness and emptiness.

"My life is a mess. I'm on medication for depression, and it's helping a little but not enough. I've had years of therapy and recovery programs, but something is still wrong. I feel so alone!"

I pull my chair closer to her.

"Shelly, tell me about your spiritual beliefs and your relationship with God."*

For a moment the black weight of depression gives way to
surprise.

"God? I . . . I don't know. I can't say I really believe in God
or have a relationship with God. I guess I believe there is
something there . . . you know, a sort of Higher Power."

She takes a deep breath.

"God feels like just another hurt. Someone else who is supposed to care and doesn't. Like even to God I'm not special
enough to be cared about."

I hand Shelly a tissue and say, "That seems so sad. What
tells you that God doesn't love you?"

She carefully blots her running mascara. Then her face red-
dens and she bursts out, "Just look at my life! There's no love
or joy. I can't get off my medication, and I'm still depressed. I
hate my job, and I gained six pounds this month. I've tried
everything and nothing helps."

I feel the depth of her despair in every anguished word. "If
you knew and felt God's love for you, do you think your life
would be better?" I ask.

"I don't know. Maybe. But I just can't do the God thing. I
can't pray to a being that doesn't help and allows so much
pain in the world yet demands my loyalty and obedience. If I
had a relationship with God, I'd have to give up me and all
that I believe and all that I know."

---

*If you are uncomfortable with the word "God," please substitute whatever term you prefer,
such as Higher Power, the Divine, Higher Self, Spirit, Universal Intelligence, the All,
Goddess, Great Mystery, Divine Love and so on.

A long moment passes before Shelly goes on.

"Actually, I feel abandoned by God. I really think God doesn't like me."

Again the tears. And the anger.

"I have to be honest . . . I hate God! I really hate God! I don't want someone out there deciding things for me, telling me how I'm supposed to be and what I'm supposed to do. And I'm sure God doesn't like me the way I am, since he's never been here for me. Obviously, I'm just not good enough to be loved by God!"

✳ ✳ ✳ ✳

Andrew, well-educated, well-dressed, fifty-two, is telling me why he is seeking my help. Unlike Shelly, his life is very full and rewarding. "I have everything I ever thought would make me happy and secure. I am highly successful in work that I love. I have a wonderful wife and beautiful children. Yet I awake each morning with anxiety, and I often feel an emptiness inside. I just can't figure out what the problem is."

✳ ✳ ✳ ✳

Though the stories my clients tell me differ in their details, the suffering they feel is similar regardless of race, gender, age, religion or sexual orientation. Sometimes the person is married, sometimes he or she is single, widowed or divorced. Some are happily married while others are not. Some have children; others are childless. Some are wealthy; others are not. Some like their jobs, and some do not. As children, some felt loved by their parents; others felt smothered or abandoned. Some were beaten or sexually abused; others were not. Some are alcoholics or drug addicts; most are not. Some are in recovery; others are not. Some had a religious upbringing, while others came from atheist households.

Despite the diversity of their backgrounds and the differences in their present circumstances, most of the people I work with have five things in common:

1. They suffer from anxiety, depression, loneliness or emptiness.

2. They do not know how to love themselves or take personal responsibility for their own feelings and needs.

3. They do not know how to love and be loved by others without becoming needy, jealous, controlling, judgmental or submissive.

4. They have tried many avenues—from therapy to prayer, from medication to meditation—but nothing has brought them the inner peace and joy they seek. Their efforts give them temporary relief but no true healing.

5. They do not have a direct personal experience of and connection with a consistent, wise, powerful and loving God.

While their outer lives may seem to be working well, on the inner level these people are adrift. They have no tether to hang on to, no strong hand to hold to keep them from feeling overwhelmed by the challenges of life. They have no one to guide them, no one to trust. They feel anxious, lonely, hurt, empty, angry, powerless or insecure. They may be filled with guilt and shame. They often feel worthless, unlovable. They

are left crying alone in the night, like...
with no warm, loving source of power and wis...

Many of us have lost our way because we don't trus...
know how to connect with God. We don't trust that Go...
really loves us personally. We don't trust God to guide us
toward our highest good. And because we don't trust and connect with God, we don't trust and connect with ourselves, our
own inner wisdom, the part of us that is God. We don't know
that we are truly lovable. We don't know that God loves us
exactly as we are. We may think that God's love is conditional upon our being a certain "right" way, that we have to
give up ourselves to be loved by God.

When I ask my clients about God, I get a lot of different
answers. Many believe in God. Some do not. Of those who do
believe, some resist the idea of having any connection to God.
They have been taught—as I once was—that God is judgmental and controlling. They think that if they open themselves to
God, they will have to give up their freedom and autonomy,
hand over their decision-making power. The last thing they
want is some outside force telling them what to do and how to
be. The last thing they want is to feel like children again.

Others believe God exists but is not there for them personally. They think they are not lovable enough, or worthy
enough or important enough to be loved by God. They have
not opened themselves to God because they think God has
already seen their flaws and slammed the door shut on them.

They are mistaken. God shuts the door on *no one*. The
truth is, God's love is unconditional, constantly available and
directed personally at every single individual on earth. It is
there for you whether you believe in it or not, whether you

.ink you deserve it or not. It is as omnipresent as the air around you. But the people who come to me cannot accept this because they do not know how to have a firsthand experience of God that would convince them—once and for all—that God's love includes them.

I have also met people who have opened themselves to God with their whole hearts, but they still do not know how to personally experience God. Never having had such an experience, they cannot know their true worth or learn how to take loving action toward themselves. Many of them do not even know that they have the right to take loving care of themselves—they think their job is to take care of everyone else. They may be exhausted in trying so hard to be loving to others, wondering when it will be their turn to feel loved. Even those who are deeply religious and have a profound love of God do not necessarily feel loved by God.

And without this deep, daily personal connection and dialogue with God, they do not know how to utilize the love, wisdom and power of God to recognize their true worth, discover their gifts and passions, take loving care of themselves and share love with others. They do not know how to create ongoing loving relationships. They do not know how to discover what brings them deep, abiding joy, fulfillment and inner peace.

If you recognize yourself in this description, and if you desire to discover how to create and maintain a daily and personal connection with God, this book was written for you. Read on.

✳ ✳ ✳ ✳

Like so many others in our society, I reached adulthood with no sense of being loved by God. I was raised by atheist parents and an orthodox Jewish grandmother who believed in a controlling and judgmental God. I rejected both my grandmother's punishing God and my parents' denial of one, but I was left with only questions, a bottomless sense of aloneness and a thirst for understanding and healing. After twenty-five years of searching for answers to my questions and relief from my suffering, I was led to discover a transformational process for connecting with God in a deep, personal and profound way—a way that moved me and my clients out of feeling like victims of our pain and into personal empowerment. My purpose in writing this book is to show you how to use this simple and life-changing process yourself.

You *Never* Have to Give Up Your Self

Each day, as I live the practice presented in this book, I receive answers to the many questions I ask of God. As we go along, I will share with you the answers God has given me. So let's start with the question that so troubled Shelly: Do I have to give up me to be loved by God?

Many of us have been taught that God wants us to act a certain way and that God's love depends upon how we act. You may also have been told that you have to put aside what you want, give up your freedom of choice and allow God to choose for you.

I can tell you from my firsthand experience of God, that is not true.

These are false beliefs, sometimes perpetuated by parents or religions that want to control you. God does not want control over you, nor does God want you to be anything other than exactly who you are. However, there is a part—a false part of you, which was created by the false beliefs you were taught— that you will have to release in order to *experience* God.

We each have two "selves"—our true Self and our false self. Your true Self is your core, the part of you that is your innate way of being—your God-given gifts and talents, your particular form of intelligence, your ability to love, your playfulness, joy, passion, aliveness, curiosity, intuition and natural wisdom. It is your essence, the light within, the unwounded aspect of your soul. It is the part of you that is God—the divinity in you.

Your false self is the wounded part of you, the part that has experienced rejection, abandonment, emotional smothering, domination, neglect, shaming and perhaps even physical or sexual abuse. It is called "false" not because it is not real, but because it is not your true nature. Your false self is the façade you created to help you survive the lack of love you may have experienced when you were young. That façade hides a frightened Inner Child, a child who feels completely alone. Your false self is your ego, your inner critic, as well as your resistance, your compliance, your anger, your blame, your withdrawal.

Your false, wounded self is the part of you that needs to be in control in order to feel safe. If you did not get the unconditional love you needed as a child—when "love" came and went with your parents' moods, busyness, or the level of alcohol in their bloodstream—you did not feel safe. But safety is essential for survival, so you created one or more false, wounded selves to give you the control you needed: to get love, avoid pain and feel safe.

After a while, you may have completely lost touch with your true self and came to believe that your false, wounded self is who you really are. What was created as a stopgap measure to ensure safety in childhood may have taken over your entire identity.

Ironically, your false self is the part of you that you are most afraid of losing. This is because your inner logic says that if you lose your false self, you will lose control. And if you lose control, you will lose your safety and whatever love you have manipulated people into giving you. So hanging onto our false selves feels crucial. Given that fact, you may think that "surrendering" to God, releasing your individual will to a higher will, means giving up your (illusory but all-important) ability to control yourself and others.

Your false self not only fears losing control over others, but may also fear being controlled by others and by God. When, thanks to your false self, you do not trust that God is directing you toward your highest good, nor that God loves you and is here for you personally, the last thing you want to do is open up to God. To your false self, surrendering to God may mean giving up your autonomy and being controlled by an outside force. If your parents were controlling, it may feel like putting yourself back into that child position, being told what you "should" and "shouldn't" do, and being shamed when you do not live up to expectations. Naturally, your false self resists with all its might.

The irony is that when the false self "protects" you by not opening up to be guided by God, you feel even more pain. No

matter how hard the false self tries to get love, you remain
overwhelmingly lonely. On you alone falls the burden of taking care of things and keeping everything under control. You
are probably exhausted from working so hard. You even have
to do double duty: making sure everything works while making sure you do not get hurt in the process.

Once you start trying to control things, life feels *anything*
but free. Instead, it feels more like a burden than the sacred
privilege that it is.

The false self puts us in a terrible dilemma. If you do not
open up and invite God to guide you, you must live with
unbearable aloneness. But if you do open up to God, you risk
being controlled by an outside force. Or you risk discovering
that God is too busy for you, that you are not worthy of God's
love. Even worse, you risk discovering that there is *nothing
there*—there is no God, you really are alone in the universe.

Our childhood experiences may have led us to make a
number of erroneous conclusions about God that may make it
difficult for us to open to and trust God. These false beliefs
not only prevent our direct communion with God, they trigger many of the dysfunctional choices we make in our adult
lives. I have encountered eight major false beliefs about God,
some of which you may harbor within your wounded self. If
so, they may underlie your difficulty in having a direct and
consistent experience of God.

1. God doesn't exist.

2. God exists, but not for me.

3. God is a controlling, judgmental man whose love is
   conditional. In order to be loved by God, I have to

change who I am, give up my freedom and be who God wants me to be.

4. I won't ever be good enough to please God.

5. God uses me to help others, but does not come to me just for me.

6. God has favorite people and showers them with blessings.

7. God made me come here to this planet.

8. If I sacrifice myself for others, I don't have to take care of myself. God will do it for me. God owes me for all the good I do.

Sometimes people on a spiritual path try to open up to God, only to find their way blocked by fear and unconscious false beliefs. You may repeat over and over, "I let go and let God," "Thy will be done, through me," "Make me an instrument of thy peace." But in your heart you cannot let go of control. You cannot leap empty-handed into the beckoning void. It is too terrifying. It requires too much trust. Who will keep you from falling if you let go of your control and there is nothing there to guide you?

But what if you knew *for certain* that you would never have to give up any part of your true Self in order to open up to God? That all you would have to give up were the mistaken beliefs and controlling ways of your false, wounded self? What if you knew *for certain* that God exists, loves you unconditionally, is here for you personally and is directing you only toward the liberation of your true Self and your highest good?

It would be a huge relief. Yet the only way you can truly know this is to have a direct personal experience of God, firsthand contact with the immense force of love that cradles the universe. The good news is this experience is not difficult to have. I will show you how you can have that nurturing, loving and joyful experience every day of your life.

The Source of All Love and Truth

Let me clarify what I mean when I use the word "God." What is "God"?

Put simply, God is love[1], and all that love encompasses. God is the source of compassion and truth, peace and serenity, freedom and joy, creativity and beauty, healing and transformation. God is Spirit, consciousness, wisdom and power. God is the learning, evolving and loving force that creates and sustains all of life.

God is not "out there" somewhere. God is always right here, within you and around you, available to you the moment you open your heart and invite God in. When you open yourself to God, you *feel* within your own heart and body the Spirit of love, light, compassion, wisdom, peace and joy that is God. You *hear* and *see* the wisdom and truth of God through an open mind. Love and truth are gifts from God that you must open to and invite within; you cannot generate them on your own. You can know God only when you can experience God, and you experience God when you literally feel within your own physical being the beauty, love and truth that is God.

Love is an energy, the energy that is God; when your heart is open to love, you become filled with this energy and can share it with others. When parents bring the love that is God to their children, their children feel safe and lovable. They know they are not alone. They know they are loved by God because their parents are bringing Divine Love through to them. They know that love exists within them because they experience it. They know themselves to be a part of God, to have the spark of God within them.

If the love of God is available to each of us, why don't more of us experience it? Why are so many of us suffering but unable or unwilling to take the hand that reaches down to us? How did we lose our trust and faith in God? Why do we turn to food, sex, TV, overworking, drugs, alcohol—almost anything—rather than fill our emptiness with the love and grace of God?

The immense suffering most people feel today is the result of the many generations of spiritual abuse in our culture. Let me explain. *A direct, personal experience of God is our birthright.* Therefore, anything that disconnects you from experiencing the light of God, from knowing that you are a part of that light and have that light within you, can be termed spiritual abuse. You may think that "abuse" is a harsh word to use in this instance—especially in cases where the abuse is not intentional—but as we take a look at the effect spiritual abuse has on children, I think you will find the use of this term is warranted.

From birth, many of us are treated in ways that disconnect us from a direct experience of God. If you were taken away from your mother after you were born and put into a hospital nursery or left alone to cry, you likely became terrified. You were so little and helpless, unable to take care of any of your own needs. You instinctively knew that if someone did not come to take care of you, you would die. Children often unconsciously translate being left alone by their parents as being abandoned by God. While most parents dearly love their children and have no intention to abuse them in any way, they may not realize how frightening it is to babies to be left alone feeling so helpless. This is how spiritual abuse, however unintentional, may begin.

Other modern child-care practices continue it. I was raised in the days when parents were taught that babies should be allowed to cry. "It will spoil them if you pick them up," the experts said. "Besides, it's good for their lungs." So my mother, wanting to be a good mother, gritted her teeth and allowed me to cry, denying the instincts that told her to pick me up. Not trusting herself (because she had also suffered spiritual abuse), she trusted the so-called experts instead. The result was that I inherited a substantial legacy of spiritual abuse and have had to spend years—and a great deal of money—recovering from the fear, helplessness, abandonment and ensuing feelings of shame that I experienced at being left alone when I needed to be held or fed.

Many of us felt so abandoned in infancy and childhood that, later in life, even if we do believe in God, we don't believe that God will be there for *us*. That we have problems feeling God's love and acceptance and opening to spiritual guidance is no surprise. How can we rely on God to be there for us when we could not experience our parents being there in the way we needed? Even very loving, well-intentioned parents may not know how to be there for their children in the way their children need. We may have ended up feeling alone even while knowing that our parents dearly loved us. My clients often say to me, "I know my parents really loved me, but I did not feel loved. They just didn't see me or understand what I needed."

For many adults, being left alone is still terrifying; it may feel as if our very survival is at stake. The buried memory of our infant aloneness, when we would have died if someone did not come to care for us, is deeply etched into our psyches. My clients have described it as feeling like they are lost in outer space with the tether to their spaceship cut, consigned to drifting in the infinite blackness until death claims them.

The intensity of this feeling of aloneness can be so overwhelming, it often triggers a host of dysfunctional behaviors—drinking, drug use, compulsive eating, compulsive shopping, gambling—which we turn to in unconscious desperation to distract ourselves or ease the pain.

This does not imply that leaving a child alone for a few minutes or leaving a child to cry for a short period of time is abusive. Nor does it imply that children left in loving day care will suffer the effects of spiritual abuse. Not only does each child respond differently to being left alone, but the intention to be loving to a child goes a long way to soften the effects of less-than-perfect situations.

Having suffered from spiritual abuse does not mean that our parents were abusers. Spiritual abuse is more often the consequence of our society's child-rearing practices than of our parents' intended abusiveness. Thus many of us ended up suffering from unintentional spiritual abuse. It is important not to blame our parents for our difficulties in maintaining a spiritual connection. Most of our parents did the very best they could, as we do with our children. It is just important to understand how our false beliefs and resulting disconnection from God may have come about.

All Abuse Is Spiritual Abuse

Spiritual abuse is more than just not holding children when they need it. It is also holding or touching them with an intent other than to love them, such as:

- To get love *from* them
- To control them
- To physically abuse them
- To sexually abuse them

In fact, all abuse is ultimately spiritual abuse, because it undermines your sense of self and your relationship with God. Giving children anything other than love and compassion is spiritual abuse because all unloving behavior toward children creates an ongoing problem in their relationship with God. Any behavior that teaches children that they must be different (smarter, more polite, more obedient) in order to be loved by God—or by their parents—is spiritual abuse. Any behavior by an adult that disconnects a child from God within is spiritual abuse. And any behavior that undermines a child's belief in God as an infinite source of love, compassion and wisdom that is *always available* to that child is spiritual abuse.

Parents are supposed to be instruments of love, bringing the love that is God to their children. Unless you felt safe in the arms of your parents, you may not know that you can safely rest in God. Unless you felt unconditionally loved as a child, you may not be able to experience being unconditionally loved by God—at least, not until you heal from your spiritual abuse.

When parents are needy and use their children to get something from them—love, security, attention, energy, a sense of power over them—children learn that they are unworthy of receiving love, that they are just objects to be used by others. They may come to believe that their worth is either in giving to others and sacrificing themselves, or in accomplishing something. If the only time they receive attention or approval is when they are "good" or when they accomplish something, they come to believe their worth is in what they do rather than in who they are. And when they feel unworthy of receiving love for who they are from their parents—their personal demigods—they feel unworthy of receiving love from God.

Many of my clients have told me that they hated being held by their mother or father. It felt to them as if the very life was being sucked out of them. Many were shamed for crying when they didn't want to be held or touched, derided with words like, "What's the matter with you? You're such a cold person." Often they have carried the mistaken belief that something was wrong with them for not wanting to be held. As they heal, they are relieved to recognize that they had good reasons for detesting their mother's or father's touch. It was a touch that *took* love, not gave it.

Parents are supposed to make sure their children are safe and healthy by setting loving boundaries, such as preventing them from running into the street or burning a hand on a hot stove. Parents are also supposed to help their children learn to trust themselves. They do this by showing their own trust of their children's ability to know what they want and don't want, as well as what feels good and doesn't feel good (when safety and health are not at issue, of course).

When parents control their children through verbal abuse (shaming, judging, criticizing, discounting, threatening) or physical abuse (hitting, beating, any violence to the body) instead of setting loving boundaries and trusting the child, children learn to feel inadequate and to distrust themselves. *When children feel inadequate, they feel unworthy of God's love. When they learn to distrust themselves, they learn to distrust others and God.* Trying to control a child through verbal or physical abuse is spiritual abuse.

Sexual abuse is also spiritual abuse. When parents or other adults abuse children sexually, they teach children that they are objects to be used. Sexual abuse deeply violates not only the body but the soul, instilling shame, fear and powerlessness, and robbing children of any feeling that they are worthy of love. When adults, who are supposed to make sure children are safe, betray them by hurting and using them, children may decide that God either doesn't exist or has betrayed them.

I have heard about a few advanced souls who came into this life remembering that the spark of God exists within them, but the rest of us had no way of knowing we were worthy of being loved by God if our parents did not bring God's love through to us. If, as we grew up, we had been able to remember who we really are—that we each have the light of God within—we would not have traded our true Selves for the bulletproof vests and steel helmets of the false self.

But we were taught that the adults around us knew better than we did about who we are. We thought that if we were lovable and worthy, we would receive love from our caregivers. We believed that if we were good enough, they would not use us or shame us or leave us alone with the deadly lost-in-outer-space feeling. We had no way of knowing that our parents were also wounded, that they did not know how to love themselves any better than they knew how to love us.

As a result of our spiritual abuse, we are left without a direct experience of God, crying alone in the night.

Fortunately, there is a way to completely heal from whatever level of spiritual abuse we experienced. Below is a very brief summary of a six-step process called Inner Bonding. In Section II, Living with God, you will learn how to utilize these steps to heal from spiritual abuse and discover your peace, joy, fulfillment and personal connection with the unconditional love, truth, wisdom and power that is God.

Step One: Choose to be aware of your feelings and choose the willingness to feel your pain. Be willing to take responsibility for the ways in which you may be causing your own pain, and accept responsibility for creating your own peace and joy.

Step Two: Choose the intent to learn to love yourself and others. Making this choice opens your heart, allows Divine Love in and moves you into your loving adult Self.

Step Three: Choose to welcome, embrace and dialogue with your wounded self and your true, core Self, exploring your painful feelings, your fears, your false beliefs and the resulting behaviors that may be causing

Step Three *(continued)*	your pain. Also explore your gifts and what brings joy to your core Self.
Step Four:	Dialogue with your spiritual Guidance, discovering the truth and loving action toward your wounded self and your core Self.
Step Five:	Take the loving action learned in Step Four—put God into action.
Step Six:	Evaluate the effectiveness of your loving action.

These steps are actually a powerful road map toward healing the false beliefs that may be keeping you limited, and toward creating your ongoing connection with God. A belief in God, however, is not necessary for this process to work. I have successfully taught Inner Bonding to men and women who do not believe in God. Instead, they call on the highest part of themselves, called the Higher Self, for their spiritual Guidance.

As you move through Sections II and III of this book, these steps will become very clear and usable to you. They will lead you into manifesting your dreams.

TWO

Life Without God

Spiritual abuse wreaks havoc within each of us and within our society as a whole. Being disconnected from God leads us to operate from an earthly perspective rather than a spiritual perspective. This causes untold individual and planetary pain. We are operating from an earthly perspective when control over the outcome of events, power over others and greed are our primary motivating factors. We operate from an earthly perspective when protecting ourselves against that which we fear—aloneness, loneliness, helplessness, rejection, being controlled by others—is more important than learning and loving. On the earthly level, our highest priorities are to get love, feel safe and avoid pain, rather than to give love to ourselves and others. Whenever you operate from your false, wounded self, you operate from an earthly perspective.

Most of our major institutions—government, business, education, some religious organizations, many families—operate primarily on the earthly level. As you can see by reading the headlines any day of the week, greed and the desire to gain power and avoid pain drive much of what happens in our society. Social problems like crime, violence, racism, substance abuse, child and spousal abuse are all motivated by the desire to avoid the pain of aloneness, loneliness and powerlessness. People achieve this end—or so they think—by attaining wealth and power over others (via crime, racism, physical abuse) or by blocking out the pain (via substance abuse). At the root of all these actions is fear. In fact, fear is both the primary cause *and* consequence of spiritual abuse.

The earthly level is the material level, the level of the day-to-day struggle for safety and survival. But external safety is an illusion. We can never be totally safe on the earthly level because our bodies can be harmed or killed through disease or injury or accident, and we can never know for sure when this will happen. Our souls, however, are eternal. While they can be wounded, they can never die and are therefore safe from permanent harm. The spiritual level is about creating *internal* peace and safety through loving, evolving and expressing the soul.

The earthly perspective views situations and events within the context of this lifetime only, while the spiritual perspective views everything on an infinite continuum of eternal consciousness. We all have many challenges on the earthly level, but if we see adversity only on this level, then we can never experience it as an opportunity and a privilege—in fact, a sacred privilege. Difficult events in our lives are here to challenge us to evolve our souls, to become more loving and compassionate to ourselves and others.

We are always being guided toward our highest good in the face of these challenges. If you see painful events such as failures, illness, loss of loved ones or loss of money purely on the earthly level, then you will see life as suffering, a burden to be endured or perhaps ended in a lonely, painful death or suicide. But when you see these extremely difficult experiences as lessons in love and compassion toward yourself and others, you will do what you came here to do—learn to love, express and evolve your soul toward oneness with the love that is God.

You operate from a spiritual perspective when evolving and loving are your primary motivating factors, your highest priorities. When you make the spiritual far more important than the earthly, you experience life on this planet as a sacred privilege.

Love, Power and Religion:
Earthly Versus Spiritual

What we call "love" on the earthly level is not love at all. "Love" on the earthly level is about *getting* something for ourselves—approval, security, attention, understanding, sex, affection. Love on the spiritual level is about giving something to ourselves and others—caring, compassion, understanding, attention, affection. Love on the earthly level is about getting our emptiness filled by things, activities, substances and people. Love on the spiritual level is about learning to fill ourselves internally through connecting with our own essence and with God, receiving the energy of love and compassion from God and sharing it with others.

Power on the earthly level is about controlling events and people; power on the spiritual level is about personal empowerment—power within. It includes the power to receive love and wisdom from Spirit, realize our creative potential and manifest our dreams. Spiritual power is the power to remain loving and compassionate *in the face of fear*.

Religion, too, can operate from an earthly perspective or a spiritual perspective.

Many people confuse religion and spirituality. A religion is a particular set of beliefs involved with a group experience, while spirituality is an individual, personal experience of God. Unfortunately, not all churches and temples operate from what I call the spiritual perspective, and much of organized religion has nothing to do with love.

Whether or not your own religious practice operates from an earthly or spiritual perspective depends upon whether you are operating, in any given moment, from your false, wounded self or your true Self. Since your wounded self is driven by fear and the need to control, when it is in charge, religion becomes just another way for you to control things. It is only when the true Self is present that religion and spirituality come together. Then religious groups can truly be instruments of God's love and compassion.

Exploring Our False Beliefs About God

Spiritual abuse, which disconnects us from God and causes us to live from an earthly perspective, leads us to the false beliefs about God listed in chapter 1.

Let's explore each of these beliefs further, except for the last false belief about controlling God, which we'll focus on in the next chapter.

1. God Doesn't Exist

When parents (or other caregivers) do not consistently bring God's love through to children because they give children disapproval or conditional approval instead and call it love, children may conclude that God doesn't exist. Few children have an inherently strong and unshakable spiritual connection as Anna did in one of my favorite books, *Mister God, This Is Anna.*[1] In this true story, Anna runs away from her abusive home at the age of four and finds a loving family to take care of her. She knows that her parents abused her not because she was bad or unlovable, but because they were wounded and unable to love. God, she knew, was "in my middle." Anna was a rare, evolved child. Nothing could sway her from her connection with God. But most children are not able to do what Anna did. In the face of spiritual abuse, they may have no reason to believe that God exists. This is especially true in homes where there is no religious or spiritual training.

Even if children are taught about God, they are often told that God is all-powerful. "But if God is all-powerful, why does God let bad things happen to me?" an abused child may ask. Even adults may ask, "Why does God allow all the bad things on the planet—the Holocaust, starvation, AIDS?"

The concept of an all-powerful God can be misleading. It is essential to understand that the Creator gave all souls free will. This means that you get to decide your own purpose in life, your deepest desires, your way of being. You decide whether you are going to be loving or unloving, responsible for your own feelings and behavior or putting the blame on others. You decide if you are going to be open to learning about your pain or avoid it with your various anesthetics—your addictions. You decide if your deepest motivation is to love yourself and others or to maintain "safety" by protecting yourself against loneliness, rejection and failure.

When your deepest desire is to be safe rather than loving, you close your heart to avoid feeling your pain. When you close your heart, you cannot feel God—God can only enter through an open heart. Free will means that God has chosen to relinquish power over your will. *Even God cannot control your intent—that is, your deepest desire in any given moment—because God has given us all free will.*

When parents protect against feeling their pain and take their woundedness out on their children, there is no doorway through which God can enter the parents' hearts. *God is an all-powerful energy that you can open to and invite into your heart, but God cannot enter your heart unbidden.* Once you shift your intent and ask God to help heal your wounds and teach you to be loving to yourself and others, then the Spirit of love, compassion and wisdom that is God will always be there for you. But it is you who must decide to open or close your heart.

When our hearts are closed to ourselves, we are also closed to the suffering of others and can cause them untold pain. Because we each have free will, God cannot force an abusive parent or a Hitler to open his or her heart. No force outside of yourself, not even an all-powerful force, can open your heart to God.

2. God Exists, but Not for Me

When parents consistently bring through Divine Love to their children, the children learn that God is there for them. When parents and other adults are trustworthy—as opposed to abandoning, smothering or controlling—then children experience God as trustworthy. But when children are taught in church or temple that God exists, yet they have no experience (through their parents or other caregivers) of God being there for them, they may come to believe that God exists but not for them. This is not unusual. Children are likely to believe that if they are not good enough to be loved by their parents or other adults around them, they are not good enough to be loved by God. *Most children project their parents' or other caregivers' feelings and behavior onto God.*

Most abused children pray to God to stop their parents from abusing them. They are too little to understand that people have free will. They do not understand that God sustains them during the abuse, but that God cannot make their abusers loving instead of unloving. They may conclude that they have been abandoned by God.

I often see adults finally face their core belief that God has abandoned them, as Shelly did. "I hate God!" they shout. "God doesn't love me! God doesn't know I exist! God doesn't help me. God doesn't hear or answer my prayers. I've prayed and prayed, but God is deaf to me. God loves everyone else but not me!" Often in facing this belief they can come to terms with a truth they have not wanted to face: God hasn't abandoned them. It is they who have abandoned God by closing their hearts to avoid feeling their pain.

3. God Is a Controlling, Judgmental Man Whose Love Is Conditional. In Order to Be Loved by God, I Have to Change Who I Am, Give Up My Freedom and Be Who God Wants Me to Be.

When our parents' approval and attention was conditional upon our acting the "right" way, we had to give ourselves up to be "loved" by them. Thus we learned to confuse *approval* with *love*. And, since most children project their parents' feelings and behavior onto God, we may have formed the false belief that we have to be a certain way to be "loved" by God. Children who are raised by stern, judgmental and punishing parents tend to see God as being the same way.

In addition, many children are told that God is a judgmental old man who will punish them if they are bad. Instead of a force of love, God was a force to be reckoned with, a Supreme Being whom we must please—or else. This, of course, is just a way that parents control their children and religious institutions control their followers.

The Bible talks about "fearing God," but the word "fearing" has been poorly translated. A more literal translation of the original text is "awe." You are told to be in awe of God, not to fear God. Throughout the New Testament you are told to "fear not," because God is always there, for God is Spirit, God is love. But parents or religious leaders who want to control their children often threaten them by saying "God will punish you," which leads to the child's false belief that God is judgmental and loves them conditionally. This "love" is not love but approval.

It is easy for some children to see God in the same way they see their parents when they are taught that God is a controlling and judgmental being. Everything changes in your perception of God when you know that God is the Spirit of love and compassion, truth and wisdom, peace and joy. Love, by definition, is unconditional acceptance, understanding and caring. Everything that is conditional—that is shaming, judgmental, critical, withholding or punishing—is not love and is therefore not God.

Once you *directly experience* God, you know that you do not have to give yourself up to be loved by God. The only way you can know *any* belief is false is to directly experience the truth, which comes from God and which *is* God. Later on, I will show you how to experience this for yourself.

4. I Won't Ever Be Good Enough to Please God

Many people grew up with parents who were never pleased with them, no matter how well they did. If they got a B in school, it should have been an A. If they received an A it should have been an A+. Their flaws were constantly pointed out. Attention was always on what they didn't do rather than on what they did do. It's no wonder so many of us grew up feeling inadequate.

If you projected your parents' negative feelings onto God, you may believe there is nothing you can ever do that will please God. You may believe that God sees you as inherently flawed, "born into sin," and there is nothing you can do to change this. You might believe that no matter how hard you try, in the end you will be punished for sin: God will never forgive you for being human. But if you are "created in the image of God," meaning that *you have the same love within you that is God*, then it is not possible for you to be inherently flawed. That would mean you were created imperfect. And God doesn't do substandard work. Nor is God unforgiving. Unconditional love is, by definition, forgiving.

5. God Uses Me to Help Others, but Does Not Come to Me Just for Me

When we do believe in God but feel ourselves unlovable and unworthy, we may believe that we can be instruments of God's love for others but not for ourselves. Sometimes children are taught that they are nothing, that their only worth is in helping others. Their goal becomes to give God's love to others so others will give love to them. This belief system fosters the giving-to-get behavior of codependent relationships. This is rampant in the helping professions. Over and over I encounter therapists and healers who tell me that they feel totally connected when helping and loving others but not when it comes to loving themselves. They can access profound truth and compassion for others but none for themselves.

6. God Has Favorite People and Showers Them with Blessings

If you grew up deprived of love and you see others who were given love as children, you may conclude that God has chosen certain people who deserve to be blessed, while ignoring others who do not deserve it. This conclusion, as with many of the other false beliefs about God, comes from seeing God as an unloving, judgmental, vengeful person rather than as an unconditionally loving Spirit or Supreme Being. People have favorite people. God doesn't. People think some people are more deserving than others. God doesn't. But when you believe God is a judgmental person, you may project your beliefs and experiences of people onto God.

All this changes when you come to experience God as unconditional love—love that is *always* there, that has *no* conditions. It is helpful to think of God as a law—the law of unconditional love—the same way you think of gravity as a law. Gravity exists for you whether you are being loving or not. (And whether you believe in it or not.) Gravity does not exist only for those who deserve it. God works the same way.

When you learn to open your heart and invite God in, you will know through firsthand experience that God's love is always here to help sustain you no matter who you are, what you've done, or what challenges and hardships you face on the earthly level. When you open your heart to God, then you know that the bad things that happen to you—such as the loss of a loved one—are not a punishment. It does not mean that you are not loved by God. It just means that bad things happen on the earthly level.

Each of us has a different journey. We cannot know why some souls learn their soul lessons through hardship, while others learn them through plenty. What you do or do not have on the earthly level has nothing to do with what you do or do not have on the spiritual level. God blesses every one of us. The love that is God merely supports your soul's journey, whatever it is you are facing and learning in this life. You cannot know what another's soul lesson is—why others are able-bodied or disabled, wealthy or poor, beautiful or plain. Just know that whatever the situation, there is much for each of us to learn about our soul's growth and much for you to learn about love and compassion in *relationship to others*.

7. God Made Me Come Here

I often hear people say "I didn't ask to be born," or "I didn't ask to be in this family with these parents." When you believe that God is a person or that God is demanding, controlling and judgmental, then you may believe that God made you come here and put you into an unloving or abusive family either as punishment (because you are inherently bad) or because God doesn't love you. This false belief relieves you of the responsibility of choosing to heal, regardless of how difficult your past, in order to evolve your soul. Your soul evolves toward lovingness through the many challenges you face on this planet, challenges that do not exist in the spiritual realm. All forms of hardship and adversity are challenges to your soul to move beyond your current limitations and beliefs into more loving behavior.

I know from my own experience that it is possible to remember life in the spiritual realm. These memories are within each of us. The more we heal, the more access we have to them. When you remember that you came here to evolve in lovingness, you will no longer say, "I didn't ask to be here," or ask "Why wasn't I born into a happy family?" When you gain an understanding of why you came here, then you understand that each challenge is an opportunity to learn and evolve. Then you understand that being alive is truly a sacred opportunity, a sacred privilege.

Life: A Sentence or a Sacred Privilege?

Let's take a look at where we are. We have seen that spiritual abuse is rampant and that it disconnects a child from God. We have also seen how this disconnection causes a person to draw many false conclusions about God and to operate from an earthly instead of a spiritual perspective.

Making life choices based on these false beliefs and this perspective is what creates most of our painful feelings and unhealthy behavior, which in turn create bigger societal problems. No wonder some people say that life feels more like a jail sentence than a privilege.

When you put all these factors together, you see that the consequences of spiritual abuse are indeed numerous and far-reaching. They include:

- Fear of death
- Lack of purpose
- Living in fear and depression
- Illness
- Core shame
- Harming ourselves and others
- Lack of personal responsibility—feeling victimized and powerless, blaming and controlling others
- Dysfunctional relationships, shattered families
- Experiencing life as a burden instead of a sacred privilege

Let's take a look at each of these and see what's really behind them.

Fear of Death

When you have suffered spiritual abuse and are disconnected from God, you do not know that your soul is immortal. You think that death is the end of everything—utter blackness. This can be very frightening. When you believe that this life is all there is, you want to hang on to it at all cost. People who want to stay on life support or have their bodies frozen in the hopes of being revived at a later date do not know that the spiritual realm is their real home and that death is about leaving this body and going home. They have forgotten about the incredible love, peace and joy that awaits them. If you could remember even a moment of your life in the spiritual realm, your fear of death would vanish. People who have had out-of-body or near-death experiences never again fear death.

The fear of death leads to the fear of really living life. When you fear death, you fear accidents, illness, victimization, old age—anything that could take away your life in this body. Fear of death often results in a much graver problem: not living life to the fullest.

The fear of death may stem from a false belief about hell. Hell, according to information I have received from my spiritual guidance, is not a place. It is a state of mind. When you do not know that God's love is truly unconditional—which means that you are loved *no matter what you've done*—you may fear death because you think you will be punished in hell for your bad deeds. But hell is not God's punishment. God has no judgment and no punishment, just love. Hell is living in fear and judgment. Hell is being disconnected from God, in life or in death.

If your childhood or present religion has very different ideas about hell, you may find this concept unacceptable. For now, I suggest you simply consider the possibility that hell is not a place God sends you for punishment. Later, when you have learned how to do the Six-Step Process, you can ask your own spiritual Guidance about hell—and any other questions you may have about how God works. I am sharing with you the information I have received from my Guidance, but I am not an authority on the universe. So you will need to find your own answers, which you will learn how to do later.

Lack of Purpose

When we do not know that our purpose here on Earth is to experience, express and evolve our souls toward lovingness and oneness with God, we may feel lost, aimless. We set goals that we believe will bring us peace and joy, such as making lots of money, finding the right job, becoming famous, losing weight, getting a bigger house or nicer car, or finding the right relationship. The problem is that many women and men who achieve all these goals—and more— still feel alone, empty and frightened. Until these people move onto a spiritual path and devote themselves toward healing those things that block love and joy, they continue filling their emptiness with addictions to substances, material things, activities and people. They continue to wonder why they wake up each morning afraid.

Discovering the most rewarding path for expressing your love and your God-given gifts is what happens when you practice the Six Steps of Inner Bonding. Your soul's purpose lies within your true Self. You cannot discover that purpose until you reconnect with your essence, the God within.

Living in Fear and Depression

The billions of dollars of anti-anxiety and antidepressant medication sold in this country attest to the prevalence of this consequence of spiritual abuse. When you have no faith that you are loved and supported by God, you feel desperately alone in the universe. The feeling is overwhelming and terrifying. It causes many people to live with knots in their stomach, numbed out on substances or dependent on prescription or nonprescription drugs to take away their anxiety and depression about feeling so alone.

The good news is we cannot live in fear and in faith at the same time. That means that the moment we move into faith that God is guiding and supporting us, our fear and desperate inner aloneness go away. To maintain faith and our personal connection with God, we must heal from our spiritual abuse by letting go of our false beliefs and embracing the truth about ourselves and God. When we do this, our anxiety and depression will likely become strangers to us.

Illness

Illness can be a consequence of spiritual abuse. That's because living with constant fear, anxiety and depression erodes the immune system. Of course, not all illness results from spiritual abuse. We have many other factors to contend with, such as processed, devitalized and insecticide-laden food, contaminated air and water, and inherited tendencies. But adding the effects of spiritual abuse on top of all this results in a very unhealthy society. The bottom line is spiritual abuse costs us billions of dollars in health-care costs.

Core Shame

Core shame is the false belief that you are fundamentally inadequate, bad, wrong, defective, unimportant and unlovable. I have never met a person who didn't have core shame. Core shame is what we feel when we did not get the love we needed as children and have not done our inner healing work. We operate from core shame when we do not experience our essence and God's essence as one and the same: "One God . . . who is above all, and through all, and *in you all*"[2] (my italics).

When we operate from core shame, we spend much of our lives trying to hide who we think we are—our false, wounded self. We cannot be authentic, honest and straightforward for fear of being found out. We live from fear instead of from love. We can never feel whole or peaceful or have sustained intimate relationships as long as we operate from core shame. The fear of rejection and aloneness that comes from our core shame causes us to act out in ways that harm ourselves and others.

Harming Ourselves and Others

When we do not know that our essence is beautiful, lovable and worthy—a spark of God—then we may not be motivated to take care of ourselves. We take care of what we value. If you value your children, your home, your car and your possessions, you take good care of them. If you do not value them, you do not take good care of them. The same is true of yourself. When you value your body and your soul, you take good care of yourself physically, emotionally and spiritually.

But when you operate from core shame, you may abuse yourself either in the ways you were abused as a child or in the ways you saw your parents abuse themselves. You may eat badly, not sleep enough, overwork, or abuse substances such as alcohol, drugs, nicotine, caffeine, sugar or junk food. You may be self-critical, shaming yourself in the ways you were shamed or in the ways you saw your parents shame themselves. You may sacrifice your own needs while caretaking others' needs. You may let others use and abuse you, not setting appropriate boundaries against disrespectful and hurtful behavior. (Boundaries are the limits that we set—or don't set—about how we treat ourselves, how we treat others and how others treat us.) You may even think about killing yourself. Adolescents often mutilate themselves because of the depth of their core shame and loneliness. Spiritual abuse can lead to self-abuse and suicide—as well as to harming others.

When you do not know that your essence is love and that your purpose is to love, and when you do not know that life is eternal and that we are all One, you can make choices that harm your soul by harming others. When you do not believe that your core Self is a spark of God, you may not cherish the core Self of others. When you feel unworthy, you may see others as unworthy. When you do not feel a sense of oneness with all living beings, then you may shame, use, threaten, hit, lie to, steal from, maim, rape or kill others. Spiritual abuse, which creates our fear and our core shame and disconnects us from God, is the great destroyer on the earthly level. *It is responsible for the increased crime and violence of our time, especially among young people.*

When you do not know that your life will continue in the spiritual realm and that you will ultimately have to feel the pain you have inflicted upon others, you may harm others without thinking. People who have had near-death experiences have said that when we leave our bodies at the time of death, we have a life review. We are asked, "How well did you love?" We then reexperience every choice we made and the consequences of them. When we chose unloving behavior that caused suffering to others, we will feel what they felt. No one sits in judgment of us. We are not sent to any "hell" for our choices. But we will feel within our souls what others felt at our anger, blaming, shaming, violence, lying and so on. You will feel all the feelings other people had as a result of every act of kindness or unkindness on your part. You will be the only judge of whether or not you fulfilled your soul's mission to love and evolve in your lovingness.

Again, if you are not comfortable accepting what I am saying here about what happens when we die, just make a note of it so you can investigate the truth later on by asking your own spiritual Guidance. My spiritual Guidance has confirmed for me that we do indeed have a life review when we die.

Many people believe that core shame is very hard to heal. Actually, it is not. *But it is impossible to heal core shame without God.* Traditional psychotherapy that excludes Spirit does not help. I have had clients who came to me after years and years of therapy, but who had not healed their core shame. Through practicing the process presented in this book and understanding that core shame is your *oldest protection*, you will learn how to heal your core shame. We'll talk more about this later.

Lack of Personal Responsibility

When, as a result of spiritual abuse, you feel alone in the universe and cannot connect with any spiritual Guidance to help you, you may not only feel inherently unlovable and have trouble connecting with others, you may also feel powerless over having these feelings. This compounds the problem.

Both these feelings—aloneness (feeling unlovable and alone in the universe) and loneliness (having no one to share love with)—are very painful. Aloneness is the black, hollow, empty feeling you have in the pit of your stomach or in your chest when you are alone *inside*. When you are not connected with Divine Love and are therefore disconnected from your core Self, you feel like a child drifting alone in a vast and indifferent universe. Loneliness, on the other hand, is the aching or burning feeling in your heart or solar plexus when you have no one with whom to share love. You can feel lonely when you are by yourself, but you can also feel lonely when you are with others whose hearts are closed.

If you are disconnected from your true Self and God, you will always feel both alone and lonely. Your heart will be closed and because of this you cannot bring God's love through to yourself or share love with others. This is the state of despair that often leads people to act out addictively.

If your heart is open, you will not feel alone because you will feel God with you, but you may feel lonely. The important thing to remember, however, is that when you are connected with God, *you are not alone in your loneliness*. You do not feel alone when you experience God's presence in your life. When you move into even deeper levels of healing and connection with God, you can feel your oneness with others even when their hearts are closed. This does not mean that you will not feel sorrow at not being able to share love with someone, but it does mean that you will be able to handle the loneliness in a way that is loving to yourself and to them. We'll look at this more deeply in the chapters on relationships (chapters 12 and 13).

Helplessness or powerlessness is the intense feeling of agitation we often experience as unbearable frustration. Because feeling powerless, lonely and alone are such awful feelings to have, we naturally want to have control over *not* feeling them. We may use addictions to block these feelings. We may also defend against them—especially the feeling of powerlessness—by trying to control others with our anger, criticism or coldness. The sad irony is, controlling behavior is one of the major causes of relationship failure, so our efforts may backfire. We may end up feeling more powerless, lonely and alone than ever.

When we operate from an earthly perspective, we tend to make others responsible for our feelings and behavior. One of my clients, Jennifer, frequently blows up at her husband, convinced that he doesn't care about her. Because she was spiritually abused in childhood, she has deep abandonment wounds that lead her to feel unlovable and victimized. Not loving herself or being able to truly love her husband, she projects these feelings onto him and becomes convinced he doesn't care about her, when in fact he loves her deeply. Whenever she suffers the consequences of not taking good care of herself—that is, of abandoning herself—she blames him for her feelings of abandonment. "You don't care about me!" she screams at him. "What about me? What about what I need? If you loved me, you would spend more time with me!" She feels like a victim of his behavior. If this goes on long enough, she may drive him away, thus confirming to herself that he never really did care about her. Sometimes she even places the blame for her feelings on her children.

Unfortunately, this is a common scenario in families. Jennifer's own unloving behavior toward herself and others perpetuates her core shame, which she will hand down to her children. She cannot experience God within her, and her own unloving behavior causes core shame in her children. Spiritual abuse breeds spiritual abuse—and all the negative consequences that follow it.

Dysfunctional Relationships, Shattered Families

Our core shame, coming as it does from spiritual abuse, cannot help but create dysfunctional, codependent relationships. In codependent relationships we hand over the job of defining our worth and lovability to someone else. We then try to control how they define us, and we feel angry and rejected when they do not make us feel worthy and lovable. Because we don't take personal responsibility for our own feelings and behavior, we end up feeling like victims and blaming others for our own pain. The consequences are misery, anxiety, depression and often illness.

A friend of mine, Lester, is a very talented healer. He is highly intuitive and very connected with the healing energy and information that comes through him from God. Like many people on a spiritual path, Lester has learned to attune to higher energies, but he has never brought that love inside to take care of himself. His connection to God has actually been his addiction, his way of *avoiding* dealing with his feelings. Because he has never done his own inner work and healed his wounded self, he doesn't take responsibility for himself and his own feelings. Instead, he makes women responsible for his sense of worth and lovability. He is a pushover for beautiful women, and each time he gets into a relationship he gives himself up by taking responsibility for the woman's feelings while ignoring his own. When he does not receive the love he believes he deserves, Lester feels trapped and resentful. He blames the woman for not loving him, never realizing that he is the one who is not loving himself. Lester is not only going through his third messy divorce, he has recently been diagnosed, at age fifty, with liver cancer. No matter how much he has prayed, how well he has eaten, how many supplements he has taken and how many people he has healed, the added stress to his immune system—caused by his not healing from his spiritual abuse and not learning to love himself or take responsibility for his feelings—may be the factor that is costing him his life.

Every day couples come to see me who are suffering from the consequences of the spiritual abuse they experienced as children. They respond to their deep fears of rejection and abandonment by controlling instead of loving. They constantly attribute their problems to their partners. Their love gets ground down to nothing as their wounded selves pound each other with their anger, blame and withdrawal. They are stuck in an earthly relationship. Without inner healing, such couples have no chance at a loving and passionate spiritual relationship. Families are shattered when the two partners leave each other to find happiness elsewhere, instead of looking within. Their fundamental error is in seeking a "better" partner when they should be seeking to *become* a better partner.

This is especially sad because when both partners are willing to do their inner healing work, very often they can repair their relationship, no matter how damaged.

Experiencing Life as a Burden Instead of a Sacred Privilege

When you add up all the consequences of spiritual abuse, it is no surprise that for some people life feels like a burden and a jail sentence instead of a sacred privilege. Having to control everything—getting love, avoiding pain, feeling safe—is an exhausting job. Believing that you have to do this yourself because God doesn't exist (or has abandoned you) makes life a misery.

Living with God

People who have a deep experience of God as love, either because they were loved as children in the way they needed to be or because they are healing from their spiritual abuse, operate at least some of the time from a spiritual perspective:

- They know that we are all spiritual beings, that our lives are eternal and that our present choices affect our souls. They do not fear death because they know the soul transcends the body. They know that life on Earth is a transitory discovery experience and that our permanent home is the spiritual realm.

- They see life on this planet as a gift from God. They have a sense of purpose. They know that they are here to express their God-given gifts and evolve their souls toward love, compassion, truth and joy, and to heal whatever blocks they have to loving and being one with God. They know that God is not a static entity but a living force that learns and evolves as we learn and evolve. They see all adversity in their lives as an opportunity to learn more about love and to experience, evolve and express the fullness of God.

- They recognize that all of us have the Spirit of God within, that we are all One, regardless of race, religion, gender or sexual orientation. They know that each of us is a unique and important part of a giant puzzle, the whole of which is God, and that to harm one harms all, including themselves. Because they operate from a spiritual perspective, they never seek to harm themselves or others.

- They see their bodies as temples for their souls. They accept the sacred privilege of caring for them by eating well, getting exercise and doing whatever it takes to be healthy.

- They see our planet as a gift and accept the sacred privilege of keeping it healthy. They care about all life.

- They have faith that God is leading their souls toward their highest good. They do not live in constant fear and do not need to attempt to control everything. They try only to express and evolve their souls, and they leave the outcome to God.

- They take personal responsibility for their own pain and joy. They do not blame God or others for their misery, knowing that their feelings are often a result of their own thoughts, beliefs and actions. They embrace the sacred privilege of spiritual growth and move continuously toward more lovingness and joy.

- They set appropriate and loving boundaries against being disrespected, used and abused by others. They resolve conflicts with others by caring about both their own and the other's highest good.

- They create balance in their lives, giving themselves time to be alone, time to pray and meditate, time to work, time to play with others and time to express their creativity, passion, aliveness, joy, laughter and love. They find work, service, hobbies and activities that joyously express their God-given gifts.

- They operate primarily in the moment, with love, rather than obsessing about the past and projecting it onto the present and future.

It would take an enlightened being to operate from the spiritual perspective all the time, and I have never met an enlightened being. But we can all be in the process of moving toward this ideal.

Learning to Love in the Face of Fear

It is easy to be loving when we have no problems, when we feel safe and secure. It is very hard to be loving when we are frightened. Yet it is our challenge—and our sacred privilege—to evolve the very fabric of love and compassion as we each learn to be loving when confronted with the hardships of being on Earth. Life on this very difficult planet gives us an opportunity that we do not have in the spiritual realm—the opportunity *to love in the face of fear*. In the spiritual realm we do not have to contend with the earthly challenges that create our fears, such as aloneness, loneliness, physical pain, hunger, disease, loss of financial security, rejection and loss of love, and physical death.

We have each courageously agreed to leave the safety of our true home, the spiritual realm, and come here to learn the things we can only learn in a body. We came here knowing full well that we would forget our original agreement with ourselves to evolve in our lovingness and have to discover it anew. We may feel lost and without purpose until we remember that we came here to help Spirit evolve by becoming beings of love and compassion.

Just as parents can regard caring for their children as a burden or a sacred privilege, so you can see your sojourn on Earth as a burden to be suffered or a sacred privilege to be fully embraced. Parents who see taking care of their children as a sacred privilege have a far deeper and richer experience than those who see it as a burden. It may be difficult at times, but those who see parenting as a sacred privilege happily learn from the hard times, while those who see it as a burden feel resentful and sucked dry by the experience.

So it is with our life here on this planet. How you see it determines your experience. We can face the hard times with the courage and determination to learn as much as we can about love, or we can run from fear and hardship by hiding behind our various addictions. Moving out of fear, control and experiencing life as a burden, and moving into love, grace and experiencing life as a sacred privilege, is a *process*, not an event. There are many paths to God, many processes for moving from fear to faith, and we each need to find the process that works best for us.

What you need to ask yourself is this: "Am I suffering enough to do something different? Am I suffering enough to learn how to experience God and take responsibility for myself? Is my primary desire to learn to be loving with myself and others and connect with God, or is my primary desire to get someone or something outside of myself to fix this for me?"

This book teaches a powerful process for moving out of the earthly and into the spiritual perspective, out of fear and into love. Those of you who have used Inner Bonding before will find it expanded here. Inner Bonding heals our false beliefs and teaches us how to live in truth. It shows us how to take loving care of ourselves and share our love with others. It enables us to recover our core Self and connect deeply with God so that we can embrace the sacred privilege of life on this planet and know, through direct experience, that we do not have to give ourselves up to be loved by God.

THREE

"Controlling" God: Traveling the Wide Road

When loving and becoming one with God isn't our highest priority, what is? If we are not willing to open to God's will, what then? What do we do when we do not choose God as our guide?

Often, we choose to follow "the wide road." In the Bible, Jesus said that we have only two paths from which to choose.[1] We can choose the wide and easy way, or we can choose the narrow way, also known as the straight gate, the challenging path or, as Robert Frost and M. Scott Peck call it, "the road less traveled." There are many other words for these two paths: earthly or spiritual, dark or light, fear or faith, low road or high road. In terms of our behavior these two roads are the choices we make to control or to love, to avoid or to learn, to close or to open, to get or to give. When we choose the wide road, we are motivated by a desire to *get* from God and others, rather than by a desire to *give* God's love to ourselves and others.

51

There is not a "right" path or a "wrong" path as far as whether or not we are loved by God; God's love is unconditional. But we will *experience* being loved by God only when we choose the narrow path, the road less traveled. That's because the narrow path leads us to God and God is the one who teaches us that we are *inherently* lovable. Our wounded, wide-road-walking minds would have us believe otherwise.

Likewise, our worth as human beings is not determined by the path we choose. Our core Self, the part of us that is an individualized expression of the Divine, is *inherently* worthy. Remember, God does not make junk. However, whether we *experience* ourselves as worthy is determined by the path we choose.

Walking the wide road leads to even further difficulties. If you are operating from your false self and do not know your own worth, you end up letting yourself be defined by others. Your highest priority becomes getting—not giving—love. If other people like or love you, you feel worthy and lovable. If they don't, you feel rejected and unlovable. This is like having a baby and, instead of loving it yourself, you keep trying to give it to other people to love. Can you imagine how this baby feels? The baby is terrified of being rejected by others because he or she has no other source of love; this innocent baby has already been rejected by you. Fear of rejection rules the baby's life. This is why the false self desperately yearns for approval, confusing it with love.

When we are desperate for something (like gaining approval), it's not enough to *try* to get it. We *must* get it. We must take *control* over getting it. It is a life-or-death matter to us. That's why the wide road is the road of control.

Earlier I asked, "When loving and becoming one with God is not our highest priority, what is?" The answer is control. Without God as our personal guide, control is what remains. We become addicted to controlling everything—maybe even God—as our way of getting the "love" we need and feeling safe.

Guy was a fifty-one-year-old screenwriter who came to see me after his girlfriend broke up with him. Although Guy said he wanted my help in learning to love himself, unconsciously he wanted me to tell him he was worthy and lovable. He started each session telling me in detail how well he was doing and how much progress he was making. Then he would wait for my response. In one particular session, my response was not what he expected.

"Guy, when you report this to me," I asked him, "what are you wanting the most?"

He thought about this a moment. "Well, I want you to know what I've been doing."

"Anything else?"

"I thought you would like it."

"Like hearing about it or like what you have done?"

"Both, I guess."

"You want me to approve of what you've done?" I asked.

"Sure."

"And what does my approval give you?"

"Well, it lets me know I'm okay. That I'm doing the right thing."

"So the only way you know you are okay is if I—or others—approve of you?"

"I guess so. I never thought about it like this before. Actually, I guess I spend a lot of energy trying to get approval and avoid rejection. But doesn't everyone? Nobody likes rejection. It feels awful, like just about the worst thing that could happen. I just don't know how to handle it. I go right back to being the little kid I was with my dad. You know, always feeling there's something wrong with me."

"Have you been doing your inner work?" I asked, purposely keeping my question vague.

"Yes, I do it every day. But nothing seems to be happening. I don't *feel* anything in my heart. I can't seem to feel the love in my heart."

"I'd like to hear what you're doing."

"Well, I pray to God for help."

"What do you say to God?" I asked.

"I say, 'God, help me feel better. Give me your love so I don't feel so alone.'"

"Guy, it sounds like you're trying to get God to fix you, to heal your aloneness for you, rather than inviting God into your heart so that you can heal yourself," I told him. "You need to open to God's love so *you* can give it to yourself."

Stunned, Guy just stared at me. He had been on a spiritual path for some time but had never realized that he was still trying to get God to do it *for* him rather than *with* him. He wanted to *get* love rather than *become* a loving person with himself and others. Guy had always played the role of caretaker in his relationships, giving to others in order to get love from them. In other words, he kept trying to *control* getting love. Even though Guy believed in God, he had never invited God into his heart. He had never decided to define and love *himself*. He always tried to get others and God to do it for him.

"This is amazing!" Guy exclaimed. "I never saw this before!"

"Are you willing to invite God into your heart so you can see who you really are and give love to yourself?"

"Yes."

And he did. In that moment, Guy shifted his deepest desire from *taking love from God* to *giving love to himself*. A surprised look came over his face, and he smiled at me.

I could see that Guy had made a new decision about what was most important to him. All his life, getting love and approval had been his goal, his deepest desire. But in that moment, sitting in my office, he had changed his mind— which we can *always* do because we have free will. Guy had decided that it was more important to give love to himself and others than to get it.

How Did We Come to Believe That We Could Control God?

Some of us were brought up by parents whose "love" was conditional. We had to earn our parents' love by acting the way they wanted us to. In the process, we learned many ways to control getting the "love" (in reality, approval) that we needed. And we probably projected our parents' feelings onto God. We believed that God's love was conditional. (It's not. It's a free and *unconditional* gift.) We believed we could win God's love by being "good" and doing things "right." This got us into even deeper water, since "good" and "right" are usually defined by parents, teachers, religious leaders and others in authority, rather than by our own inner spiritual Guidance. In reality, "good" is whatever is truly loving to ourselves and others.

Children are often systematically taught to try to win love from others and God. We train them in the art of control by controlling them and by rewarding their various attempts to control us (by giving them candy or kisses when they are good, for example). Parents try many ways to control their kids: anger, threats, sarcasm, punishment, criticism, judgments, withdrawal, physical violence, treats, money, shame and smothering. Kids, in turn, may try to get parental approval or attention by being nice, by caretaking (giving themselves up and doing what parents want them to do), overachieving, becoming invisible, becoming ill, acting out or having temper tantrums. Anytime we role-model controlling behavior by trying to control our children or reward their manipulative behavior with our attention, we teach them the soul-deadening art of control.

Some of our most famous children's songs teach kids that they can control the outcome of things by being "good," like the one that tells them Santa knows when they've been good or bad. This song not only teaches the art of control by telling kids how to make Santa do what they want, it practices it, too, by telling children they will only get gifts if they are good. By implying that Santa Claus sees *and judges* all, the song aims to keep children in line. Some parents don't realize that children generally learn right from wrong by watching the behavior of the adults around them.

Some children see God the same way they see Santa Claus. They believe they can manipulate God into loving them, too, by being good or doing things right. Until they learn that the love of God is a *free gift* and cannot be bought or bargained for, they will find endless ways to try to get it. They will say their prayers, try to be perfect, follow all the rules, rigidly keep the Ten Commandments, be polite, always be right—or righteous. Being good may mean suppressing their sexuality. Being the right way may mean dieting or throwing up to the point of starvation to look right. Being right may even include beating up people who are smaller and weaker. When parents beat their children for being "bad," they role-model that it's okay to hit someone smaller when it's "for their own good."

Being good may even include children denying their own feelings and taking responsibility for others' feelings: Children are routinely told that focusing on themselves is "selfish." (When people with this kind of training grow up, they may continue the pattern by following the rules of a church, being a community do-gooder or being self-sacrificing, not because they are moved from their hearts to do so, but in the hope of earning others' and God's approval.)

All of this training in how to control others in order to get the "love" we need ultimately leads to the avoidance of personal responsibility for our needs, feelings and behavior, and the absence of loving, compassionate behavior toward ourselves, others and God.

Loving Versus Controlling Behavior

Loving behavior is personally accountable behavior that nurtures and supports our own and others' spiritual growth and highest good. It is behavior that is consciously intended to *give* something helpful—like support, compassion or understanding—to ourselves and others. Controlling behavior, which is often unconscious, attempts to *get* something (like safety, love or attention) or to *avoid* something (like rejection, disapproval or loneliness). Loving behavior is satisfying in itself and is not attached to an outcome, to getting something back. Controlling behavior always has an expectation of a certain outcome attached.

For example, you can give to your children because it gives you joy to do so, or you can give because you want them to love you, take care of you when you are older, or have others see you as a good parent. You can have sex with your partner for loving or for controlling reasons, too. You may want to share and express your love; or you may want to get loved, distracted or affirmed; or avoid your partner's anger or disappointment. You can donate money to worthy causes purely for the satisfaction it gives you, or to get publicity, a tax break or a place in heaven. While the action of giving to your children, having sex or donating money is the same, the energy behind a controlling intent feels totally different to the receiver than the energy of a loving intent. Loving behavior feels nourishing while controlling behavior feels lonely, smothering or draining to the receiver.

In the same way you attempt to control the outcome with others, you may attempt to control the outcome with God. You might pray, go to church or temple, tithe or do volunteer work in order to make God love and protect you, rather than for the pure joy of doing so and from the deep desire to serve God. Have you noticed that even some religious dogma is based on an attempt to control God? For example, some Christians believe that *only* if you "confess Jesus Christ as your personal Lord and Savior" will you go to heaven. This gives them a sense of control over God: I only have to believe the "right" thing and I am safe. Each religion has its rules—don't work on Saturday, give away a certain percentage of your earnings, don't divorce, sacrifice yourself for others—to ensure God's grace. The problem is that none of these rules has anything to do with love and compassion. Worse, they teach you that you do, indeed, have to give yourself up—that is, deny your own inner truth and follow someone else's teachings—to be loved by God. In fact, they teach that it is *only* in giving yourself up that you will be loved by God. While this may give you a sense of safety, it does not move you along your spiritual path toward becoming more loving and compassionate.

The doctrines and dogma of *religion* have nothing to do with opening to the will of God, which is what *spirituality* is all about. Opening to God does not mean giving yourself up in the sense of ignoring your own needs and your own truth or going along with what other people want or what they tell you God wants. Opening or "surrendering" in the *spiritual* sense means that you release the will of your wounded, false self and invite in the will of love, compassion, truth and wisdom—the will of God. You cannot surrender and attempt to control the outcome of things at the same time. Letting go of the outcome does not mean that you do not decide what you want and do everything in your power to get there. It means that you come from the faith that God supports your highest good at all times and that you cannot always know which outcome is best for your soul's growth toward wholeness and oneness with God.

I have often been asked, "How can ending up homeless or losing loved ones to death or disease be in our highest good?"

Can you consider the possibility that the homeless person has soul lessons to learn through the experience of being homeless? Or that he or she is giving others an opportunity to learn soul lessons through offering their help? On the earthly level it makes no sense, but on the spiritual level it makes total sense for the journey of that particular soul. Sometimes a very evolved soul will agree to a life of illness or poverty in order to give others the opportunity of *evolving through helping*. Judeo-Christian religious training doesn't seem to have this point of view, although Buddhism and Hinduism do.

When we are devoted to the rules and dogma of religion, the wounded part of us often operates from judgment instead of compassion. We may judge the homeless person as somehow bad, wrong or undeserving. This concept is well put in *Meeting Jesus Again for the First Time* by Marcus Borg. Borg describes what he calls "the purity system"—the belief that women, the poor and sometimes the ill are considered "impure"—which started with the ancient Hebrews and continued into Christianity:

> *In parts of the church there are groups that emphasize holiness and purity as the Christian way of life, and they draw their own sharp social boundaries between the righteous and sinners. It is a sad irony that these groups, many of which are seeking very earnestly to be faithful to Scripture, end up emphasizing those parts of Scripture that Jesus himself challenged and opposed. An interpretation of Scripture faithful to Jesus and the early Christian movement sees the Bible through the lens of compassion, not purity.[2]*

Unfortunately, many Christians do not come close to following the teachings of Jesus in this matter. The purity system has nothing to do with love and compassion. It is based on judgmental concepts of right and wrong that serve the wounded self's desire for control:

"It is right to be heterosexual and wrong to be homosexual."

"It is good to be white and bad to be a person of color."

"It is right to stay married and wrong to divorce."

"It is wrong to use birth control."

"It is wrong to masturbate."

"It is right to suffer and sacrifice, and wrong to bring yourself joy."

These are all examples of the frightened, wounded part of ourselves speaking, the part that believes that if we know for sure what is right and wrong and if we follow the rules, we will be able to control God and the outcome of things.

When compassion has a higher value than control, we do not judge things in terms of right and wrong. Instead, we look at our own and others' behavior and try to understand the values and preferences behind this behavior. We try to understand the *very good reasons* we all have for feeling, believing and behaving the way we do. We try to *learn and understand* rather than *judge*. (As far as I have been able to determine, there is only one value that is common to all religions: Love thy neighbor as thyself. Some form of this value is found in all the writings on which the world's religions are based. If we followed this one value, we would never harm each other.)

To be on a spiritual path is to accept that you need to put aside your concepts of right and wrong, good and bad, and embrace instead compassionate learning, understanding and acceptance as your way of being.

Sadly, control rather than compassion has become the most prevalent way of life. Through the ages, certain techniques for controlling God have become set in concrete in our lives:

- Penance, suffering and self-abuse
- Prayer
- Giving to get
- Self-sacrifice
- Shame
- Victimhood and blaming
- Resistance

Penance, Suffering and Self-Abuse

If you believe that God wants you to suffer to prove your love and devotion, then you can feel safely in control of God's love by simply suffering. When I was in Mexico as an adolescent, I often saw people inching toward church on bleeding knees. I was appalled to see this self-abuse and could not understand it. Later I read about priests and nuns who ritually flagellated themselves to prove their love of God. While some forms of self-abuse may be ways people have learned to put themselves into an altered state in order to connect with God and attain clarity of mind, often these rituals are really just attempts to control God. Hours and hours of prayer or chanting when you are hungry and tired may bring clarity and connection—or it may be an attempt to win God's "love" through suffering.

Likewise, doing penance when we have done something we believe was wrong may also be a way to control God. Often confession and doing penance are ways to get back into God's grace so that we can go ahead and do what we want again—get drunk, hit our spouse, have an affair, cheat someone. If we were truly sorry for our behavior, we would make amends and get the help we need so that we never do that particular behavior again.

When your heart is truly open and you receive a direct experience of God, you know that the last thing that God wants is suffering. The Spirit that is God wants to express itself through us as love, compassion, joy, peace, creativity and beauty. Suffering and self-abuse, other than when strictly biologically based, often come from fear, not love.

Prayer

More and more people are recognizing the power of prayer, and many ask, "How do I pray? What is the best way to pray?" The "how" of prayer is not nearly as important as the "why" of prayer. Our *intent* is what matters most.

We either pray from an open heart—our true Self—or a closed heart—our wounded self. Think of your prayers for a moment. Who prays? Your core Self or essence, or the false self that wants to get some blessing or remedy from God? When your intent is to get something or prevent something, your prayers are simply an attempt to control God. These are the demanding, begging and bargaining prayers, and the prayers we do because we think we "should." Since the wounded self always has an outcome in mind and wants control over this outcome, all these prayers have an expected outcome attached to them. We pray in the hope of getting God to fix things for us. These are the prayers that will always go unanswered because they do not come from a desire to give love.

Prayer coming from love is quite another matter. Here the intent is to invite God into your heart, to surrender your individual will and become an instrument of Higher Will. You are not asking God to fix things for you. You are asking for help in becoming one with Divine Love so you can bring love, compassion and truth through to yourself and others. Instead of trying to *get* something, you are offering to *give* something. Prayers that come from love always include a period of contemplation, of listening to God so you can hear God's instruction to you. God is always speaking to us, but most of us never take the time to listen.

I have discovered that prayer is far more powerful when I thank God for what I have and for what I know is on the way rather than when I try to get God to give me something. One of my personal challenges has been to trust my inner knowing about what is true for me. It seems easier to trust my knowing about what I know is true for others. For example, a number of years ago, my dear friend Erika was very ill. For a while we thought she was dying. As she lay in bed feeling so sick, God told her of her life's purpose—to start a service organization called Hope America, whose primary purpose would be to help the homeless. Erika was shown pictures of her and other chaplains trained in Inner Bonding, traveling the country in motor homes, helping people living on the streets who needed help. This vision was the beginning of Erika's healing. She began establishing the nonprofit organization[3] having no idea how she was going to get the first motor home. I had a deep sense of knowing that when Erika was well enough to go on the road, the motor home would be there for her. I told her, "Don't worry, it will be there," and went about thanking God for the motor home that I knew was on the way. And sure enough, the motor home showed up, the gift of a very generous man.

When it came to trusting my knowing for myself, however, it was not as easy. *What if I was wrong?* I thought. What if my inner knowing told me something, but it never happened? I hadn't worried about this with Erika because I knew God would show up for her, but what about me? I realized that I believed in the power of my prayer for others, but not for myself. I finally decided to start trusting my knowing for myself and to pray in gratitude for what I had and for what I knew was coming. This has made an enormous difference in my ability to surrender to the will of God. By trusting my deep sense of knowing, I am trusting God.

I used to pray for help in healing the darkness within me— the fear, anxiety, anger and judgment—and to become an instrument of God's love and compassion. Now I also pray in gratitude, knowing that this is *already* true, even though I don't realize it 100 percent of the time.

Our prayers of gratitude are already answered, and our prayers for help in learning what is loving toward ourselves and others will always be answered. Our prayers for help in facing whatever darkness is in the way of our being pure instruments of love and compassion will also be answered. Whenever you invite God into your heart, you will be presented with what-ever lessons you need to continue on your spiritual path. Spirit always supports your highest good—not necessarily in the earthly, material sense but in the spiritual sense of your soul's evolution. You may not get what you want in the earthly sense—getting into the school you want, getting the job or the house or the relationship you want, getting pregnant when you want to, getting the money or prestige you want—but you will always get the information and the lessons you need to evolve your soul toward love.

Your loving prayers for others—the prayers for their high-est good—will also be answered, but, as with prayers for your-self, you need to accept that you do not know what is in their highest good. If you pray for someone to heal from an illness, but it is time for them to leave this planet, you may believe that your prayers have not been answered. You need to recog-nize that when you pray for a specific outcome, you may not get what you want because it may not be in your, or another's, highest good.

As I write this, I am in an airport in Springfield, Missouri. My flight has been delayed, which means I will probably miss my connecting flight from St. Louis to Los Angeles. It is fairly important for me, on an earthly level, to arrive in Los Angeles early, so I am certainly hoping to make my connecting flight. But I also know that I have no control over the outcome and that whatever the outcome, I can learn something. Learning something, whether it be letting go of more of my attachment to time on the earthly level or accepting my powerlessness over the situation, may be more supportive of my highest good on the spiritual level than arriving on time in Los Angeles.

So, while I hope to make my flight, what I am praying for is simply my highest good, which I cannot always know. I pray the first part of the Serenity Prayer:

> God grant me the serenity to accept the things I cannot change,
> The courage to change the things I can,
> And the wisdom to know the difference.[4]

By praying these words, I am asking for God's help in keeping my inner peace and in making inner peace more important than arriving on time. And, by thanking God for all opportunities to learn and evolve my soul, I manage to stay light-hearted instead of feeling put out by the vagaries of air travel.

The more you pray from gratitude, love and faith instead of fear and the desire to control, the more powerful your prayers are. We are in fear when we do not have the faith that we are being spiritually guided. We are in fear when we operate from our wounded self, feeling separate from God. We are in faith when we invite God's will into our hearts. Our challenge on this planet is to move out of fear, anger, shame, judgment and hurt, and into faith and love.

Giving to Get and Self-Sacrifice

Self-sacrifice comes from the false belief mentioned in the last chapter: "If I sacrifice myself for others, I don't have to take care of myself. God will do it for me. God owes me for all the good I do." This belief always reminds me of the joke about Joe, whose house was flooded during a huge rainstorm.

First a neighbor came by in a rowboat and called to Joe, who was standing on a table.

"Come on, I'll row you to safety."

"No," said Joe. "I have been praying to God and doing good deeds my whole life. God will save me."

Soon the water was up to the second floor. Another neighbor came by in a powerboat and the same thing happened. The water rose still further. Joe was standing on his roof when a helicopter came by. Again he refused help. Then Joe drowned.

When he got to heaven Joe was furious. "God, I have been praying to you and sacrificing for you all my life. Why didn't you save me?"

"What do you mean?" God said with a puzzled look. "I sent you two boats and a helicopter."

There are two different motivations for giving. When you give for the pure joy of giving, when you are filled with love and the love flows over, giving is a wonderful expression of your true Self. Often, however, many of us *give to get*, which is just another way to control. Sometimes it takes the form of praise, affection or sympathy, which we offer others as a way to win their attention and approval. The same can be true of volunteering time or giving time to charities. It all depends on our intent.

Many religious doctrines teach that being a good person means self-sacrificing, and if you do not sacrifice yourself for others, you are selfish. This is backwards. What's truly selfish is trying to control others into sacrificing themselves for you.

Many of the people I work with ask me, "If I do what I want and someone else is upset by it, aren't I being selfish?" I tell them the story of my grandmother who, being an orthodox Jew, believed we shouldn't do anything on Saturdays. She lived with us and took it upon herself to make sure I was a "good girl." When she caught me breaking her rules by doing my homework on a Saturday, she shamed me unmercifully, shaking her head while making a "tsk, tsk" sound with her tongue. "How can you do this to me?" she would say. "You are so selfish." I quickly learned that anytime I did what I wanted, even with no intent to harm anyone else, I was considered selfish if someone was upset by it. It was only after I grew up and started healing that I realized that it was *she* who was being selfish by expecting me to give myself up to fall in line with her beliefs.

Our society's definition of "selfish"—which parallels my grandmother's—often makes it difficult for people to take responsibility for themselves. Instead, they are praised for sacrificing themselves and taking responsibility for others. The result is a nation of people embroiled in dysfunctional, codependent relationships.

Since God's love is a free gift, it cannot be won by self-sacrifice. It is far healthier for each of us to stop trying to control others and God by sacrificing ourselves for them. Instead, we need to take responsibility for ourselves, for making ourselves peaceful and joyous. Then we will naturally give because it feels so good and makes us happy to do so, not out of fear, obligation or guilt.

Shame

It can be a little difficult to see how feeling ashamed is a form of control. Let's start by reviewing how core shame—the false belief that you are essentially bad—begins. When, as infants and young children, we were neglected, shamed or physically or sexually abused—all of which constitute spiritual abuse—we had only two choices about how to see things. We could see the truth, which was that our parents were wounded and did not know how to love us, and that we were helpless to do anything about it. Or we could believe the abuse was our fault—that we were defective, inadequate, unworthy and unlovable.

Because admitting we were helpless might have filled us with the deepest despair—especially as infants when having some power over getting our needs met was a matter of life and death—most of us chose to avoid the truth. Instead of blaming our parents, we blamed ourselves. We developed core shame ("It's my fault they don't love me. I'm worthless") as a brilliant defense against that despair. After all, if we believe that it is our fault we are not loved—that we are so bad we *cause* others to be unloving to us—then the power to change this, to get love, is in our hands. We can try to be good. Thus, we can control getting the love we need from others. (Or so we think.) We do the same thing with God.

Operating out of shame—believing that you are inherently bad and inadequate—may be your way of trying to get God to do things for you. If you really believe you are inadequate, then you obviously cannot take care of yourself. Someone else—or God—has to do it for you. This is how core shame absolves you of personal responsibility.

As long as we hang on to our false belief in our unworthiness, we can convince ourselves that we can fool others and God into loving us by hiding our shame and trying to do things right. We become *addicted* to shame because it protects us from the truth that we really have no control over others and God. We can't *make* them love us. While we can *influence* whether others like us or approve of us, we have no actual *control* over them. Yet, if we operate from the false belief that our *best feelings* come from others loving us and giving us what our parents didn't, we will continue to try to control getting this. Until we know that our best feelings come from giving ourselves the love we need and sharing that love with others, we will continue to try to get what we need from others, driven by the pain of our core shame.

Until we give up our illusion of control over others and God, we will never understand what we do have control over: our own choices and our own intent. Personal power, which is knowing what we *do* have control over and taking action, eludes us until we accept that we are helpless over other people and God. The paradox is that we cannot move into personal power until we accept our powerlessness over everything but ourselves.

Giving up control becomes easier when you open to God and discover how irrelevant trying to make God love you is. *There is nothing you can do to earn God's love and nothing you can do to stop it, other than shutting it out of your consciousness.* You can abandon God, but God will never abandon you. God's love for you is as ubiquitous as the air you breathe. When you know you are loved no matter what, control becomes superfluous.

Despite what some religions say, knowing God and feeling shame are mutually exclusive. When you know God, you also know that the perfect love that is God exists within you, that the essence of your soul is God, is love. When you know that you *are* love, you move beyond shame and beyond the need to try to manipulate anyone or anything into loving you.

Shame may also serve as a defense against being confronted with things about yourself that you do not want to look at. I once had an employee who used her shame to control people in this way. If ever I was the slightest bit unhappy with something she did, she felt terrible about herself and started crying. This made it very difficult to let her know when something needed to be done differently.

We may use shame the same way with God. Feeling ashamed is one way of not hearing God's lessons and instructions for us. "God won't talk to me. I am nothing. I am not good enough." By clinging to our shame, we protect ourselves from learning God's will for us and escape having to take loving action based on it. Our shame may actually be our wounded self's way of avoiding not just personal responsibility, but also spiritual growth.

For years I attempted to help people heal their core shame, yet over and over I found they could not get free of their awful feelings. Affirmations didn't help. Therapy didn't help. Nothing seemed to help. One day when one of my clients was expressing her feelings of shame, I got the sense that shame was not the root feeling. Then I heard my spiritual Guidance telling me that the woman's shame was a protection against far more painful feelings: helplessness and loneliness. I was told that the reason this woman's shame was so hard to heal was because it was an addiction. An addiction is anything we use to protect ourselves from what we deeply fear.

Shame is simple to heal, but it is not necessarily easy to heal. Your shame will vanish when:

1. You have the courage to feel your loneliness when someone's heart is closed toward you rather than attempting to control feeling the depth of that loneliness by deciding it is your fault that the other is closed to you.

2. You have the courage to feel and accept your helplessness over whether someone opens or closes his or her heart to you.

3. You are willing to take responsibility for compassionately managing—with God's help and the help of others—your feelings of loneliness and helplessness and to gratefully accept this opportunity to evolve your soul.

Victimhood and Blaming

Being an emotional victim—as opposed to being physically victimized, such as getting mugged—means that we choose not to recognize that, as adults, we have choices. When we are being victims we deny the fact that we have free will to choose our path and that our feelings—our anger, hurt, anxiety, depression or misery, as well as our peace and joy—are a result of the path we chose rather than the result of others' or God's choices. The moment we think our pain is being caused by something outside ourselves, we choose to be victims.

Caroline Myss, in her wonderful book *Anatomy of the Spirit*,[5] states: "Managing the power of choice, with all its creative and spiritual implications, is *the essence of the human experience*. All spiritual teachings are directed toward inspiring us to recognize that the power to make choices is the dynamic that converts our spirits into matter, our words into flesh. Choice is the process of creation itself."

As with shame, choosing to be an emotional victim and denying that, as adults, we have choices absolves us of personal responsibility for those choices and their consequences. As long as we believe we are victims, we believe we are not responsible for healing our present misery.

The seeds of victimhood and blaming are planted when we try to control God and others. Ironically, the fruit of those seeds is that we end up with the very feelings that our control tactics were designed to prevent: aloneness and loneliness. We feel alone because we cannot connect with God when we try to control God, and we feel lonely because others back off from us when they sense that we are trying to control them. Next, we blame God and others for our painful feelings instead of seeing that our feelings are the consequences of our choice to control instead of to love. Finally, we believe that if only we feel miserable enough, God and others will see our misery and bail us out by giving us the love we want.

Believing you are a victim and blaming always go hand in hand. If you believe you are a victim of others' or God's choices, then it is their fault you feel so badly. When you blame someone, you make them responsible for what is going on inside you. Until you accept the truth that *your* wounded-self feelings come from *your* choices and that *you* are responsible for *your* thoughts, beliefs and actions which create these feelings, you will be stuck on the earthly level.

One of our greatest challenges is to understand what it means to take personal responsibility for our own feelings and behavior. It is especially difficult to do this when someone is behaving in a way that feels hurtful—attacking, blaming, lying, shaming and the like. We want to think that our feelings of anger, hurt or guilt are caused by the other person's behavior (or from God bringing that person into our life). How often have we said or thought, "You make me so mad!" or "You hurt my feelings"?

But if you pay close attention to your feelings, you will discover that it is not others' behavior that creates your distress, but your own thoughts and behavior in response to them. For example, let's say my friend Mary is angry with me because I haven't called her in a long time. The truth is, I don't feel a real connection with her and I haven't been motivated to call. One day Mary calls and says, "You don't know how to be a friend. I have to do all the reaching out. If I didn't call, we would never talk. I don't think you even care about me."

I've learned that how I respond to Mary and how I end up feeling is a direct result of whether I come from fear or love. If I come from my fearful, wounded self—the part of me that fears disapproval and defines my worth through others' eyes—then I, too, will use blame and shame in an attempt to regain control over how Mary sees me and treats me. I may attack back: "How dare you blame me for the problems in our friendship? Whenever I do call you it takes you forever to return my call. You're just projecting your own lack of caring onto me." Or I may pacify: "Mary, please don't be angry with me. You're right, I haven't been a very good friend lately. It's not that I don't care about you." Or I may become defensive: "Look, Mary, I've been overwhelmed. Things are really difficult for me right now. If you were really a good friend, you would find out what is going on in my life before getting angry at me."

Once we end the conversation, I may feel like a victim of Mary's attack or I may berate myself for not calling her more often. I will either blame her or myself. I may also blame God for bringing into my life people who treat me badly.

Regardless of who I blame, I end up feeling bad—hurt, abandoned, angry or guilty—and I believe that how I feel is a result of Mary's anger at me, that I am a victim of her choices and God's choices.

But what if instead of coming from fear, I come from love? Then I have the choice to open my heart to my spiritual Guidance, asking for help in responding to Mary in a loving way. I have the choice to surrender to God's will and allow my response to come *through* me from God instead of from my wounded self. In this case, I might say, "Mary, I understand that you're feeling hurt and uncared for by me, and I'm open to hearing your pain. Can we talk about it without the blame? I do have some very good reasons for not calling you, and if you'd like to explore this with me, perhaps we could resolve this in a caring way. If you just want to blame me, then I'd rather talk about it when you're not angry."

By setting a boundary against being blamed and not taking responsibility for Mary's feelings, while letting her know that I am open to resolving the issue, I respond in a way that is loving to both of us. If Mary refuses to stop blaming me and is unwilling to open up and explore her desire to blame, then I can disengage from the conversation. "Mary, I'm unwilling to continue a conversation when I am being blamed. Please call me when you are open to resolving this with me."

Continuing the conversation when I am being shamed and blamed is not good for me—or for Mary. Even though she may feel furious that I will not allow her to blame me, this is still the most loving action I can take for both of us. I may feel sad that Mary will not open up to me. I may feel a pang of loneliness about it. But I will not feel angry, hurt or victimized. By taking responsibility for myself through staying connected with my own feelings and with my spiritual Guidance, I am able to take loving action for myself—as well as support Mary's highest good by refusing to accept her unloving behavior. This leaves me feeling empowered instead of victimized.

As adults, we are no longer helpless over ourselves, over how we feel (though we are—and always will be—helpless over others). Whenever I allow others to treat me disrespectfully, I feel victimized. I have discovered that whenever I do not set good limits against being treated badly or respond with anger or blame to another's anger or blame, I feel awful. And it is easy to think that I feel awful because of how I have been treated instead of how I am treating myself and others. The moment I set loving boundaries against disrespectful behavior and refuse to treat the other person with disrespect, I feel powerful, lovable and worthy.

None of us likes to think of ourselves as victims. Therefore, it comes as a shock to most of us to realize how often we allow ourselves to be victims. We are victims any time we give another person the power to define our worth. We are victims any time we make our addictions to approval, sex, substances, things or activities responsible for our feeling happy and lovable. We are victims any time we blame another or God for our feelings of fear, anger, hurt, aloneness, jealousy or disappointment. When we define ourselves *externally*, we hand away our power to others and then feel controlled by their choices. When we define ourselves *internally* through our connection with God, we move into personal power and personal responsibility.

We always have two choices: We can try to find our happiness, peace and safety through our addictions—including our addiction to trying to control others and God—or through our connection with God, bringing love to ourselves and others.

The wounded part of us hates and fears the thought of being controlled by others or by God. When there is no loving adult to set appropriate boundaries against being controlled, the wounded self protects itself by going into resistance. Resistance is a form of control—over not being controlled. This is such a big subject and has such a powerful effect on so many of us, we'll need to spend some time with it. So the final chapter in this first section of the book is The Resistance Syndrome: When Resisting Is More Important Than Loving.

FOUR

The Resistance Syndrome: When Resisting Is More Important Than Loving

Gregory was raised by a mother who tried to program his every thought. There were rules for everything, from the right way to speak to her to the right way to wipe his bottom. The moment Gregory did not do things her way, his mother withdrew her love, becoming a block of ice. Because Gregory's father was not around much, his mother was all he had. He needed her to survive. So Gregory capitulated. He gave himself up in order to get her love. He did everything her way. He allowed her to control him, to take over his life until almost nothing of the real Gregory was left.

But a tiny part of him refused to give in. It found little ways to resist, to keep him safe from being completely consumed. One of these was dawdling. Not only would Gregory dawdle, but when he finally did what his mother wanted, he did it badly, always making some mistake that drove her crazy.

Now, as an adult, Gregory finds himself procrastinating, even over things he *wants* to do, such as connecting with

God. This is especially difficult since Gregory is a minister. The moment Gregory knows God's will for him, he finds himself procrastinating. He puts off acting on God's will. He just doesn't get around to it. He dawdles. When he does get around to acting on it, he makes mistakes. And because Gregory doesn't understand why he procrastinates and makes so many mistakes, he can't change his behavior. He is stuck.

Whenever God speaks to him, Gregory (and his wounded Inner Child, who is really running the show) hears his mother's voice, and he automatically resists. His mother's need to dominate him—which came from her own unhealed spiritual abuse—left Gregory with a terror of being consumed by anything or anyone, *including* God. His resistance is so pervasive, in fact, that he even resists his own good intentions for himself.

The old power struggle between little Gregory and his mother is now being reenacted inside the adult Gregory. The part of him that wants to stay safe from control struggles with the part of him that wants to open to God's love and get things done well and on time. Until Gregory becomes aware of this battle, his resistance will keep winning.

❈ ❈ ❈ ❈

People who resist learned early on that resisting was the only way to maintain their integrity in the face of invasive, controlling parents or other caregivers. This may have been true when they were children, but it's not true now. In fact, when you are driven to resist out of fear of being controlled, you are not free to make your own choices. You are not even free to do the things you know are best for you. Paradoxically, *you are actually controlled by your resistance.* What used to safe-guard your integrity now cheats you out of your personal freedom and sabotages your ability to grow and change.

The problem goes even further. As we saw with Gregory, people who had to resist controlling parents often transfer this resistance to their relationship with God. They then find it impossible to surrender to God—and God's love—for fear of being controlled and consumed by God the way they were by their parents. They believe on the deepest level that they would have to give up themselves to be loved by God.

I discovered this pattern while working with clients who seemed to be stuck in their healing process. I call it the Resistance Syndrome. It occurs when your fear of being con-trolled is so great that resistance becomes your identity, your essential way of interacting with the world. In the same way that a fish cannot see the water it swims in, you may not even be aware of your resistance. You cannot see it, but on some level you believe you must have it to live.

The Resistance Syndrome is often why people get stuck in their recovery, why their healing seems to go just so far and no further. It is a key reason why people have not been able to open to God and experience God's love firsthand. But, despite how powerful and pervasive the Resistance Syndrome is, I have not seen it described in this way before. We'll spend this chapter looking in depth at the syndrome and seeing how it plays out in different people and different situations. As you read, see if anything rings a bell for you. In my experience, the simple act of recognizing the Resistance Syndrome at work in our lives and choosing not to continue it is like taking an express train to emotional and spiritual well-being.

There are six symptoms of the Resistance Syndrome. Most people who are caught up in this syndrome will identify with at least three of them.

1. *Being stuck:* No matter how much therapy you have, how many different healing processes you try, how many self-help books you read or how many workshops you attend, you don't feel better. Nothing is working. You are stuck in your unhappiness, your relationships, your work, and you often feel alone and misunderstood.

2. *Having had controlling parents:* One or both of your parents were controlling—invasive, overprotective, engulfing, consuming, physically or sexually abusive, shaming or critical.

3. *Wanting to change but not taking meaningful action:* You seem to have the best of intentions to really take care of yourself in new ways. You decide on some new actions you'll take, but somehow you never seem to carry them out for more than a few days or a few weeks at the most. No matter how many resolutions you make to follow through, you never do.

4. *Denying your real motivation:* You say you want to change—to become loving, successful, happy, responsible, spiritually connected, slender, sober, healthy, on time, organized and so on—yet it never happens. You are in denial about the fact that you have a more important goal, which is not to be controlled by anyone or anything, not even by your own good intentions.

5. *Resenting the goal:* While you say you want to be loving, successful, responsible, healthy, organized and so on, you

resent the very thing you say you want. You may even, at times, judge it as being an unworthy goal: "People who jog are too obsessed with their appearance. Why are looks such a big deal in our culture?"

6. *Getting satisfaction out of others' frustration with you:* When people react negatively to your lack of action or your obstinate behavior, you feel gratified, like a rebellious adolescent who is winning the power struggle with his or her parents. You might even feel a gloating satisfaction when your therapist is not able to help you get "unstuck." You might feel this same satisfaction with regard to God, who also cannot get past your resistance.

* * * *

Why is having control over not being controlled so important to us? How did resistance become so much more important than loving in our lives? Resistance is one of the consequences of spiritual abuse. If our connection with God (and with our true Self, the God within) was cut off in childhood, we do not have a consistent source of love and safety in our lives. And if God isn't there to protect us, to reassure us that we are safe, we must protect ourselves. We may do so by resisting all forms of control.

This is especially true if your parents were extremely invasive and consuming in their attempts to control you. Such children often feel overwhelmingly helpless, alone and lonely. As we saw earlier, these are almost intolerable feelings, especially for a child. (In fact, the purpose of all addictions is to avoid these feelings.) So you came up with little ways—or sometimes big ways—to resist your parents, to assert your power, to hang on to some tiny part of yourself. Over time, this resistance came to be the only thing that made your wounded Inner Child feel safe. You became addicted to it. Resisting became part of your identity.

As we saw in Gregory's case, the Resistance Syndrome can sabotage your relationship to others, to yourself and to God. Let's look at resistance to others first.

Resistance to being controlled by other people falls into two categories: overt resistance and covert resistance. Overt resistance includes all the ways we openly try to stop others from controlling us: explaining to them why they should not be treating us the way they are,[1] defending our position, blaming them for their behavior and getting angry at their invasiveness. Covert resistance includes all the surreptitious ways we try to thwart others' efforts to control us: withdrawing our attention or fading out, digging in our heels and being stubborn, giving them the silent treatment, procrastinating, forgetting, doing the opposite of what is being requested of us, getting tired, falling asleep, lying—and denying that we are doing any of the above.

Behind Every Stuck Person
Lurks Resistance

Let me tell you about my first clear experience with what I now recognize as the Resistance Syndrome.

Elisa had been working with the Inner Bonding method for a few years and had done much healing around her past abuse issues and with her family, especially her abusive mother. Her work and her relationships were going well. From the outside, it looked like Elisa had everything, but inside she felt anxious, empty and sad much of the time. When she was with others, she frequently got angry and irritated at them about minor things. She found this especially disturbing because it was exactly the way her mother had treated her.

Elisa clearly heard her inner voice asking for what it wanted (such as less stress and more sleep), but she didn't respect its wishes or take responsibility for her feelings of anxiety, sadness and emptiness. She also heard the voice of her spiritual Guidance, yet she rarely asked it for advice and even more rarely took action on what she was told. As to her wounded Inner Child, Elisa knew that she existed and needed her love, yet she persisted in hating her. When Elisa looked at her life, she was completely mystified at her inability to love herself and to take meaningful and loving action on her own behalf. She was truly stuck.

Elisa attended one of my five-day Inner Bonding intensives to try to break through her stuckness. On the fourth day she was working one on one with me and feeling frustrated with her lack of progress.

"I hate my wounded child," Elisa told me. "I think she is bad. I don't want to love her. I can't love her. I know I should. I know I'm supposed to. I know no one else can do this for me, but I don't want to."

As I listened to these words, something in Elisa's voice and manner suddenly struck me—she looked and sounded like a rebellious adolescent secretly gloating over the fact that her parents could not make her do what they wanted. "Ha, ha, you can't make me" was the feeling I picked up. I later came to recognize this gloating satisfaction as one of the six symptoms of the Resistance Syndrome.

"Elisa," I asked, "do you feel resistant?"

"Yes!" she shouted. "That's exactly what I feel."

Knowing her background, I was aware that Elisa was brought up by an extremely controlling mother.

"Elisa, what do you think your mother wanted from you the most?"

"She wanted me to love her," she promptly replied.

"So you did everything she wanted you to do. You gave in to her control, except in this. She could not make you love her. Is that right? She could not control you in this area?"

"That's right! I remember being seven and deciding that I would never love her. I knew that no matter what she did to me, she could not make me love her. And it was not just her she wanted me to love. She wanted me to love my sister and be loving in general. She wanted me to be a sweet, loving girl."

"So this is where you took your stand against being controlled? This is where you said 'No, you can't make me'?"

"Yes!" Elisa's hands tightened into fists. "She could make me do everything else, but she couldn't make me be loving."

"So in order for you to be loving now to your Inner Child, you would have to give in to your mother's demands? You would have to let her think she has won?"

"Oh my God! That's what has me stuck! I can't be loving because my mother will think she has control over me, and I can't stand that thought."

"So you would rather be miserable than let your mother think she won?" I asked softly.

Elisa was silent for nearly a minute. Then she looked directly at me and said, "That is exactly what I've been doing, but I didn't realize it. And you know what? I don't want to do that anymore."

"What if your mother thinks she has finally gotten control over you?"

"Well, that makes me feel kind of sick inside, but it would be better than being irritated and angry so much. Yes . . . I think I can live with her thinking she has control over me."

"Maybe you've been in a power struggle with your mother all this time without even realizing it—one that you seem ready to let go of. Do you think that by resisting being controlled by your mother, your life has been controlled by the power struggle?"

"Yes," Elisa said. "I see that now. It's like I've been controlled by my own resistance!" Excitement had flooded her cheeks with color. "This makes so much sense. I feel like a door is opening in me."

I saw the shift in Elisa as she sat before me, and I knew that this insight would profoundly change her ability to love others. But Elisa would have to address a second part of her resistance before she could fully heal.

"Elisa," I continued in a gentle voice, "being a loving person also means loving yourself. And that means loving your wounded Inner Child, the part you keep saying you hate."

"Oh, yeah. The bad part." She frowned. "What does that have to do with resisting my mother?"

"Well, the part you call 'bad' is just like your mother— angry, irritated, even controlling sometimes. Really loving yourself means dropping any judgments you have made about yourself and your mother and healing that wounded child, the child who got so hurt by your mother yet learned to be like her in many ways. You have been very resistant to loving this wounded part of yourself."

"I get it. Because my mother tried to make me love her, I resisted, and that meant resisting loving any part of myself that was like her. The thing is," Elisa continued, shaking her head, "I do love my mother, even though she is still controlling sometimes. And I really am just like her sometimes. So I guess I can learn to love that part of me if I don't have to resist her control anymore." She let out a deep breath. "Whew . . . I feel so relieved!"

Elisa's face broke into a radiant smile I'd never seen on her before. She was shining, bubbling over with joy. When I saw her the next morning, she was still exuberant, laughing, hugging other people in the workshop, overflowing with joy. Her soul was beginning to taste freedom after all those years of bondage to the power struggle inside her. Resisting control, instead of loving, had been Elisa's savior, her God, albeit a false one. Now she was free to choose the path of love, the love that truly *is* God. Watching her from across the room as I sipped my tea, I realized that Elisa looked like she had just been let out of prison.

The next time I noticed the Resistance Syndrome at work was at another five-day intensive a few weeks later. I was working with Annette, whom I had just met. Annette had not used Inner Bonding before, but she had sought out many other forms of healing for her misery. Like Elisa, she was stuck.

As Annette sat with me on the second day of the intensive, attempting to explore her issues, she kept collapsing into tears—the helpless, miserable tears of someone who feels like a victim. Looking at her, something did not feel right to me. Here was a very attractive, obviously bright and talented woman in her forties, with an aura of power about her and a loving and generous heart—yet she was very unhappy. She felt victimized. Something was definitely wrong with this picture.

I suddenly realized that Annette was resisting something. Remembering my experience with Elisa, I asked, "Annette, was one of your parents controlling with you?"

"Yes, my mother was very controlling. Everything had to be her way."

"Did you give in to her?"

"Yes, I was a good girl."

"What do you think your mother wanted from you the most?"

Without hesitation Annette answered, "To be happy. She used to point her finger at me and say, 'Be happy. Just be happy.' I think she felt if I wasn't happy, she wasn't a good mother."

"Were you happy?"

"No, I never was."

"So you gave in to your mother's control in everything else, but this is where you took your stand. This is where you tried to maintain some sense of self, some sense of integrity. In this one way your mother could not control you. She could not make you be happy."

"That's right! Wow! I just remembered throwing stones in the creek one day when I was about ten and vowing to myself that there was nothing she could do to make me be happy!"

"So all these years you have been in a power struggle with your mother, refusing to be happy, believing on some deep level that you were maintaining your integrity and sense of self by resisting being happy?"

"Yes. I really have . . . . That's pretty ironic!" Annette said, giving me a wry grin. "I'm the one who's suffering from not being happy, not her!"

In that moment, I saw the dark cloud under which Annette had lived her life start to lift. I sat there stunned at the seemingly instant transformation. Annette's tears dried up and her wry grin was replaced by a beatific smile that slowly spread across her face, a smile that I would see often during the remaining three days of the intensive. After thirty-odd years of resistance, Annette was finally free to be happy.

Is It Really That Simple?

On the flight home after the intensive, I thought hard about what had happened with Annette, and earlier, with Elisa. Their healing seemed so quick, so magical, like opening a jail door and freeing the soul. Had I stumbled onto something wonderful, something that could help people who were stuck? Was it really that simple? Did people only have to *recognize* the resistance that had been running their lives to be free of it?

In the weeks and months that followed, I started seeing the Resistance Syndrome everywhere, every time someone was stuck in their healing process. And I noticed that while some people who recognized the power the syndrome had over them were freed from it, others had a harder time choosing true freedom over the illusion of freedom from control.

Neil, a young man in his mid-twenties, was an example of someone who had this difficulty. His mother, who tried to completely run his life, had always wanted him to be thin, while his highly critical and financially successful father wanted him to make a lot of money. When Neil came to see me, he was immobilized in his life. As you might guess, he was seriously overweight, emotionally shut down and unwilling to find meaningful work even though he had a brilliant mind. Resisting his parents had become far more important to Neil than getting unstuck and taking good care of himself.

Unfortunately, recognizing how the Resistance Syndrome was controlling his life did not even begin to free Neil from it, as it had with Elisa and Annette. Instead he made the conscious choice to continue to resist. In Neil's case, resisting his parents—and thus getting back at them for trying to control him—was truly more important to him than loving himself. Being right about how awful his parents were, and punishing them for it, was more important than being happy.

Looked at in these terms, doesn't Neil sound more like an angry seven-year-old than a grown man? That's exactly what's going on behind the scenes. When your wounded Inner Child is in charge of your life—as Neil's was—you may eat doughnuts for dinner, get to work an hour late and skip your exercise routine. The next day, however, you may do just the opposite. You may force yourself to get up an hour early, have a green salad with no dressing for lunch and jog four miles instead of two. This Dr. Jekyll-Mr. Hyde behavior is due to the fact that, at any given moment, your wounded self is being either permissive or authoritarian, just as your parents were. Both kinds of behavior are based on false beliefs and both are unloving.

This is how the Resistance Syndrome makes us resist even ourselves. Any time your wounded self tries to exert power over you with rigid rules, internal criticism and unilateral decisions that ignore your feelings, you are trying to have control over yourself. This sets off a power struggle between the authoritarian part of you that wants control and the permissive, indulgent part that resists being controlled with all its might.

Let's say your authoritarian part lays down the law:

"From now on, I'm cutting out fats."

"I will write down everything I eat."

"No more drinking. It's ruining my marriage and it's time to stop."

"Tomorrow morning, I will start my new exercise program."

"I'm putting myself on a budget right now. No more extras."

"I will get up early tomorrow."

What usually happens when you do this? Your good intentions are short-lived, aren't they? They don't result in long-lasting change. That's because they get sabotaged by your permissive part, which experiences any attempt at control—even self-control—as life-threatening. It will fight tooth and nail to repel it. This makes sense when you remember that when you are caught in the Resistance Syndrome, resistance has become your identity. Any assault on your identity feels like a deadly attack.

So your permissive part responds to the authoritarian part with fury:

"You can't tell me what to do! I can eat whatever I want."

"One drink won't hurt."

"I'm the boss of me. I don't have to do what you say. I don't like exercise."

"Leave me alone. I'm really tired. I need to sleep late."

The result of this power struggle is a standoff. Neither side wins. The voices of the authoritarian part and the permissive part are equally loud and equally convincing. And behind each of them is a compelling set of false beliefs. For example, your authoritarian part may believe: "I have power. I can control what and how much I eat, drink, smoke and spend money. I can control my health, my weight and my addictions. I can do this by myself, without help."

In the meantime, your permissive, indulgent part believes: "I am nurturing myself and rewarding myself when I eat whatever I want, drink whenever I want, sleep in or watch TV instead of exercise and buy whatever I want. The only way I can be my own person is to resist what is demanded of me, even if I am resisting myself."

Paradoxically, the goal of both parts is to keep you safe. But it's a goal you can never reach without giving up the very strategy you think is protecting you.

❊ ❊ ❊ ❊

Being willing to give up your lifelong resistance can be very frightening. I saw this clearly in a client named Brittany. Brittany and I had worked together for a number of months and she had done a lot of growing, but now she was stuck. Her friendships and love relationships were not going well and her employer was constantly yelling at her, as had most of her previous employers. Her connection with God was sporadic.

One of the symptoms Brittany and I had explored at different times was that she seemed to fade out whenever difficult feelings came up. Sometimes she would even fall asleep during her work with me. This, combined with the fact that

Brittany had a controlling father, suggested to me that she might be stuck in the Resistance Syndrome.

"Brittany," I asked her one morning, "what do you think your father wanted from you the most?"

"He wanted me to listen to him."

"So you gave in with everything else, but he couldn't get you to listen?"

She broke into a sheepish, yet self-satisfied smile. "Yeah. It drove him crazy. He would end up yelling at me, 'Why don't you ever listen?'"

"So this was where you drew the line? He could not force you to listen. He could force you to do a lot of other things, but not to listen."

Laughing, Brittany said, "Yeah, that's right!"

"What does your employer say when she is yelling at you?"

Brittany's eyes widened. "I can't believe it—she says the same thing! She is always saying to me, 'Brittany, why can't you just *listen?*' It drives her crazy." Again came the gloating, self-satisfied laugh.

"What about in here, in our sessions?" I asked. "Do you think I am trying to control you when I bring up difficult issues?"

"I guess so," she conceded, shifting in her chair. "It feels like you are invading me somehow."

"So you just fade out?"

"Yeah, but that doesn't make sense. I'm here to get help."

"Maybe resisting what you perceive as control or invasion feels safer. Maybe it's more important to feel safe than to get help."

"But it's ruining everything—my work, my relationships. Nothing is going right."

"That's true. But your first priority seems to be keeping yourself safe by resisting control. Until you decide it's more important to be loving to yourself and others—which means being willing to listen and learn, even if it feels like you are being controlled—you will keep fading out."

"But that's crazy!"

"Not to your wounded self. To the wounded part, it makes perfect sense to resist, to hold the line against being totally consumed."

"Margie, I feel like going to sleep right now."

"I guess your wounded child doesn't like being talked about."

"Well, I know I've got to deal with this for my life to get better, but I sure can feel the part of me that would rather fade out, no matter what the cost."

Brittany shifted her gaze and stared out the window. After a few moments, she said in a small voice, "The idea of giving up this resistance feels so scary. It feels like I'm going to die." Tears filled her eyes. She looked terrified.

❊ ❊ ❊ ❊

The desperate intensity of Brittany's reaction made perfect sense to me, and I have since seen it in many people who are confronting the need to drop their resistance. I think there are three reasons for it.

First, if you have used resistance all your life to keep yourself safe, giving up resistance must feel, at first, like opening the door to a lynch mob. Unless you have learned how to set loving boundaries against being invaded by others, it is just too scary to give up your resistance. In addition, you may have spent so much time resisting that you have no idea who you are other than a person who resists. You may even fear that underneath all the resistance you are empty, dark, full of holes. That you have no core Self, no essence. If so, losing your identity as someone who resists—even if it's a false identity—will always feel life-threatening. Finally, because resistance was the primary way you protected yourself from the pain of feeling powerless to prevent invasion, it came to be an addiction. And, as many of us know, giving up an addiction that is keeping our pain at bay (or so we think) feels like dying.

Brittany faces a hard decision. She can give up her resistance and start to listen to other people, thus accepting the fact that she may feel at first as if others are controlling her. Or she can continue to create a façade of safety based on her resistance and her refusal to listen, thereby accepting the fact that she will continue to suffer problems in her work and her relationships. She has to decide which is more important to her: resisting control or being loving. Of course, what Brittany wants—what we all want in our wounded self—is to continue to resist while enjoying the results of being loving. If she persists in her denial, lying to herself that this is possible, she will stay stuck.

Revealing the Hidden Agenda

Being stuck in your life, work or relationships is a painful way to live. Yet time after time, when I speak to new clients, they tell me "I decided to work with you because I am stuck. I am repeating the same patterns over and over again, both at work and in my relationships. I can't seem to find my way out of this rut I'm in. There must be more to life than this." The truth is that while they think they truly want to get unstuck from weight problems, health issues, power struggles with a mate, debt, alcohol, anger or depression, they actually have a hidden agenda.

See if this fits for you. Consciously, you want to get unstuck, be free from the pain in your life, but unconsciously something else is far more important to you. Getting unstuck means that you need to change your mind about your deepest desire, your deepest motivation, your intent. You have to move off the wide road, the earthly path, and onto the narrow road, the spiritual path.

You may say that your desire is to be loving and open to learning, growing and taking responsibility for yourself and for your own feelings. You may say you are on a spiritual path, eager to evolve your soul and connect with God. However, the fact that you are stuck indicates that you have a deeper desire, a more prevailing intent *to have control over being controlled*. As long as safety from being controlled is more important to you than loving yourself, others and God, you will stay stuck.

As you can imagine, the Resistance Syndrome can wreak havoc with intimate relationships.

Suzanna came to see me because she was unhappy in her marriage. She had been married to Jason for thirty-one years and was very confused about why she was so unhappy since she knew that she still loved him. Not only was Suzanna depressed, she was sick much of the time and couldn't seem to discover the reason.

As we talked, it became apparent that Jason was very stuck, both in his neediness and in the Resistance Syndrome. As a child, Jason had a very invasive mother and an absent father. He had withdrawn early in life to protect himself from being engulfed by his mother's invasiveness. While Jason professed great love for Suzanna, his actions were not caring. He was either pressing her to meet his needs—being as invasive as his mother had been—or he was resisting giving Suzanna what she wanted, especially caring, empathy and emotional intimacy—just as he had resisted giving in to his mother. While Suzanna saw that she sometimes *was* controlling, she also saw that Jason perceived her as controlling even when she wasn't.

Over time, Suzanna worked hard on letting go of her controlling behavior, hoping that Jason would then be able to drop his resistance, but things got even worse. As soon as Suzanna disengaged herself from her unhealthy struggle to control him, Jason felt abandoned. His alarm bells went off and he started pulling on Suzanna for time, sex and attention. Then, as soon as she started coming toward him again, he retreated emotionally. She couldn't even offer a suggestion to Jason without his shutting down and resisting. Suzanna finally realized that Jason saw her as his mother, no matter what she did.

Jason was trapped between a rock and a hard place, between fear of engulfment and fear of rejection. He was stuck and didn't want to do the inner work necessary to get unstuck. In the end—and much to Jason's dismay—Suzanna made the difficult decision to leave the marriage.

Everyone who is unhealed has both of Jason's fears in varying degrees, depending upon the level of spiritual abuse they suffered. People who have a terror of engulfment have an underlying and even deeper terror of rejection. As children, they suffered from unbearable rejection when they did not capitulate to their parents' invasive demands. And, because they were not taught they were unconditionally and inherently lovable, they do not know that their very essence is love. In fact, they let others define their essence, their worth. In doing so, they become dependent on someone else's definition of who they are and thus put themselves at risk for even greater rejection. *Fear of rejection is a direct result of not having defined our own worth, not knowing our own light and lovability.*

When you are intimate with someone, fear of rejection can make you think you have to give yourself up, do everything they want, and take responsibility for their feelings. Naturally, this triggers the fear of engulfment. In the heat of this fear, you withdraw and shut down, as Jason did, cutting off the very connection you seek. The person on the other end of your behavior gets confused. First they see you desperately wanting to connect with them and pulling on them in various ways to get it. But if they open up to connecting with you, they experience you pulling away.

Sonya and Ian had a relationship similar to Suzanne and Jason's, but with a much better outcome. They came to one of my intensives, during which Ian recognized his own Resistance Syndrome. He even remembered making the decision early on in his life to not do what his mother wanted him to do, no matter what it was. Ian would act like he was complying, but each time he found some way to sabotage his performance.

When Ian interacted with Sonya, whom he loves very much, his wounded self was in charge. He would shut down to whatever she wanted from him, which resulted in a total lack of affection and connection toward her. Ian also professed to want affection, yet he pulled away whenever Sonya reached out to him. When she then withdrew, he called her cold. Sonya ended up feeling confused and frustrated. She just couldn't win. When she voiced her frustration, Ian would tell her that it was her fault because she was so controlling.

At the intensive, Ian gained a clear understanding of the Resistance Syndrome and how it was affecting his relationship. But I did not encourage him to release it. Instead, I told him to continue to resist but *to choose resistance consciously rather than unconsciously*. This, as I will explain below, is the first step out of the resistance trap.

When Ian watched himself *choosing* to resist, he stopped operating on automatic pilot. Suddenly a new choice became available to him. He could choose to resist or choose to act a different way. For the first time ever, he was able to reach out to Sonya with love rather than holding back out of fear of engulfment. There wasn't a dry eye among us as we witnessed their love being openly expressed.

Ian learned another crucial lesson that day. He discovered that when he stopped resisting being controlled by Sonya, he started being able to connect with God. He no longer resisted God.

For resistant people, the answer to the question, "Do I have to give up me to be loved by God?" is a resounding "Yes!" The thought of surrendering to God and being controlled by some outside force is terrifying to them. It triggers all their old fears of engulfment. This presents a terrible dilemma: You cannot know who you really are, the love that is your very essence, without a connection with God; yet in connecting to God you fear losing your own essence. Fear of rejection plays a big role in resistance to God as well: You might feel you have to let God control and consume you in order to win God's love, and that God will reject you if you don't do it right.

If your parents didn't bring through Divine Love to you, the only way to know your own light and lovability is by receiving that information from your spiritual Guidance. Yet you cannot connect with your Guidance when you are resisting being controlled by God! And without a spiritual connection, you have no consistent source of safety and love in your life. So you must protect yourself. And that means resisting all forms of control, which means you can't connect with your Guidance.

Is this really a vicious circle? Or is there a way out?

The Freedom to Choose Differently

There are three things you can do to break the cycle of resistance that prevents you from having a firsthand experience of God's love and wisdom:

1. Notice that resistance is a choice and notice yourself making that choice.
2. Notice the consequences of that choice.
3. Make a new choice that becoming a loving human being is more important than whether or not you are being controlled.

Once you have accomplished these tasks, you will be able to successfully use the Six-Step Process to have a deep daily dialogue with God—and learn once and for all that you do not have to give yourself up to be loved by God.

The first task is to be willing to notice—*without judging yourself*—when you choose to resist. This may sound simple, but it represents a huge shift in consciousness. When you really see that resistance to any given situation is a choice, you no longer operate on automatic pilot. You have taken the first step out of denial and into awareness. In that very moment, you start seeing that you can make other choices, such as choosing love instead of control. Noticing when you choose to resist is the beginning of changing your intent.

If you find you resist seeing your resistance—that is, if you resist the awareness that resistance is a choice—back up a step. Start watching yourself, noticing your feelings kindly and without judgment. Notice how you feel when someone wants something from you. Do you feel uncomfortable? Do you think those feelings are being caused by the other person? See if you can tune in to the fact that your feelings arise from your own fear of being controlled, not from what the other person is saying or doing. No one can *make* us feel anything. They may trigger certain feelings in us, but we ourselves are the source of our feelings. For example, if someone calls you a cheapskate and you know you are not, you may laugh or simply dismiss the remark. But if deep inside you feel you really *are* a cheapskate, that person's remark may bring up feelings of anger or shame. Your reaction is *your* responsibility. So how do you end up feeling when your fear forces you to resist? How do you end up feeling when you make resisting control more important than loving?

Now ask yourself this. Are there things that you want for yourself but resist because someone else also wants them for you? Notice what happens inside if someone urges you to do something you actually want to do, such as be on time, eat well, exercise, pray or take time for yourself. Watch yourself procrastinate and notice how you feel when you do. Do you feel like a child who's winning a game or an adolescent who's getting away with something? Later, once your procrastinating self has won, do you still feel like a winner? Or do you end up feeling like you are the one who lost?

If you are honest with yourself, you will discover that instead of maintaining your integrity, you have lost it. You will see that the belief held by your wounded self that resisting maintains your integrity is false. *In fact, you maintain your integrity only when you make choices based on spiritual Guidance, on what is truly loving to yourself and others, not based on your fear of losing yourself.*

* * * *

Once you notice that your resistance is a choice, you are ready for the second task in conquering the Resistance Syndrome: noticing the consequences of your choice to resist. Choosing to live from fear forces us to walk the wide road, the earthly path. It closes our hearts and ruins our relationships. It pushes us into addictions and makes us turn to others for attention and approval.

You may be reading this book because you yourself are stuck. Being stuck is the direct consequence of choosing resistance instead of growth and spiritual connection. Look at your life. In what areas is it not working? Is your love relationship thriving? Are you satisfied at work? Do you have a caring circle of friends? Do you take exquisitely good care of your body? Do you want to change but nothing works? Now ask yourself if resisting control is really worth all that pain. Or would you consider making a new choice?

Now that you have noticed the *choice* you are making and have been honest with yourself about the *consequences* of that choice, the door is open for you to take the final step to getting unstuck. The power to free yourself from the invisible shackles of resistance is entirely yours.

The third and final task in breaking through the Resistance Syndrome is to make the conscious decision that becoming a loving human being is more important to you than protecting yourself from being controlled (or from someone's thinking they control you). In other words, you actually need to be *willing to be controlled* without putting up your wall of resistance. This does not mean, however, that you will be controlled.

That's the paradox of giving up the Resistance Syndrome: When being a loving human being is more important to you than resisting being controlled, *you don't ever get controlled*. That's because when you choose to be loving, you can move into the Six-Step Process through which you will experience Divine Love, heal your wounded self, and learn to set healthy, loving boundaries (instead of the hostile, controlling boundaries seen in overt resistance). When you are in resistance, you only focus on what's happening externally—someone is trying to control you, and you've got to get safe by resisting. When you change your intent and choose to make loving more important, you focus on what's happening internally.

You create safety for your Inner Child and do whatever you need to do to take care of yourself. (You will learn the specifics of how to do this later in the book.) You no longer have to resist to avoid being controlled. Instead, you learn to handle engulfment and rejection in ways that are loving to yourself, and to set appropriate boundaries against being invaded, consumed and controlled by others.

Until you are willing to accept that you cannot control others' attempts to control you and choose to make love a higher priority than fear, you will stay stuck in your resistance to yourself, others and God. Your constant fear and vigilance against being consumed will keep you occupied with the darkness. You will not turn toward the light and true spiritual growth until it becomes more important to evolve your soul into oneness with the love and compassion that is God than whether or not you are controlled by others or by God.

There's a boomerang effect with the Resistance Syndrome. The more our wounded self tries to make us feel safe, the more unsafe we feel. And the more we try to protect against loss of freedom, the more unfree we end up feeling. The problem is that true safety and freedom can never come from trying to control and resisting control. In fact, the more you control and resist control, the more unsafe and insecure you end up feeling. *That's because each time you choose control instead of love, you undermine your sense of self.* Attempting to control others not only violates them, it violates your true Self, which is love. Since your true Self—and the true Selves of others—is an individualized expression of God, whenever you do anything that harms yourself or others, you violate God. This violation of your true Self is what creates the lack of safety, security, peace, joy and freedom you experience.

True safety and freedom result from developing a spiritually connected, loving Adult self, who is able to make loving choices for you, set loving boundaries with others and freely give to others without feeling a loss of self. When you allow yourself to be guided by God instead of your resistance-prone, wounded self, you will discover your personal power and true integrity.

Becoming a person who honors and welcomes God instead of resisting God is a vital part of the spiritual journey of evolving the soul.

SECTION II

Living
with
God

This section describes the newly expanded
Six-Step Inner Bonding process for healing
your false beliefs and having a direct personal experience of the unconditional love,
truth, wisdom and power that is God. As
you use this Six-Step Process, the false
beliefs that create your fears of being controlled or rejected by God are replaced by
truth. Shame is healed as you learn to love
yourself through experiencing the limitless
and unconditional love that is God.

FIVE

Inner Bonding: Beginning the Six Steps

In the first four chapters, we saw what life without God looks—and feels—like. You understand now *why* you don't have to give up yourself to be loved by God. You have seen the harm that trying to control others and God can wreak, and you may have identified the Resistance Syndrome at work in your life. Now we are going to start to change things. You are going to experience the Six-Step Process of Inner Bonding that I have used with literally thousands of people to help them have direct daily contact with God and thus know their own divine worth.

First, I want to share with you how Inner Bonding came into my life.

The Path of Discovery

I was born on a farm in upstate New York. I have clear memories of being outside in my playpen when I was around eight months old, communing with nature and feeling what I would now describe as a oneness with God. I remember the warmth of the sun, the freshness and openness of the air, the smell of the grass and the exquisite beauty of the butterflies that drifted past. I remember the feelings of joy and peace and the connectedness I sensed with everything around me.

My grandfather, who lived on the neighboring farm, used to come and sit with me. I felt our deep love and connection with each other. My grandfather was a very wounded person. No one liked him and, until I came along, he had never deeply loved anyone. But he was gentle with me. His heart opened and the love flowed between us. As a little child, I interpreted this to mean that I had *caused* him to open his heart. Looking back, I can see that because of this, I developed the false belief that I could heal wounded souls by causing them to open their hearts, too. I also believed it was my responsibility to do so. These false beliefs set the stage for much of what I later did in my work and my relationships, behavior that resulted in much pain for me until I discovered these beliefs and healed them.

When I was thirteen months old, we left the farm for Los Angeles. I never saw my grandfather again. Our country was at war, and fear hung over the city. I recall lying on a bed in a crowded, dingy apartment complex and looking up at the air. I could see the denseness and darkness of the energy—babies often see things that adults can't see. I had lost the brightness and clarity of the air in the country. I had lost the warmth of the sun and the smell of the grass. I had lost my grandfather, and I had lost my sense of connection with God.

Soon after coming to Los Angeles, I got very sick and

almost died. At that time, I established the second false belief that governed much of my behavior in my relationships: If I am not connected with someone I will die. As a result, much of my behavior became motivated by my desperate need to control getting this connection with others.

Looking back, I can see that the search for connectedness drove my actions from the time we left the farm. I hated being an only child. I used to beg my parents to give me a brother or sister. My deepest desire was always to connect with others, to feel our oneness instead of my loneliness and fear. My parents were very loving, but I was a mystery to them. Unable to connect with God or themselves, they could not connect with me in the deep way I needed.

My profound desire to connect with others, combined with a deep belief that life was more than what it seemed on the surface, motivated me to begin a spiritual search in my early twenties. This search took me into many different forms of therapy—psychoanalysis (four days a week for four-and-a-half years), Jungian, neo-Reichian, Ericksonian, humanistic-existential therapy, Transactional Analysis, psychosynthesis, rebirthing, Rolfing, past-life regression and hypnosis. I joined a meditation group, and I worked with various healers in my attempts to connect with myself, others and God.

Each experience was beneficial but none brought me the inner peace and joy I sought. Why was the deep connection I longed for so elusive? What was I missing?

I married and struggled for years trying to discover how to have a loving relationship. The marriage brought me wonderful children and much learning, which my former husband and I wrote about in our book, *Do I Have to Give Up Me to Be*

Loved by You? But something was still missing. I still had no personal connection with God, and my connection with my husband was sporadic. No matter how hard I tried, I couldn't keep my heart open to others during conflict. I wanted so much to be loving, but I was often angry, critical and controlling. As a result, my ability to maintain a deep connection with others was limited.

I tried prayer and meditation, but that didn't seem to be the answer either. Sometimes, when I prayed with others, I got a fleeting sense of God's presence and was filled with hope. Then it would be gone. Try as I might, I couldn't make that connection on my own. I just didn't know how.

During those years I also grappled with illness, going from doctor to doctor, from chiropractor to homeopath, trying to understand why I was exhausted and hurting so much of the time. I studied nutrition, ate only organic foods, took supplements and exercised. I rented an art studio and took two days off a week to pursue painting, something I had always loved. Yet I was often in a puddle of tears in my art studio, feeling sick, miserable, lonely, wondering what could be so wrong.

By 1984, I had run out of things to try. On the outside, things looked fine. I was married, had three beautiful children, a career I loved, a successful book, an art studio and enough money to do what I wanted, and I'd had tons of therapy—but I still wasn't happy. I just felt lost. Like it or not, I had to face the fact that I needed more help than I knew how to get for myself. So I prayed for a teacher to come into my life, someone to lead the way, someone I could learn with and learn from.

It has often been said that when the student is ready the teacher appears. I guess I was ready. A few months later, I met

Erika Chopich, Ph.D., who has since come to be my dear friend, my coauthor and my companion on the spiritual path. Erika had half the Inner Bonding process, and I had the other half. Together Erika and I developed Inner Bonding. I wrote a book by that name, and we wrote two books together, *Healing Your Aloneness* and *The Healing Your Aloneness Workbook*.[1]

Most importantly, however, it was through Erika that I finally learned how to have a direct personal experience of God.

✳ ✳ ✳ ✳

One morning in late 1992, Erika called me in a panic. She had moved the previous year to Santa Fe, New Mexico, and was living in a beautiful house on pristine land.

"I think I'm going nuts!" she told me. "I must be hallucinating!"

"Why? What happened?"

"This is really crazy. Last night I got into bed and there at the foot of my bed was an old Indian woman. I got scared, thinking she was a homeless person who had somehow got in. I asked her who she was and why she was in my house. She said, 'I am your spiritual Master Teacher.'"

"That's great!" I replied. Among the many things I'd tried in order to heal my own emptiness was contacting my spiritual guides, messengers of God who could bring me Divine Love and wisdom and let me know God's will for me. It had never worked.

"No it's not!" Erika shouted. "I told her I didn't want a teacher. This is all too hooey-wooey for me."

I smiled, thinking of Erika's medical training and her scientific mind.

"Don't tell her to leave!" I said. "You aren't crazy. She's here to teach you."

"Margie, I don't want this stuff. This is too weird."

Well, of course her Teacher came back. No protests from Erika could stop it from happening. Finally, Erika accepted that her Teacher was here to stay and let herself learn from her.

In my own attempts to meet my spiritual guides, the closest I had gotten was when I painted. Each time I stood before a blank canvas, I saw a beautiful silvery-haired woman smiling down at me and radiating light. So I painted what my "artistic imagination" saw. She is in almost all of my paintings.

One evening, after Erika had learned how to contact her Teacher, we were talking on the phone. I wasn't feeling very well and was lying on my bed.

"Erika, do you think you can see my Teacher?" I asked.

"I don't know," she answered, "but I'll try."

There was silence on the phone for a few minutes. Then I heard, "Oh my God. This is really weird!"

"What?"

"I'm here in my house, but I think I'm also in your house. I see your Teacher working on your body. Are you lying on your bed? Wearing a pink sweatsuit?"

I was—and I was stunned.

When Erika described my Teacher, I recognized her instantly. She was the radiant silver-haired woman whose beloved image already hung in every room in my house.

I longed to know more. "I only see her when I paint," I protested, "and she doesn't talk to me. Erika, ask her how I can see her and hear her when I'm not painting."

There was a short silence. Then Erika said, "She says that to connect with her you must be in the same creative state that you are in when you are painting. She says . . . well, she says to try it in the bathtub."

❄ ❄ ❄ ❄

As peculiar as this suggestion was, it proved to be a life-changing piece of information. The first time I relaxed in a tub of steaming hot water and tried connecting with my guide, it worked. As I lay there and imagined myself painting, the radiant image of my Teacher suddenly filled my mind. I was thrilled. I held the image in my mind, and I realized that when the image of my Teacher came to me while painting, I had never thought to ask her a question. So now I asked her question after question, and I was overjoyed to receive clear answers—some in words, some in pictures and some through feelings. I now converse with my Teacher each morning when I walk and throughout the day when I need guidance. Through her, I gradually learned to feel God within and around me each moment.

Having this contact with Spirit has completely changed my life. I am no longer exhausted. Writing used to be hard. Lecturing and teaching seminars used to be hard. Even my hobbies, drawing and painting, used to be hard. Now they are easy, due to my very tangible and direct connection to God. My relationships are thriving and I walk through my day knowing I am a beloved child of God. The sick, miserable aloneness I lived with for so long is gone.

In addition to having a personal experience with God, I often receive information from other people's spiritual guides in the form of pictures and words. This is how I do much of my work with my clients now. I also help my clients connect with their own spiritual mentors, guides, Teachers or angels. I have done this successfully with clients ranging from construction workers and housewives to artists, physicians, lawyers and accountants. I will teach you how to do this, too, if you desire to have a guide. However, it is not necessary for you to "image" a guide in order to have direct contact with God. There are many ways of establishing this contact, which you will learn in a later chapter.

Inner Bonding has changed my life. As you can see, I struggled for years to find happiness. I prayed to be shown how to overcome the shame, fear and false beliefs that ran my life and kept me separate from God. I yearned to evolve my soul and become an instrument of God's love on this planet. I prayed for a process that would teach me how to rediscover my core Self, my essence, and connect with the unconditional love and truth of God.

God answered my prayers by bringing Erika into my life and helping us, through our Teachers, to develop the Inner Bonding process. Erika and I have been evolving Inner Bonding for the past fourteen years. As each year passes, Erika and I receive a deeper understanding and experience of this profound process.

God gave us Inner Bonding for a purpose. God puts each of us on this planet to be an expression of Divine Love. Being God's pencil (as Mother Teresa put it) means being God's loving hands, voice, intent and actions. Through our loving actions we bring the divine spirit of love and compassion through us, and we express God on this planet. The Six Steps of Inner Bonding will show you how to evolve your soul and become an instrument of God's love.

Inner Bonding Definitions

Let's start by defining six terms you'll need to master before using the Six Steps. Some of these I have referred to in previous chapters. Here I present them in detail. This section will also serve as a review of the key points you need to understand for the Six-Step Process of Inner Bonding to work.

Intent

Our *intent* is what governs how we think, feel and behave. Our intent is the most powerful and creative force we have; it is the essence of free will. Your intent is your deepest desire, your primary motive or goal, your highest priority *in any given moment*. There are only two primary intents:

- To learn about loving yourself and others, even in the face of fear and pain.
- To protect yourself from fear and pain with addictive, controlling behavior and thereby avoid responsibility for your feelings and actions.

When your intent is to learn to love, you are willing to face your fears and feel your painful feelings in order to understand how you may be creating them and discover what you need to do differently. The deeper purpose here is to become one with

God. When you open to learning, you move toward God. No fear gets in the way. When your intent is to learn to love, your deepest desire is to find your safety, peace, lovability and worth through an *internal* connection with God.

When your intent is to protect yourself from fear and pain, and avoid responsibility for your feelings, your deepest desire is to find your safety, peace, lovability and worth through *externals,* such as attention, approval, sex, substances, things and activities. When you believe that others and God are responsible for how you feel, you try to control them in order to feel safe and worthy.

In every moment, each one of us chooses our intent either to feel safe by controlling or to learn to become God's emissary of love upon this planet. When you deeply desire to heal from your spiritual abuse so as to become one with the love that is God, you choose the spiritual path, the path of the heart, the path of courage—the intent to learn to love. While the choices that others make may influence you, no one but you has control over your intent. Not even God can control your intent, since that would negate your free will. In each moment, you choose what is most important to you, and in each moment you have an opportunity to change your mind.

Ultimately, it is the wounded self that decides whether to learn or to protect. Some part of our wounded self hits bottom and says, "I've had it with living like this. It's not giving me what I want. It's not working. There must be something better out there, and I want to find it."

Now here's an important distinction. The *intent to know* is not the same as the *intent to learn.* The intent to know comes from the wounded self wanting to know what to do and how to do it "right" in order to have control over getting what it wants—attention, approval and so on. People can even get addicted to gathering information; they think it will give them more control. Having the intent to learn means that you do not have to know what to do. You only need to open to your spiritual Guidance, and you will be directed.

Core Self and Wounded Self

We have already talked a little about the core Self (also called the true Self or essence), as well as about the false, wounded self. It is helpful to imagine the core Self as a bright and shining child, the natural light within that is an individualized expression of God. This aspect of ourselves is actually ageless—it always has been and it always will be; it evolves through our life experiences. Our core Self contains our unique gifts and talents, our natural wisdom and intuition, our curiosity and sense of wonder, our playfulness and spontaneity, and our ability to love. This is the unwounded aspect of the soul. It can never be harmed. It was never touched by the spiritual abuse we suffered. Instead, the core Self was hidden away. It waits to be retrieved through a healing process. Because of this unbroken part in each of us, complete healing can occur. Your healing is complete when you have fully retrieved and deeply know this aspect of yourself, who you really are—a child of God.

The wounded self is also a child, a wounded child who learned to be an unloving Adult. Another term I use for this aspect of ourselves is "child-adult," because this part of the self is like a child who had to learn to be a little adult, who had to take care of things that should have been beyond his or her responsibility. This is the wounded aspect of the soul. Our child-adult is often a mirror image of one or both of our parents. Even though we may have said, "I'll never be like that," our wounded self learned to be just like our parents.

Your wounded self is the aspect that was harmed by the spiritual abuse, and it carries all the fears, false beliefs and controlling behavior that result from spiritual abuse. While these fears, beliefs and behavior cause us pain in our adult lives, they were the only way we could feel safe when we were children. Your wounded self—your child-adult—can be any age in any given moment, depending upon how old you were when you learned a particular false belief, addiction or way to control.

Your wounded self has many parts that were developed to handle various aspects of abuse, especially if there was severe physical or sexual abuse. You may have a mean, angry or violent part, a withdrawn part, a lewd or obscene part, and a "nice" part who learned to be a "good" boy or girl. You may have a part that uses food, drugs or alcohol to numb out fear and loneliness. All the parts of the wounded self need healing, and they can be healed only through compassion, acceptance and unconditional love. Once you understand that these wounded parts of yourself were your survival mechanisms in childhood, you can feel grateful and compassionate toward them instead of judgmental. Your challenge is to learn to love the parts of yourself that you usually judge.

The wounded self is always trying to protect against a perceived threat of rejection or engulfment, a threat experienced in the past and projected onto the present or future. Through anger, blame, resistance, capitulation or withdrawal, the wounded self hopes to ward off and control that which it fears. In addition, the wounded self is in denial—protecting against experiencing the pain that results from *its own choices*. The wounded self always sees itself as a victim of others' or God's choices. It believes others or God cause its pain.

Almost any activity can be used as a protection against your pain. It depends on your intent. For example, meditation can be used as a way to connect with God and learn about loving, or it can be used to bliss out and avoid dealing with your feelings every time your anxiety comes up. There are many people who have meditated for years without improving the quality of their lives because they have used meditation as a way to avoid pain rather than a way to learn. Likewise, reading the Bible can be a way to help you open your heart and move into your lovingness and your desire to learn, or it can be used as an anesthetic, an addiction, a way to avoid yourself and your fear. When the Bible is used this way, it often becomes a tool to control others and God, to make God love us more or reward us. Neither the ancient Hebrews nor Jesus intended this sacred text to be used to manipulate and control.

The intent to protect—the choice to control others and God rather than to open to spiritual Guidance—automatically closes your heart. When your heart is closed, you cannot bring through truth and Divine Love, and you cannot give and receive love with others. You are alone inside and this terrible aloneness then drives your wounded self to try to have control over getting love to stop the painful feeling of aloneness. Can you see what a vicious circle this is?

One of the major false beliefs of the wounded self is that we, as separate egos, cut off from God, can have power over ourselves and others. We can, to a certain extent, control others' behavior (although not their feelings), but not without violating ourselves and others. The wounded self is willing to violate the core Self and others to have this control. As wounded child-adults, we violate ourselves through substance and process addictions.[2] We violate others through controlling (and sometimes violent) behavior. Whenever we violate ourselves or others, we are act from our wounded self.

Your wounded self is codependent; that is, it depends upon others to define its worth. It does not know your core Self, the spark of the Divine within you, because it does not know Divine Love. Like Jennifer in chapter 2, who yelled at and blamed her husband for her aloneness, and Guy in chapter 3, who pulled on me and others for approval, you hand the job of defining your worth over to others—and continue the cycle of woundedness by trying to control getting others' love, approval and attention in order to feel worthy.

False Beliefs

In chapter 2 we looked at the eight major false beliefs about God that are held by the wounded self. But the wounded self has *hundreds* of other false beliefs, many of which we adopted when we were very small. A false belief is a belief about ourselves, others, the world, the universe or God that limits and disempowers us, causing us to fear. Our false beliefs are the conclusions we drew about ourselves, others, the world, etc., as a result of our spiritual abuse. Our false, self-limiting beliefs cause much of our pain *and* much of our behavior that causes us pain. For example, if you concluded (falsely) from your childhood experiences that you are bad, unlovable or unworthy, then you will generally behave as if this were true. Your resulting behavior, such as anger or withdrawal, which is geared to protect you from the rejection or engulfment that you fear, may actually result in others rejecting you—which is just what you expected. This brings you pain and reaffirms your false belief about being unlovable. In addition, the very act of choosing to protect rather than to love is an abandonment of your core Self and further reaffirms your belief in your unworthiness.

Our false beliefs are the lies we have learned that cause us unnecessary fear, anxiety and pain. We know a belief is false when the belief itself causes us fear, anxiety and pain. We then protect against the fear, anxiety and pain *caused by our false beliefs* by sinking into our various addictions.

The following chart lists some of the false beliefs carried by the different parts of the wounded self. Remember, these are the wounded parts of us that need welcoming, embracing and healing. As you read this list, be sure to put your judgments aside and compassionately embrace the parts you identify with.

False Beliefs of the Wounded Self

The Domino Effect of Core False Beliefs

- I am a victim. I am not responsible for my own feelings and behavior. Others' or God's unlovingness to me causes my feelings and behavior.

- God is judgmental, controlling, too busy or nonexistent. God doesn't love me, just as my parents/caregivers don't love me. I project my parents' feelings and behavior onto God and conclude that God has abandoned me.

- Therefore, I am alone in the universe and I cannot handle the pain of aloneness. I won't survive if someone I love/need disconnects from me.

As a child, unable to bear the helplessness and despair of this aloneness, I concluded:

- It is my fault I am not being loved because I am intrinsically flawed, defective, damaged, bad, wrong, inadequate, unimportant, unlovable or unworthy [development of core shame].

Without God to define me, others are responsible for defining my worth and lovability. Therefore:

- I must and can have control over getting the love I need to feel worthy and avoiding pain to feel safe.

- I must and can control people, my feelings, God and the outcome of things to feel safe and worthy.

- I can have control by hiding my flaws through looking good or doing everything right.

The wounded self develops many controlling aspects that come from the victim and core shame beliefs.

Defender
- BELIEF: I can explain to others how they should see things and get them to see me the way I want to be seen. I can talk them out of seeing me as bad or wrong.

Fixer/Lecturer
- BELIEF: I know what is right and it is my job to point out to others when they are wrong. My worth is in advising and fixing people and in being right.

Blamer
- BELIEF: I can intimidate others with anger and blame into feeling afraid or guilty enough to give me the love, attention, affection, sex or approval I want/need.

Critic/Judge
- BELIEF: By criticizing and judging myself and others, I can get myself and others to change and be the way I want.

Complainer/Martyr
- BELIEF: If I complain verbally or with silent suffering, others will feel sorry for me and give me the love, attention or sympathy I want.

Pleaser
- BELIEF: If I compliment others, do nice things for them and smile a lot, they will give me the approval I need.

Caretaker/Rescuer
- BELIEF: I'm responsible for others' feelings and behavior.
- BELIEF: If I sacrifice myself to take care of others, they will give me the love and approval I need.
- BELIEF: I am selfish if I take care of myself.

(Chart continued on following page)

Taker • BELIEF: I can control getting the love, attention, sex or approval I want by invading others' boundaries with touch, anger, invasive or needy energy, incessant talking or emotional drama.

Bully/Predator • BELIEF: If I physically control others through threats, violence or rape, I can get what I want from others and feel powerful and safe from being violated and controlled by others.

Avoider • BELIEF: I can find a way to feel good if I deny my pain, my fear and the truth about myself and others.

Worrier/Obsessor • BELIEF: If I think long and hard enough, or if I perform certain rituals, I can control how others feel and act and the outcome of things. If I worry enough, I can stop bad things from happening.

Clown • BELIEF: If I can be funny enough, I can control getting others to give me the approval and attention I need, and I can prevent them from withdrawing, getting angry or disapproving of me.

Perfectionist/ Performer • BELIEF: If I look perfect, act perfect, say the right thing, achieve and perform right, I can control how others feel about me and treat me.

Resister • BELIEF: I can stay in control and avoid being controlled by others, by God, or even by my own inner critic by numbing out, spacing out, forgetting, withholding or procrastinating.

• BELIEF: Resisting being controlled is essential to my integrity.

Addict • BELIEF: I can fill the emptiness, avoid pain or feel safe if I can fill up from outside or numb my feelings with food, drugs, alcohol, sex, approval, love, spending, connection with others, things or activities such as TV.

False beliefs can have a devastating impact on our natural spirituality, as we see in the following true story told to me by my friend Don Eaton, a teacher, singer and songwriter.

A girl was born deaf at the time when nothing could be done medically to restore her hearing. Like all children, she was born with a strong connection to God's love and was naturally happy and loving and open and curious. People loved her in an especially compassionate way because they saw her as "handicapped" because she was deaf. People noticed how loving she was toward everyone in her life. Her parents took her to church and Sunday school, but she could not, of course, hear the sermon or teachings of the adults.

One day, when she was eight, a "miracle" happened. Medical advances made it possible to restore her hearing. Her parents took her to have an operation and her hearing was restored. Everyone thought she would be happy to be able to hear—and she was, at the time. But when she became an adult, she looked back and realized what she had lost when she gained her hearing.

Being able to hear the words of other people powerfully affected the little girl. She heard whom she should play with and whom she shouldn't, who the "good" people were and who the "bad" people were (which seemed to depend upon the color of their skin, what church they belonged to, what their parents did for a living or what neighborhood they lived in). She learned to fear people. She learned whom to love and whom not to love, and who would love her and who wouldn't. She learned about sin, hell and being thrown out of a garden that she thought she had been playing in all this time. She learned about a God who was harsh, strict and judgmental—a God who was completely different from the one she had known inside herself as a child.

She tried to be a good girl, so she learned all of the "right" beliefs about herself, others and God, and over time she learned not to trust her own experience of life. Eventually, the "right" beliefs that she was taught became her reality.

Now, as an adult, she is challenging that reality. She knows that everything she learned from hearing the adults in her life was the *opposite* of what she had experienced as a deaf child. She sees that although she gained her hearing, she lost her joy, her natural loving spirit and her God. And she is working to turn that around, to become deaf to all of those "right" beliefs that robbed her of her joy and her connection with God. She knows now how powerful beliefs can be, and that what you believe is what you get. She is on the path of love that will lead her back to her original experience of oneness with herself, others and God.

Inner Child

When I use the term "Inner Child," I am referring to *both* the wounded self and the core Self. Imagine a child—perhaps a sad, lonely, frightened or angry child. Imagine that within that wounded child is a beautiful light, the light of the core Self. But the wounded child does not know that this light is within. This wounded child operates from the false belief that he or she is inadequate, flawed, wrong, unlovable, unworthy—that his or her core is dark instead of light. Only when we are able to bring the love that is God through to the Inner Child will the wounded child heal enough to discover the light within.

Your Inner Child is an infallible communication center. It lets you know through your feelings what is good or bad for you, right or wrong for you. The feelings you may experience coming naturally from the core Self are the joy, peace and love that, as an adult, are the result of being loving to yourself and others. The core Self also has the natural feelings of sadness and sorrow (over people's inhumanity to each other, for example), loneliness (when you have no one with whom to share love), grief (over loss), helplessness (over others' choices), outrage (over injustice), as well as fear of real and present danger. The feelings that come from the wounded self are anxiety, depression, anger, hurt, aloneness, neediness, emptiness, misery, guilt, shame, fear (of a perceived rather than an actual threat), and so on.

When we are in faith, we will not feel the fear of the wounded self. However, even when we are in faith, we will continue to feel the fear of real and present danger. This is a natural physical reaction—the fight or flight response—to help us handle danger. Too many of us, however, are often in the fight or flight response over perceived and imagined danger. This is the feeling of anxiety that troubles so many people.

All of your feelings let you know whether what you are doing and thinking is right or wrong for you. They let you know whether someone is open or closed, dangerous or safe. The tightness in your stomach in reaction to someone's threatening anger tells you something important, as does the safety you feel when someone is being truly giving. Your anxiety, anger or depression tell you that you are not taking loving care of your Inner Child, while your peace and joy let you know that you are being truly loving to yourself. Trusting these feelings and discovering what they are telling you will help you take personal responsibility for your own feelings.

Because I grew up being a caretaker as my primary way to control (and therefore feel safe), whenever my stomach was tight around others, I took this as a sign that something threatening was happening that I needed to fix. I would immediately attempt to pacify the other person so he or she wouldn't be upset with me. This would give me a temporary feeling of safety—which disappeared as soon as someone else got upset with me. Now I know that my tight stomach is my Inner Child telling me to take care of her. Instead of trying to fix others so I can feel safe, I take action for myself. My feeling of inner safety is no longer temporary and no longer dependent upon others.

The Loving Adult

The loving Adult is the vehicle through which the Spirit of love and compassion that is God thinks and acts. It is God's emissary, receiving love, truth and power from Spirit and then taking loving action in the best interests of the Inner Child. In other words, the loving Adult puts God's love into motion.

Many of us do not yet have a powerful, spiritually connected loving Adult who knows how to nurture and truly protect us and love others without trying to control them. Many of us do not have a loving Adult who knows how to set appropriate inner boundaries against our harming ourselves with addictive behavior. Nor do we have a loving Adult who knows how to set loving boundaries against harming or being harmed by others. This is because we may have had little or no role modeling on how to be a loving Adult. If your parents and their parents before them were wounded child-adults, doing the best they could from their wounded selves, they could not provide the necessary role modeling.

You, however, have the opportunity to practice a healing process that creates a powerful loving Adult. If you do not have role models for loving behavior, do not despair. We can all learn to access our guides in the spiritual realm as role models for loving action. In the next chapter, you'll start learning to access this guidance.

Until we develop a loving Adult, the wounded child-adult is in charge of our intent. There are only two circumstances under which the child-adult decides to open to learning. One is when we are in a lot of pain and realize that our protections are not working to bring us the safety, peace and joy that we want. The other is when we remember that we came here to this planet to love and evolve in our lovingness. *The memory of our soul's mission is within each of us.* Spirit attempts to remind us each day of our soul's mission in the hope that we do not have to hit bottom to shift our intent. Those of us who learn to hear the voice of Spirit may then open to learning.

Let's put together all of the terms and points we've covered and look at the two life paths you can choose and the consequences of each path. The first section of the Life Paths chart that follows shows the choice, purpose, desires and intent of the wounded self on the Earth path of fear, and the loving Adult on the spiritual path of love and courage. As you can see, the intent determines whether the heart is open or closed.

Life Paths

EARTHLY PATH OF FEAR		SPIRITUAL PATH OF LOVE/COURAGE
CONTROL in the face of FEAR	CHOICE	LOVE in the face of FEAR
To get love and avoid pain	PURPOSE	To give love to self and others
Find happiness, safety, lovability and worth through EXTERNALS such as people, sex, things, activities, substances	DESIRES	Find joy, peace, safety, lovability and worth INTERNALLY by connecting with God's unconditional love
To protect against pain and avoid responsibility for feeling it	INTENT	To learn to love and take responsibility for own pain and joy
THE HEART CLOSES		**THE HEART OPENS**

The next section of the chart shows how the wounded self reacts to fear.

THE HEART CLOSES		**THE HEART OPENS**
You turn to ADDICTIVE, CONTROLLING BEHAVIOR	REACTION TO FEAR	
ADDICTIONS TO MANIPULATING OTHERS Anger, blaming, interrogating, criticizing, judging, shaming, perfectionism, threatening, violence, withdrawing, resisting, denying, caretaking (giving in order to get), people-pleasing, complaining, demanding, defending, lying, analyzing, convincing, lecturing, pulling, explaining, telling feelings to blame, drama, illness		
ADDICTIONS TO PEOPLE Attention, approval, love, connection, romance, sex		
ADDICTIONS TO ACTIVITIES AND THINGS TV, computer/Internet, busyness, gossiping, sports, exercise, sleep, work, making money, spending, gambling, shopping, worry, obsessive thinking, self-criticism, talking, telephone, reading, gathering information, meditation, religion, crime, danger, pornography, masturbation, glamour, beautifying		
ADDICTIONS TO SUBSTANCES Drugs, alcohol, nicotine, food, sugar, caffeine		

Sometimes it is confusing to people to see reading listed as an addiction. As we saw earlier, when we talked about meditation, whether or not any behavior, thing, activity or substance is an *addiction* depends upon your *intent*. You can read for pleasure and learning, or you can read to avoid your pain. You can watch TV for the enjoyment of it or to avoid your anxiety. You can eat for nutrition and pleasure, or you can eat to numb out your feelings of aloneness. The *substance* or *the process* itself does not define the addiction—*the intent behind it does*.

The last section on the left side of the chart shows the consequences of choosing the earthly path of fear. These consequences will always result from using addictive, controlling behavior to avoid responsibility for pain.

Life Paths

EARTHLY PATH OF FEAR		SPIRITUAL PATH OF LOVE/COURAGE
CONTROL in the face of FEAR	**CHOICE**	LOVE in the face of FEAR
To get love and avoid pain	**PURPOSE**	To give love to self and others
Find happiness, safety, lovability and worth through *EXTERNALS* such as people, sex, things, activities, substances	**DESIRES**	Find joy, peace, safety, lovability and worth *INTERNALLY* by connecting with God's unconditional love
To protect against pain and avoid responsibility for feeling it	**INTENT**	To learn to love and take responsibility for own pain and joy

THE HEART CLOSES		THE HEART OPENS

| You turn to ADDICTIVE, CONTROLLING BEHAVIOR | **REACTION TO FEAR** | |

ADDICTIONS TO MANIPULATING OTHERS
Anger, blaming, interrogating, criticizing, judging, shaming, perfectionism, threatening, violence, withdrawing, resisting, denying, caretaking (giving in order to get), people-pleasing, complaining, demanding, defending, lying, analyzing, convincing, lecturing, pulling, explaining, telling feelings to blame, drama, illness

ADDICTIONS TO PEOPLE
Attention, approval, love, connection, romance, sex

ADDICTIONS TO ACTIVITIES AND THINGS
TV, computer/Internet, busyness, gossiping, sports, exercise, sleep, work, making money, spending, gambling, shopping, worry, obsessive thinking, self-criticism, talking, telephone, reading, gathering information, meditation, religion, crime, danger, pornography, masturbation, glamour, beautifying

ADDICTIONS TO SUBSTANCES
Drugs, alcohol, nicotine, food, sugar, caffeine

FEAR INCREASES		

| You feel UNSAFE and INSECURE | **RESULTS** | |

WITHIN SELF
- Sad, depressed, alone inside, lonely
- Victimized, powerless, helpless, fearful, anxious, desperate
- Empty, numb, hopeless, unfulfilled, purposeless
- Angry, hurt, jealous, envious, insecure, untrusting
- Ashamed, guilty, unlovable, unworthy
- Trapped, stuck, going in circles

IN RELATIONSHIPS
- Codependent: taker/caretaker system, dependent
- Disconnected, distant, unsupportive
- Conflicted, angry, blaming, locked into power struggles
- Violent, violating, disrespectful
- Unsexual, unable to give or receive love
- Dishonest, suspicious, undermining

When you choose the spiritual path of love and courage and open to learning about loving yourself with God, then your reaction to fear is to move into doing the Six Steps of Inner Bonding.

Life Paths		
EARTHLY PATH OF FEAR		**SPIRITUAL PATH OF LOVE/COURAGE**
CONTROL in the face of FEAR	**CHOICE**	LOVE in the face of FEAR
To get love and avoid pain	**PURPOSE**	To give love to self and others
Find happiness, safety, lovability and worth through *EXTERNALS* such as people, sex, things, activities, substances	**DESIRES**	Find joy, peace, safety, lovability and worth *INTERNALLY* by connecting with God's unconditional love
To protect against pain and avoid responsibility for feeling it	**INTENT**	To learn to love and take responsibility for own pain and joy
THE HEART CLOSES		**THE HEART OPENS**
You turn to ADDICTIVE, CONTROLLING BEHAVIOR	**REACTION TO FEAR**	You turn to THE SIX STEPS of INNER BONDING®

THE HEART CLOSES

You turn to ADDICTIVE, CONTROLLING BEHAVIOR

ADDICTIONS TO MANIPULATING OTHERS
Anger, blaming, interrogating, criticizing, judging, shaming, perfectionism, threatening, violence, withdrawing, resisting, denying, caretaking (giving in order to get), people-pleasing, complaining, demanding, defending, lying, analyzing, convincing, lecturing, pulling, explaining, telling feelings to blame, drama, illness

ADDICTIONS TO PEOPLE
Attention, approval, love, connection, romance, sex

ADDICTIONS TO ACTIVITIES AND THINGS
TV, computer/Internet, busyness, gossiping, sports, exercise, sleep, work, making money, spending, gambling, shopping, worry, obsessive thinking, self-criticism, talking, telephone, reading, gathering information, meditation, religion, crime, danger, pornography, masturbation, glamour, beautifying

ADDICTIONS TO SUBSTANCES
Drugs, alcohol, nicotine, food, sugar, caffeine

THE HEART OPENS

You turn to THE SIX STEPS of INNER BONDING®

STEP 1 **Willingness** to feel pain/fear and take responsibility for your feelings and security.

STEP 2 **Choose the intent to learn** about love and fear; invite Spirit into heart—open heart to compassion.

STEP 3 **Welcome and dialogue** with wounded selves, exploring fears, false beliefs, memories and resulting behavior that is causing the pain. Explore gifts and what brings joy to core Self.

STEP 4 **Dialogue with spiritual Guidance,** exploring truth and loving action toward Inner Child.

STEP 5 **Take the loving action**—put God into motion.

STEP 6 **Evaluate** the effectiveness of your action.

In putting it all together, you can see what the eventual results are of practicing the Six Steps.

Life Paths

EARTHLY PATH OF FEAR		SPIRITUAL PATH OF LOVE/COURAGE
CONTROL in the face of FEAR	**CHOICE**	LOVE in the face of FEAR
To get love and avoid pain	**PURPOSE**	To give love to self and others
Find happiness, safety, lovability and worth through *EXTERNALS* such as people, sex, things, activities, substances	**DESIRES**	Find joy, peace, safety, lovability and worth *INTERNALLY* by connecting with God's unconditional love
To protect against pain and avoid responsibility for feeling it	**INTENT**	To learn to love and take responsibility for own pain and joy

THE HEART CLOSES		**THE HEART OPENS**

You turn to ADDICTIVE, CONTROLLING BEHAVIOR	**REACTION TO FEAR**	You turn to THE SIX STEPS of INNER BONDING®

ADDICTIONS TO MANIPULATING OTHERS

Anger, blaming, interrogating, criticizing, judging, shaming, perfectionism, threatening, violence, withdrawing, resisting, denying, caretaking (giving in order to get), people-pleasing, complaining, demanding, defending, lying, analyzing, convincing, lecturing, pulling, explaining, telling feelings to blame, drama, illness

ADDICTIONS TO PEOPLE

Attention, approval, love, connection, romance, sex

ADDICTIONS TO ACTIVITIES AND THINGS

TV, computer/Internet, busyness, gossiping, sports, exercise, sleep, work, making money, spending, gambling, shopping, worry, obsessive thinking, self-criticism, talking, telephone, reading, gathering information, meditation, religion, crime, danger, pornography, masturbation, glamour, beautifying

ADDICTIONS TO SUBSTANCES

Drugs, alcohol, nicotine, food, sugar, caffeine

STEP 1	**Willingness** to feel pain/fear and take responsibility for your feelings and security.
STEP 2	**Choose the intent to learn** about love and fear; invite Spirit into heart—open heart to compassion.
STEP 3	**Welcome and dialogue** with wounded selves, exploring fears, false beliefs, memories and resulting behavior that is causing the pain. Explore gifts and what brings joy to core Self.
STEP 4	**Dialogue with spiritual Guidance,** exploring truth and loving action toward Inner Child.
STEP 5	**Take the loving action**—put God into motion.
STEP 6	**Evaluate** the effectiveness of your action.

FEAR INCREASES		**FEAR RESOLVES**

You feel UNSAFE and INSECURE	**RESULTS**	You feel SAFE and SECURE

WITHIN SELF

• Sad, depressed, alone inside, lonely
• Victimized, powerless, helpless, fearful, anxious, desperate
• Empty, numb, hopeless, unfulfilled, purposeless
• Angry, hurt, jealous, envious, insecure, untrusting
• Ashamed, guilty, unlovable, unworthy
• Trapped, stuck, going in circles

IN RELATIONSHIPS

• Codependent: taker/caretaker system, dependent
• Disconnected, distant, unsupportive
• Conflicted, angry, blaming, locked into power struggles
• Violent, violating, disrespectful
• Unsexual, unable to give or receive love
• Dishonest, suspicious, undermining

WITHIN SELF

• Empowered, self-trusting, free
• Grace-filled and spiritually growing
• Authentic, integrated, service-oriented
• Grateful, at one with Spirit and others
• Joyful, peaceful, serene, aware of intrinsic worth
• Creative, curious, passionate, alive, playful, spontaneous

IN RELATIONSHIPS

• Part of a spiritually-growing circle of love
• Able to resolve conflicts lovingly
• Interdependent, supportive, empowering each other
• Intimate, honest, trusting
• Respectful, kind, gentle
• Passionate, creative, playful

Living Under the Safe Umbrella or the Love Umbrella

Imagine that over each side of the Life Paths chart is an umbrella under which you can choose to live. Imagine that the Earthly Path of Fear is covered by the "safe umbrella," while the Spiritual Path of Love and Courage is covered by the "love umbrella." It would look something like this:

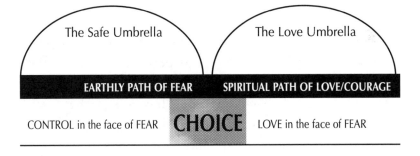

You can choose which umbrella you want to shelter you. People who choose the path of love, as well as people who choose the path of safety, will be loving when they feel safe. Both will stand under the love umbrella. When they are frightened, both kinds of people will run under the safe umbrella to protect themselves against pain. The difference is that people who are devoted primarily to their own safety will huddle in fear under the safe umbrella *until other people come and make it safe for them* to risk loving again. People who are devoted to the path of love, on the other hand, want to move back under the love umbrella as soon as possible, so they *take responsibility for making it safe* for them to do so.

When your devotion is to safety, you operate from the false belief that your emotional safety is based on things outside yourself, so you try to have control over making other people make it safe for you to be open and loving. In your heart, you believe that *others* are responsible for your feeling safe. When your devotion is to love, you know that your emotional safety comes from having a loving inner Adult taking care of you. You do your own inner work to make it safe for yourself to be loving again with others. In your heart, you know that *you* are responsible for feeling safe.

People who live under the safe umbrella open their hearts only when there is an external, dependable source of love. They depend upon others to be their source of love because they either don't believe in God or they believe that God is controlling or rejecting. Because they have no internal spiritual source of love they can depend on, they will close their hearts as soon as their external source of love is cut off, even if only temporarily.

When you feel as if you have to "walk on eggshells" around certain people, it is because they have decided to live under the safe umbrella and will retreat to their anger, blaming or complaining as soon as you do something they don't like. They will stay in a bad mood until you comply with what they want. Everyone around them has to make it safe for them to be nice again by doing everything "right." They take no responsibility for their own feelings and behavior. One of my clients described her childhood as "always trying not to wake the bear." The children had to tiptoe around, trying to avoid upsetting her father so he wouldn't yell at them.

People who live under the love umbrella are actually much more secure than the people who have chosen the safe umbrella. They are in the process of developing a loving Adult who connects to God as their dependable source of love.

Inner Bonding Versus Traditional Psychotherapy or Traditional Spiritual Practices

Traditional psychotherapy deals with healing the wounded self: remembering the past, talking it out, releasing anger and grief, and gaining insight. But it usually ignores the spiritual aspect of healing and therefore does not help us develop a loving Adult. I have worked with many clients who have given up on traditional psychotherapy. It is my experience that the wounded self cannot be healed without a spiritual connection—the grace of God.

What about traditional spiritual or religious practices? Can they provide full healing? While many spiritual practices do help us connect to God, bringing a momentary sense of peace, they generally ignore the Inner Child and the crucial healing of the wounded self. Inner Bonding unites the effects of psychotherapy and spiritual practice by healing the wounded self *and* freeing the core Self through bringing Divine Love inside to the Inner Child and expressing it via the actions of the loving Adult.

In many cases neither psychotherapy nor traditional spiritual practice improves the quality of our lives significantly. But practicing the Six Steps of Inner Bonding on a daily basis *does*. It accomplishes this by giving you a direct daily experience of God and enabling you to experience life more frequently from a state of grace—that complete feeling of love, peace and joy within.

Inner Bonding does not exclude any other therapeutic or spiritual practices. Rather, it provides a framework that includes all other processes and practices. It works no matter what your concept of God is. It works even if you do not believe in God, because you can begin using Inner Bonding by accessing the highest part of yourself, often called the Higher Self, for your Guidance. Eventually, if you keep practicing, you will have a firsthand experience of God.

Step One of Inner Bonding, the willingness to feel your feelings and take responsibility for them, can include any therapeutic modality that helps you access your feelings. This includes all forms of bodywork and breathwork, yoga, energy work, shamanic journeying and soul retrieval, dream work, movement and art therapy, as well as the more traditional forms of psychotherapy. In Step Two, moving into the intent to learn, you can use any process or meditation for opening your heart to learning. The Six Steps can be adapted to any religious or spiritual system and to any other healing process.

Inner Bonding works to heal deep past and present wounds as well as to resolve minor everyday problems. It works with both children and adults, providing there is no psychosis (there must be some grounding in reality to begin the process). No matter how deep your spiritual abuse, Inner Bonding can bring you into truth and into loving yourself and others. The Six Steps of Inner Bonding provide a clear road map to healing and loving.

Understanding, through the intent to learn, what your Inner Child needs to feel loved by you and then taking the action necessary to heal past and present pain and bring in joy and connection with God, is the heart of Inner Bonding. It is a powerful process for moving you out of the false, limiting beliefs that lead you to violate yourself and others. By learning about your false beliefs and replacing them with the truth experienced directly from God, you eliminate the causes of your fears and anxiety, thus eliminating the need for your addictive and controlling behavior.

Inner Bonding is a process that creates communion with God and opens you to your buried essence, your core Self, your untarnished and innocent soul. It is a profoundly creative spiritual process that allows you to heal the wounded self and move ever deeper into actualizing your potential and becoming a truly loving and joyful human being.

SIX

Growing Your Consciousness: Steps One and Two

I will now show you how to use the Inner Bonding process to have a direct, daily experience of God. This chapter takes you through the first two steps of the process. Steps Three through Six are covered in chapter 7. Although the Six-Step Process is simple, it is not always easy, so I am going to spend some time explaining it to you. Once you understand it, you will probably find that, with practice, it is relatively easy to use and can often be done very quickly.

For example, let's say you have a run-in with someone at work. Maybe someone has said something that you felt was rude or disrespectful. You may react by feeling hurt or angry. That happens to all of us. Most people just let feelings of hurt or anger dissipate in the course of the day. But if you are willing to take full responsibility for your feelings and spend ten minutes—or more, if necessary—to do the Six Steps, you can learn what is at the root of your upset. Once you have done that, you will know what action you need to take (which may or may not involve the other person), and you will quickly move back into an inner sense of safety and peace.

Naturally, if you have a big upset or uncover some very deep, very old feelings that hugely impact your life, you will need to spend a longer block of time with them, and maybe get some help with them. And you will probably find that these old feelings will show up again and again when you do the Six-Step Process. That doesn't mean you are doing it wrong. That means that you are slowly learning about and healing the deep wounds inside you.

You can also choose to use the Six-Step Process as an open-ended inner exploration, without waiting for there to be an upset in your life. As I walk you through the whole process, I will give you tips on how to do this.

Step One

Choose to be aware of your feelings and willing to feel your pain. Be willing to take responsibility for the ways in which you may cause your own pain, and accept responsibility for creating your own peace and joy. Make use of somatic (body-based) therapies like breathwork and deep massage to access your feelings.

You cannot begin a journey without the *willingness* to do so. Without the willingness to do whatever it takes to heal from your spiritual abuse, you will not begin the journey of healing and evolving your soul. Doing whatever it takes means that you are ready and willing to feel, understand and take full responsibility for the whole range of your feelings—from fear, anger, hurt, shame, depression and loneliness to safety, worth, lovability and joy. Willingness also means that you are ready to see how you are responsible for many of your own feelings by becoming aware of creating them with your thoughts, beliefs and actions.

Willingness is a huge step forward in your spiritual growth. It means that you have decided to face your fears, your demons, that shadow side of yourself you hide from everyone. It also means you are ready to stop hiding *from yourself*, in other words, to stop being in denial about the pain you are in. It means you are willing to see how much you want control over your pain, over others and over God. Until you are willing to see, *without judgment*, how much you want to control everything, and all the overt and subtle ways you try to have control, you cannot open your heart.

Finally, willingness means that you are ready to ask for help from God—and from others who can bring God's love through to you—to help you heal. It means that you have admitted to yourself that you cannot find the safety you seek without spiritual Guidance, that you are ready to invite Spirit into your heart to nurture and guide you. It means that you have embraced the journey, the sacred privilege of learning about love.

When I tell people that they need to be willing to feel their pain, they often say to me, "What's the big deal about that? I feel my pain all the time." But there is a world of difference between feeling pain and having the *willingness* to feel it in order to learn from it. Willingness includes the capacity to stay with the pain, explore it, own it. There is no healing in just feeling and expressing your pain. You can cry and rage forever, but if you are not willing to take responsibility for your pain, you will be stuck with it forever.

Sometimes people respond with, "Why? Why feel my pain? What's the point?" They believe that feeling pain—especially the pain of childhood—is a waste of time. "Why cry over spilled milk?" they argue. "Why can't we just try to find our joy and skip the pain?" The answer is: *because joy and pain are in the same box.* When you put a lid on your pain and stuff it back inside, you put a lid on your joy. You choose to live an emotionally stunted life. You also close your ears to the information that pain brings you.

Pain is how your Inner Child lets you know that you are behaving in ways that are not in your highest good. Pain is also your teacher in other ways. For example, if you are sawing a piece of wood and you accidentally slice into your finger, the physical pain you experience tells you to stop sawing! The same is true of your emotional pain; it tells you to stop doing the thing that is causing you pain. If you do not pay attention to your emotional pain, you will go on thinking and acting in ways that cause you pain. What's more, you will develop unhealthy, even harmful, mechanisms for *not* feeling your emotional pain: addictions to substances, people, manipulations, activities and things.

Ask yourself this. When you want to binge, eat sugar, drink alcohol, use drugs, smoke, blame, hit, appease or resist someone, run away, turn on the TV, gamble, shop, masturbate with pornography, demand sex from your partner or compulsively act out in any way, *what are you feeling?* Look back at the Results listed on the Earthly Path half of the Life Paths Chart in Chapter 5 on page 135. Are your actions driven by any of these feelings? Are you turning to your addictions to distract you from feeling lonely, sad, angry, unworthy, etc.? Can you commit to feeling these feelings *without* blocking them with addictive behavior?

Before I learned how to do this Six-Step Process, I was willing to feel my pain only about 10 percent of the time. Now it's more like 85 percent. I am telling you this so you don't think that perfection—being willing to feel your pain 100 percent of the time—is your goal. We are all human. What you want to strive for is simply to be *more* willing, *more* open, *more* aware than you are now. As I said, I can't stay open to loving all the time, and I don't know anyone who can, but moving toward that is the most worthy goal I know.

The idea of feeling your long-suppressed emotional pain may be very scary to you. The truth is, you can handle it. Your fear of those feelings is based on the beliefs about pain that you acquired in childhood, *beliefs that are false now that you are an adult*. Let's take a look at some of them.

False Beliefs About Pain

When we were very small, we could not handle our pain alone. Our little bodies were too small to endure the huge energy of physical and emotional pain, so unless we had loving parents there to help us when we were in pain, we learned various ways to numb out and endure it. As adults with grown-up bodies, we can now handle the big energy of emotional pain. Most of us don't realize this. Nor do we realize that we are no longer victims. We now have choices about staying in painful situations, choices we didn't have when we were young. We can leave a painful situation, call a friend or therapist for help, and learn to bring through Divine Love to handle our painful feelings.

What beliefs do you have about your pain? See if any of these rings a bell.

- I can't handle my pain. It's too much for me. I'll go crazy or explode into a million pieces and die from it.
- If I open to my pain, it will be unending, a bottomless pit with no way out. Better to keep a lid on it.
- There is no point in feeling my pain.
- No one wants to hear my pain. If I open to my pain, I will end up alone.
- Feeling and showing my pain is a sign of weakness and will lead to my being rejected.
- Feeling my pain makes me too vulnerable to being controlled by others and by God.

To move beyond these false beliefs, you must be willing to test them, to *prove* them false. And to test them, you must resist the urge to blunt your pain with addictions (which includes controlling behavior). You see, until you stop numbing out in the face of your pain, you will never know that you *can* feel your pain without going crazy or dying, that your pain is not endless, and that it can actually be a source of information and strength rather than weakness.

In all the years I have been working with people in pain, I have never had anyone die, explode or go crazy from opening to their pain. I have never met anyone whose pain was unending. Nor do people kill themselves from feeling their pain when they are willing to learn how to heal it, and when they reach out for the appropriate help. It is not opening to

pain and learning how to manage it lovingly that causes sui-
cidal feelings; it is sitting in pain with no inner and outer help
that causes a person to take his or her own life. Suicide may
be how the wounded self avoids taking responsibility for the
emotional pain of the Inner Child. A loving Adult would
never think of killing a child, which is what some acts of suicide are—killing the Inner Child who carries the pain. When
you open to feeling, learning about and healing your pain,
and learn how to manage and release deep pain, there is no
longer a need to avoid it.

Breaking Old Patterns

Even when we are willing to feel our pain, it can take some
practice to actually do so. Many of us are so used to ignoring
our feelings that the moment we feel a twinge of fear, anxiety
or loneliness, we open the refrigerator, pour a drink, grab a
cigarette or turn on the TV. We may even find ourselves
doing this before we *consciously* know we've had a feeling. In
order to break this pattern and learn about your feelings and
what you believe, think and do to cause them, you have to be
willing to feel what is going on inside your body.

This means learning to pay attention to the physical sensations within your body—the tightness, fluttering, heaviness,
emptiness or burning in your stomach, chest, legs, jaw, throat
or anywhere else in your body. Remember, feelings are physical sensations within your body. Old feelings and memories
from childhood are often stored in the musculature of the
body. So are feelings from the present. Because the wounded
child-adult tends to treat you the way you were treated by

your parents (or the way your parents treated themselves), some of your present-day painful feelings come from the thoughts and beliefs you learned in the past. For example, if you believe, "I have to do everything right or I will be rejected," you will probably feel anxious, maybe even panicky. Therefore, some of the anxiety in your body may be old, coming from past rejections, but some of it is current, coming from the pressure you put on yourself and your *expectation* of rejection.

Whatever the origin of your pain, you are the one who is responsible for feeling it and healing it. If you need help to feel your feelings, you can use various therapies. You might try regressive work,[1] dream work, yoga, meditation or bodywork[2] such as massage, Trager, Rubenfeld Synergy, Feldenkrais and Rosen. Or you may have spent so many years numbing out and ignoring your body that you will need some deeper form of somatic therapy such as Holotropic Breathwork (a form of deep breathing that takes you into memories and feelings) or deep tissue work (a deeper, more focused form of massage) before you can begin to tune into your feelings. If your feelings overwhelm you, you can seek out energy work, such as EMDR (Eye Movement Desensitization and Reprocessing) or TFT (Thought Field Therapy). These forms of therapy release patterns that are stored in the energy system of the body.

Some people have such deep pain from childhood abuse that they will not be able to endure opening to it until they have a solid, loving, spiritually connected Adult in place. (I will show you how to do this in Step Two.) It is not advisable to attempt to open to the pain of severe abuse on your own. If you suspect that you may have deep buried pain or if you have not succeeded in feeling your pain despite a genuine willingness to do so, it is imperative that you receive therapeutic help while practicing the Six Steps of Inner Bonding.

* * * *

Brian came to see me because he was severely depressed and addicted to masturbating with pornography and acting out sexually with prostitutes, despite the many therapies and processes he had used to deal with these problems.

The first thing I noticed was that Brian was seriously out of touch with his feelings. When he tried to talk to his Inner Child, nothing happened. It was as if there was no Inner Child in there. I assured him that he did indeed have one, but there was some good reason his Inner Child did not want to talk to him right now. Instead we concentrated on helping Brian develop his loving Adult.

Every day Brian practiced talking with his spiritual Guidance, learning what it meant to take care of his Inner Child. As Brian strengthened his spiritual connection and his ability to take loving action in his own behalf, he began to sense that his Inner Child was filled with pain. Eventually, when Brian's Inner Child felt safe that a loving Adult was there to handle the pain, he let Brian know about the severe physical and sexual abuse that had occurred before the age of six at the hands of his father.

Brian had dissociated during the abuse, leaving his body in order to endure the pain, both emotional and physical. As a teenager he learned to use sex to numb out the old pain he carried. He could not stop his sexually compulsive behavior until he knew what it was that this behavior was protecting him from, and he could not open to the old pain until he developed a loving Adult. Once the loving Adult was in place, Brian was able to feel the depth of his pain and heal it. Once his Inner Child felt seen, heard, understood and loved, Brian no longer felt depressed nor needed to act out sexually.

✳ ✳ ✳ ✳

No matter what therapy you use to become aware of your feelings, remember this: It will not work unless you are truly willing to *learn* from your feelings, not *avoid* them. I cannot emphasize this enough. Willingness means being ready to learn to love rather than *ignore* or *judge* the wounded parts of yourself that carry your painful feelings.

This can be a tall order. Don't be dismayed if you don't succeed immediately. Letting go of our controlling behavior and breaking the habit of numbing out with substance and process addictions takes time, but when you are willing to feel and take responsibility for your own feelings, and you pray daily for help from God, you can slowly learn to move inward and attend to the signals that your Inner Child sends you in the form of painful feelings.

Of course, you do not have to be in pain before listening to your feelings. You can practice Step One by regularly tuning in to your body to see how you are feeling. Remembering to do this is the challenge. You can set the alarm on your watch to go off every fifteen minutes to remind you or you can put notes on your mirror, your refrigerator and your dashboard. Remembering to tune in is a major challenge because most of us have practiced tuning out for most of our lives.

As you practice turning your focus inward and becoming

aware of your inner experience, you will find yourself more acutely aware of what is going on around you as well. Your feelings can tell you whether you are safe or not, whether someone is being loving or unloving with you, and whether someone is lying or telling the truth. The more disconnected you are from your feelings, the more disconnected you are from your experience in the world and from what you need to do to feel safe, happy and peaceful.

You can even strive to do Step One all the time. This means that you continually attempt to become more and more aware of what you are feeling in the moment. In fact, the whole Six-Step Process can be done at any time—not just when you are in pain. The more you do it, the better you will become at it and the more loved your Inner Child will feel. The more loved your Inner Child feels, the safer you will feel, and the less you will act out addictively. It's the very opposite of a vicious circle. You might call it a victorious circle.

If you are still not willing to feel your pain, you can pray to God daily for willingness and God will help you *become* willing. If you are still not willing to feel your pain and are unwilling to pray for willingness, then you are not ready to heal. God cannot help you until you ask for help. But please remember that God's love is *always* here for you whether or not you are willing to feel your pain, to receive spiritual help or to heal your spiritual abuse. God's love is always here for you whether or not you *believe* it is. God's love is unconditional, but you will not *feel* that love until you are willing to invite God into your heart.

And without willingness, you cannot move to the next step on your healing journey—opening to learning about love.

Step Two

Choose the intent to learn to love yourself and others. Making this choice opens your heart, allows Divine Love in and moves you into your loving Adult. Use any meditation or spiritual practice— or anything else—that helps you surrender and opens your heart to oneness with Spirit.

Once you can feel your painful feelings, you can consciously choose to learn what you may be thinking or doing to cause them. Knowing this will enable you to make new choices that will be more loving to yourself. It is choosing the intent to learn to love that releases your individual will and allows God into your heart so that you operate as a loving Adult. You cannot learn unless you are a curious, loving Adult, and you cannot be a loving Adult unless you surrender to God. Surrendering your individual will, letting go of control over the outcome of things, and inviting the presence of God into your heart are the results of moving into a true intent to learn with God about loving your Inner Child.

Lots of people are uncomfortable with the word "surrender," so let's talk about what surrender is—and what it isn't. Surrender is not an act of acquiescence, but an invitation to God to use your being as a vessel of love, compassion and truth. Surrender does not mean that you give up the things that are important to you. It does not mean that you have no personal goals and just wait to see what God does with you. Nor does it mean relinquishing your free will or giving up your "normal" life for a more ascetic life.

Surrender means that the wounded part of you, the part that is usually running your life, steps aside, relinquishing the controls and letting Spirit take over, so that you, as a loving Adult, can *embrace* your wounded self rather than *be* your wounded self. It means opening your body, mind, heart and soul to the presence and action of your spiritual Guidance. Surrender means letting go of attachment to the outcome and opening to an exciting journey of discovery.

The idea of choosing to learn to love sounds simple, yet doing it is not always easy. We saw that with Elisa's struggle in chapter 4. Elisa realized that in order to put love first in her life, she would have to give up her resistance to being controlled, which she acted out by refusing to love her very controlling mother. She saw that she would have to be loving to her mother, even if doing so made her mother think that she had control over Elisa. This is true for all of us. In order to let God into our heart, our desire to learn to *love* must be stronger than our desire to *protect* ourselves against the pain of rejection, engulfment, helplessness, loneliness or whatever else we fear. We must be willing to decide that loving is more important to us than anything else, even being controlled, hurt or manipulated by others.

Even when we say we want to surrender control and let go of attachment to outcomes, blame, anger and misery can get in our way. When we feel victimized, we are usually unwilling to open our beings to Spirit and learn about ourselves because we do not believe that we are the ones causing our own pain. As long as your focus is on blaming your past, others or God, you have no power to do anything about your pain. As we saw in Step One, although your childhood spiritual abuse may have caused you much pain and created your false beliefs and resulting behavior, those beliefs and behavior are now *yours*. They—not the past—are what cause you pain in your life.

Bridges to Learning

When you are stuck in the anger, blame or numbness of your wounded self, you need to find a bridge that will take you into a state of openness to learning. Bridges are things you can do to open your heart. Of the many bridges you can use, prayer, especially a prayer of gratitude, is probably the most powerful bridge. Prayer can take many forms, such as dialogue, meditation, recitation or song. The choice is up to you. I have found that repeating a simple prayer of gratitude throughout the day helps me stay open to learning. I use some version of the following:

> *Dear God, sweet Spirit of Divine Love, I will to will thy will. I deeply desire to be an instrument of your love and compassion. Thank you for helping me heal all blocks to being this pure instrument. Thank you for helping me support my own and others' highest good. Thank you for the challenges in my life that provide me the opportunities to learn and evolve my soul toward love.*

Generosity is another bridge to opening the heart. Many of us focus on how we can get what we want or avoid getting hurt. But one of the quickest ways of moving out of a closed heart and into openness is to ask God: "What can I *give* to myself and others?" The moment you sincerely ask this question—with no attachment to its outcome—your heart will open and Divine Love will rush in. We know this will happen because the very nature of God's love is abundant, unconditional and always there for you when you ask for help.

Everything changes when you decide to go through life thinking about how and what you can give instead of how to get what you want or avoid the things you fear. For example, if you are going to a party where you don't know anyone, you can create a lot of anxiety for yourself by worrying, "How can I get people to like me? How can I avoid being alone?" However, if you walk in thinking, "What can I give? I can give people my smile, my interest, my acceptance and my sense of humor," you will feel great. The moment you decide to give, your heart opens and God fills you with love and peace.

How can we know this is true? Many of us fear that nothing will happen if we open—that God will not show up for us. The problem is that the wounded self does not believe that God is here for us and believes that if we let go of trying to get what we want, we will just end up feeling very alone. Our fears of being rejected and feeling alone, being controlled by God, or even dying from being alone and helpless (the old infant feelings) may be so strong that we are unwilling to open our hearts to see if God is really here for us. Until you are willing to take a "leap of faith" and open your heart through the intent to learn, you will not know God.

Sometimes, people are too stuck in their woundedness and can't pray from the heart, or they don't believe in prayer. When this is the case, they need to try other bridges that will open their heart to learning about love. These include:

- Listening to music
- Taking a walk
- Being in nature

- Talking with a friend
- Reading spiritual literature
- Journaling
- Drawing or doing other artwork like sculpture or collage
- Dancing
- Attending Twelve-Step or other support-group meetings
- Playing with a child or a pet
- Being held by a loving person
- Letting yourself cry
- Releasing your anger by yelling and pounding

Remember, though, that these bridges will only open your heart when your intent is to learn to love. If your intent is still to protect against pain and fear, no bridge will work.

The Anger Process

Were you surprised to read that releasing anger can help you open your heart? Releasing your anger will work only when your intent in releasing it is to learn about what you do that causes your angry feelings. If you just want to use your anger to blame, control and justify your position, you will stay stuck with a closed heart. This three-part anger process moves you out of victim mode and into openheartedness.

1. Imagine that the person you are angry at is sitting in front of you. Let your wounded child yell at him or her, saying in detail everything you wish you could say.

Unleash your anger, pain and resentment until you have nothing more to say. (The reason you don't tell the person directly is because this kind of cathartic, no-holds-barred "anger dump" would be abusive to them.)

2. Now ask yourself who this person reminds you of in your past—your mother or father, a grandparent, a sibling? (It may be the same person. That is, you may be mad at your father now, and he is acting just like he did when you were little.) Now let your wounded child yell at the person from the past as thoroughly and energetically as in part one.

3. Finally, come back into the present and let your wounded child do the same thing with *you* expressing your wounded child's anger, pain and resentment toward you for your part in the situation or for treating yourself the way the people in parts one and two treated you. This brings the problem home to personal responsibility, opening the door to exploring your own behavior.

Anger at another person is generally a projection of your wounded child's anger at you for not taking loving care of yourself. Recognizing your anger at others as a projection can move you into an intent to learn.

Exploring Your Good, Compelling Reasons

There is another essential aspect of the intent to learn: You must believe that there are *good, compelling reasons* for your present feelings and behavior. These reasons may be the false beliefs of your wounded self, or they may be the promptings and desires of your core Self. Understanding that you have good reasons for your feelings and behavior is the opposite of being judgmental. It is being compassionate. Your Inner Child will not open to you if you are shaming and judgmental of his or her feelings or behavior. And if your Inner Child doesn't open to you, you will not be able to learn what you are doing or thinking that is causing you pain.

There *are* times when we have to make judgments about things, but there is a big difference between judgment intended to *discern* what is in your highest good and judgment intended to *condemn*. If you approach an actual child and ask, "What are you feeling?" in a condemning tone, the child will not feel safe in giving you an honest answer. If you ask that question in a compassionate tone, the child will probably tell you. The same is true of your Inner Child. *Compassion is the natural result of understanding that you and others have good reasons for your feelings and behavior.* You cannot be judgmental and compassionate at the same time. Accepting that you and others always have good reasons for your feelings and behavior will move you out of judgment and into the open heart of compassion.

Subtleties of the Intent to Learn

A true intent to learn is not driven by the wounded self. It is not focused on an outcome—such as getting rid of the pain or changing yourself so you can find a mate. Your wounded self may like to think that you are open when you strive for answers, but often this is just an information addiction based on the false belief that finding the "right" answer will give you more control.

A true intent to learn is a surrender, an opening, an invitation to Spirit to enter your being and "enlighten" you. You must be willing to be in a process of adventure and discovery rather than striving for a certain result. *The only outcome we are looking for when we are in a true intent to learn is to become a more loving human being.* We are not trying to get rid of pain, win love or get a new job; instead we are just trying to do what we came here to do, which is to evolve in our lovingness. If you have any goal other than that, you will not be in a true intent to learn. Sometimes people decide to learn to be a loving human being so they can find a mate. When they don't find one, they are angry because they didn't get the result they expected. Being in a true intent to learn means we want to learn to be loving, period!

Often in my work with people, they think they are in an intent to learn, but my experience of them is that they want answers. Their wounded self believes that I have the answer for them and when they find out what it is, their pain will stop. As long as they are focused on ending their pain and as long as they think the answers are outside themselves, they are not truly open to learning.

Other times in my work with individuals, they think they are in an intent to learn but really they are trying to control how I see them. Because they have not defined themselves as worthy and lovable, they depend on me to do so. If they think I like them, they feel worthy, and if they think I don't like them, they feel inadequate. They may interpret my offering them information about themselves as condemnation and go into resistance, closing down instead of learning about themselves. My work has shown me that the wounded self always hears information about itself as an *attack* while the loving Adult hears it as a *gift*.

Until these people are willing to define their own worth, they will have a hard time being open to learning. Often, when I help them connect with their spiritual Guidance and see their Inner Child through the eyes of God rather than through the eyes of their parents and their own wounded self, they suddenly find that they can hear, with curiosity and interest, the information I am offering. It is a profound experience for me to see how quickly a person can move from defensiveness into curiosity when they connect with the love and truth of God.

Often the people I see just want my approval or sympathy. They are unwilling to give themselves these things because they believe that getting *another person's* approval or sympathy will make them happy or heal them. If I give it to them, I enable them in being codependent with me, and if I don't, they are angry and feel I do not care about them. But when these people allow me to help them connect to their own spiritual source of approval and compassion, they begin to learn and heal.

The Practice of Learning

Moving into and maintaining an intent to *learn* (instead of *protect*) is one of life's greatest challenges. Had we been brought up in loving families with parents who were consistently spiritually connected and in their own intent to learn, we would naturally be in this state. But since many of us had parents who were themselves wounded child-adults trying to control in order to feel safe, that is what we learned. It takes time and practice to remember that we have the option of moving into the intent to learn about what our wounded child really needs from us when feelings of anxiety, fear, anger, depression and aloneness come up. For thousands of years people have responded to their painful feelings with various defenses. These patterns are not easily broken. But unless we break them and become role models for our children and their children, we will continue to suffer the consequences of our controlling behavior: fear, anxiety, anger, aloneness, unloving relationships—and the crime, violence, substance abuse and process addictions that result from them.

Each time I remember to open to learning, especially when I am distressed, that choice is easier to make the next time. The results of being open to learning are so satisfying to me that the more I do it, the more I want to do it. As my self-esteem and inner peace increase (thanks to my connection with my core Self and God and, consequently, to the resolution of so many of my false beliefs), I find it easier to move directly into the intent to learn whenever I experience internal or external conflict.

Becoming a loving Adult is a process. It is a skill that takes practice, the same kind of practice you would need to become a fine musician or an excellent athlete. When it comes to practice, however, many people run into a problem: Until you either hit bottom or remember your soul's mission to love and evolve in your lovingness, your wounded self will resist the process at all costs because it does not want to lose its power. It is the age-old battle between love and fear, between God and the devil. Your wounded self is like a little demon sitting on your shoulder, whispering in your ear, telling you that you will be hurt too much unless you act out in your addictive and controlling ways. It is often very hard to hear the quiet voice of the little angel (your core Self) sitting on your other shoulder, urging you to be open to learning with your Inner Child and God. You may find yourself grabbing a candy bar or yelling at someone before you even recognize that you are in pain. Your pain becomes a trigger for your wounded self to instantly initiate your protective behavior. As we saw in Step One, it takes time and effort to break this immediate response to pain and instead move into learning. Sometimes, the only way to break it is with help.

I have many clients who, for the first three to twelve months of their work with me, are able to practice being a loving Adult only in my office, with a lot of help. Sometimes the only way they can open is if I am holding them and being a vessel of Divine Love for them (we'll cover this in chapter 9). Eventually they develop enough of a loving Adult to be able to choose to do the process of Inner Bonding on their own.

The steps of Inner Bonding build upon each other. You will not be able to move into the intent to learn (Step Two) until you choose to be aware of your painful feelings and take responsibility for them (Step One) instead of protecting against them by acting out addictively. And you cannot move into Steps Three and Four, the important dialogue processes, until you are in an intent to learn.

SEVEN

Evolving Your Soul: Steps Three to Six

The final four steps in the Inner Bonding process bring you into dialogue with your Inner Child and with God, and ask you to act on what you have learned in these dialogues by taking effective loving action to evolve your soul.

Step Three

Choose to welcome and learn with the wounded self and the core Self. Embrace and dialogue with your Inner Child, exploring your painful feelings, your fears, your false beliefs and the resulting behaviors that may cause your pain. Also explore your gifts and what brings joy to your core Self.

In Step Three, we open our arms to all aspects of ourselves—our wounded aspects as well as our core Self. Although one of the goals of Inner Bonding is to integrate all parts of ourselves, we first need to separate the various parts of the wounded self and heal them individually. Eventually the energy from these parts unites with our core Self and our loving Adult. Some of the immense energy that once went into protecting and avoiding is free to go into playing and creating (activities of the core Self) and some will go into taking loving action (the role of the loving Adult). The more you operate from your core Self and loving Adult, becoming a vessel of God, taking loving care of yourself and sharing your love with others, the more integrated you become.

Look at this as an exploration into the layers of yourself. Welcome rather than judge or condemn anything that comes up. Here are some of the aspects of your wounded self that you might invite to dialogue with you:

• Victim	• Taker
• Defender	• Predator/Bully
• Fixer/Lecturer	• Avoider
• Blamer	• Resister
• Critic/Judge	• Obsessor/Worrier
• Martyr/Complainer	• Clown
• Pleaser	• Perfectionist/Performer
• Caretaker/Rescuer	• Addict

When you talk to these wounded parts, you ask them to tell you what they feel, and you welcome and embrace those feelings, *whatever they are*. It helps to imagine these feelings as coming from a hurt child or adolescent, and your job is to welcome him or her into your loving embrace so you can learn what you may be doing that causes these painful feelings. Remember, no feelings are ever wrong or bad. All the feelings you have are for good reasons, and by using Step Three's dialogue process gently, with great compassion, you will be able to discover the information these feelings have for you.

Sometimes it's hard to know exactly what you are feeling, especially if you have spent much of your life avoiding your feelings. Here are some of what my clients and I have felt in the wounded parts of ourselves:

- Fearful
- Terrified
- Anxious
- Insecure
- Panicked
- Trapped
- Helpless
- Angry
- Jealous

- Murderous
- Alone
- Empty
- Numb
- Depressed
- Guilty
- Ashamed
- Unworthy
- Unlovable

- Inadequate
- Unimportant
- Damaged
- Hurt
- Needy
- Lonely
- Excluded
- Abandoned
- Disappointed

The next part of Step Three is to explore—with love, compassion and curiosity—these feelings and whatever related false beliefs, behaviors and memories you might have. This is what I call dialoguing with your wounded self. For example, you would ask him or her about the events in childhood from which your false beliefs arose. Tears and anger may come up as you do this. For some people, using a doll or stuffed animal acting as a surrogate Inner Child is very helpful; you can hold this surrogate child and bring yourself comfort when painful feelings come up. You can dialogue with various aspects of your wounded self, as well as various ages, from a young child to an adolescent.

When you dialogue with your wounded self, ask questions like this:[1]

- What would you like to talk with me about?
- What are you feeling right now?
- Are you angry with me? I'd like to hear what it's about.
- Why are you so sad (or frightened, depressed, etc.) today?
- Does this person or situation remind you of something that happened when you were little?
- What have I been thinking or doing to cause these feelings?
- Have I let you down in some way?
- How do you feel about how I am taking care of you?
- What do you need from me right now?
- Are you happy or unhappy with the work we do? With the relationship we are in?
- What are some of the things you've always wanted to do, but have never done? Have I kept you from doing them?

In this dialogue, you can also explore your wounded self's false beliefs (it might help to refer to the chart of false beliefs in Chapter 5, pages 124–126). If you don't uncover those beliefs by asking your Inner Child questions like those above, get more specific. Ask questions like this:

- Why do you think God doesn't love you?
- Why do you feel you have to be nice to everyone?

- What would happen if someone didn't approve of you?
- What are you afraid will happen if we take care of ourselves instead of everyone else?

Sometimes the pain you explore will turn out to be about the past, and you will find yourself delving into old memories and the false beliefs that long ago resulted from them. Other times the pain will be from the present, a result of your own unloving choices. The present illuminates the past, and the past illuminates the present. Healing your pain means healing the false beliefs from the past that create your unloving behavior toward yourself and others in the present. Step Three is primarily about uncovering these false beliefs.

✳ ✳ ✳ ✳

So far, we have talked only about dialoguing with the wounded aspect of your Inner Child. But a vital part of Step Three is to also embrace, dialogue with and learn about your core Self. It, too, has wisdom to share with you, and its answers will help you know what's beautiful and true about yourself. You can also dialogue with your core Self to keep yourself company when you are feeling healthy grief, sorrow or loneliness over the difficulties we all face in our lives.

Here are some questions you might ask.

- What are my gifts and talents?
- What brings me joy?
- What is my calling?
- Where does my passion lie?

- What genuine sorrows do I carry?
- How can I express my creativity?
- What will fulfill my soul?

Hints for Successful Dialoguing

A very important aspect of dialoguing with your wounded parts is to be aware of who is asking the questions: Is it your loving Adult or your wounded child-adult? Are you really in a compassionate intent to learn (your loving Adult) or are you asking the questions from your fear and woundedness (your child-adult)? Do you want to learn about how you may be causing your pain (your loving Adult) or are you just trying to get rid of it (your child-adult)? You will not receive helpful or accurate answers when your wounded child-adult asks the questions. This is why it is *imperative* to do Steps One and Two before starting to dialogue.

When you begin, it is best to dialogue with your Inner Child out loud or in writing so that you don't get lost in your wounded self. A written (or taped) record of your dialogue can also be helpful later, when you look back at your early process. After a year or so of regular spoken or written dialoguing, most people find that they can dialogue silently.

Were you surprised just now when I said a year? I have been doing the Six Steps of Inner Bonding myself for more than a decade, and the wonderful thing about this process is that it is not just a quick fix. It is a way of life. It is a way of creating and maintaining a daily connection to your innermost self and to the sacred. As you grow and your life goes on, more and more challenges will come your way. You can use this Six-Step

Process for dealing with all of them, the big ones and the small ones. Some of these challenges will bring up old pain from childhood events. You can use this Six-Step Process to address those feelings, too. In learning Inner Bonding, you learn a tool that you can use again and again to connect to God's guidance and the wisdom of your core Self.

Listening to the Answers

When you are ready for your Inner Child to answer your questions, move your attention into your body. The answers will come from deep within you rather than from your head. When you explore blaming, anger, fear, aloneness, depression and anxiety, you are dialoguing with your wounded self. When you explore sadness, sorrow, loneliness and what brings you fulfillment, peace and joy, you are dialoguing with your core Self. (Remember, both the wounded self and the core Self are aspects of your Inner Child.)

If you can remember to use Step Three whenever you feel hurt or lonely or angry, you won't have to act out addictively. Instead, you will be able to find out what you *really* want by dialoguing with your Inner Child. You might ask, "What is it you are *really* seeking or feeling hungry for?" The wounded self always grabs for a short-term fix—new clothes, sex, Scotch, cocaine. But by embracing and listening to your wounded self, you can discover what your Inner Child *really* wants and needs.

Of course, the answer is always love. Your Inner Child, which includes both your wounded self and your core Self, wants to experience Divine Love coming to him or her through you (that is, through your loving Adult). It is only when you learn to bring through the love that is God to yourself that the hunger, emptiness and aloneness you experience gets filled. Until you address the issue of your inner aloneness and emptiness—the aloneness and emptiness that you have been filling with your various addictions—you cannot begin to address the issue of the loneliness you may feel either with others or from not having others around. You will feel both alone and lonely until you heal your aloneness, your separation from God. Using Step Three, you can discover the fears and false beliefs that are in the way of receiving God's love.

Often, people tell me that they have been dialoguing with their Inner Child but they don't seem to be getting anywhere. When I ask them to show me exactly what they have been doing, I invariably discover that they have not taken the time to first open to learning by inviting God into their hearts. They *think* they are open because they are asking their Inner Child questions, but the tone of their questions is curt, bored, condemning or embarrassed. I gently remind them to go back and do Steps One and Two so they are in a true intent to feel their feelings and learn to love their Inner Child.

If your Inner Child still refuses to talk to you, that's okay for now. Go ahead and skip to Step Four. Eventually, when you have developed a solid, loving Adult, your wounded self and your core Self will open to you.

Step Four

Dialogue with your spiritual Guidance, exploring the truth and loving action toward your Inner Child.

Once you understand which of your false beliefs and actions cause you pain, you are ready to learn the truth about those beliefs and discover what new, loving action you need to take on your own behalf. This information will come to you through a dialogue with your spiritual Guidance.

Accessing the Spiritual Realm

All matter vibrates at a specific frequency. This has been confirmed by science. The spiritual realm exists at a higher frequency—a higher vibration—than the earthly realm. One of the best explanations of "frequency" that I have heard comes from Erika, and I want to share it with you. Erika writes:

> *The book you are reading, your body, the furniture around you, all subtly vibrate from the movement of the electrons in the molecules. This vibration has a frequency; therefore, all matter resonates at various frequencies. People are different from objects because our frequency changes throughout the day in a rhythmic pattern. The pineal gland regulates our frequency. For the most part, this is an involuntary function. It is possible, however, to learn to control the pineal gland and raise your frequency at will. I often compare this to blood pressure. We don't normally think about it as it rises and falls throughout the day. If we need to, however, we can learn to control our blood pressure through biofeedback and meditation techniques. I have the ability to raise and lower my frequency at will. When my frequency is high, I can contact my Teacher. When it goes even higher, I can see someone else's Teacher.*

Another way to understand "frequency" is to imagine a room filled with people who are sharing love and joy with each other. This room has a feeling of lightness—a high frequency—whereas a room filled with angry, tense people has a feeling of heaviness—a low frequency.

In order to access the higher frequency of the spiritual realm, you must raise your own frequency. There are numerous things you can do to raise your frequency. First, though, you must truly have the intent to learn with God about loving yourself and others. *When you have a true, pure intent to learn, your frequency automatically raises. None of the actions I suggest below will raise your frequency without this intent.* However, once you have this intent, the following actions can help to further raise your frequency.

- *Move into your imagination.* Your imagination is a gift from God. When you move into your imagination, you raise your frequency and tap into the source of your creativity and inspiration. As you might recall, at first I was only able to see my spiritual Teacher when I was painting. As soon as I stood in front of a blank canvas, I moved into my imagination. Our willingness to move into and trust our imagination is essential to being able to connect with our personal spiritual Guidance. When you first begin to utilize your imagination to increase your frequency and connect with God, you might feel as if you are just using your imagination to make things up. However, as you take the risk of trusting what you think you are "making up," you will discover that it really is coming *through* you from God rather than *from* you.

- *Keep your body clear.* Your body is an energy system. If your body's energy is clogged with drugs, alcohol, nicotine, caffeine, sugar, heavy foods, too much food or foods contaminated with pesticides, preservatives, artificial sweeteners or any of the thousands of chemicals that are added to foods, your frequency is lowered.

- *Pray.* Sincere prayers of gratitude and asking God for help in healing all blocks to loving can raise your frequency.

- *Chant.* Repetitive prayers (such as the rosary), chants and mantras can open you to higher frequencies, as can singing in general.

- *Dance.* Rapid repetitive movement, such as Native American drumming dances, may open you to higher frequencies.

- *Spend time in nature.* The frequency of a city is far lower than the frequency of nature. Being among trees and flowers, near a river, creek or lake, at the ocean, in the desert, or on a mountain can all raise your frequency.

- *Listen to classical or spiritual music,* such as Bach, Vivaldi, Handel and some of Mozart's work, as well as Kitaro, Taizé, and Gregorian and Indian chants. Throughout the ages music has been used to raise the frequency.

- *Do creative, artistic activities,* such as painting, drawing mandalas or working with clay. Moving into your creative imagination raises the frequency.

- *Use incense or do smudging.* Incense has been used for centuries to raise the frequency and invite spiritual connection. "Smudging" is using the smoke from various dried plants such as sage, pine, cedar and lavender to clear the energies in a room and raise the frequency. Smudging has been used for thousands of years by indigenous peoples throughout the world.

- *Light candles*. Candle light also clears the energies in a room and raises the frequency.

Connecting with Your Guide

So what does dialoguing with your spiritual Guidance mean? Naturally, it means different things to different people. Our spirituality is as individual as we are. Some people find they can dialogue directly with God, whatever their concept of God is: a person, an energy or simply light. Others dialogue with a personal Teacher (also called a Master Teacher); an Ascended Master; a religious figure like a saint, a guide or a guardian angel; a beloved deceased relative, friend or pet; an inner mentor; a power animal; or with an image of the highest part of themselves. Even young children can contact their Guidance by imagining a coach, a teacher or a fairy godmother.*

If you would like to create a personal guide or mentor to dialogue with, try the following exercise. Put on some beautiful music and have someone read the following visualization to you, very slowly (or tape it for yourself and play it back).

---

*(Numerous schools are teaching Inner Bonding. By leaving out the spiritual aspect, which is not allowed in public schools, children learn to dialogue with an inner mentor, teacher or coach. They not only learn to self-nurture, but they improve their self-esteem and grades as well!)

Close your eyes and imagine that you are sitting some-where in nature in a place that is very beautiful for you—the mountains, the desert, a forest, a brook or waterfall, a lake, a meadow, the ocean. . . . Imagine that you can hear the sounds around you, smell the smells, feel the temperature of the air on your skin. . . . Use your imagination to see, hear and feel your surroundings. . . . Imagine yourself feeling content and peaceful, surrounded by love. . . .

Sometimes it is hard to imagine the energy of love, so pretend that it is the color violet. . . . Imagine that what you need to feel filled and to flourish is the color violet. . . . Imagine that throughout your life you have been seeking to get bits of the color violet from others and from accomplishments. . . . Now imagine that the space around you is filled with violet, and all you have to do to be filled with it is to open to learning about loving yourself. . . .

Allow the light, the love, the color violet to fill your whole body, within and without . . . surrounding you in a cocoon of violet, a cocoon of love. . . . Imagine yourself resting, relaxing into this love. . . . Breathe it in and breathe it out in a circle of light. . . . And imagine that circle of light connecting with Divine light, Divine Love, the source of all light, the source of all love. Breathe it in and breathe it out. Each breath in and each breath out allows you to go to a deeper place of spiritual peace and relaxation. . . . Deeper and deeper . . . surrendering the control as you relax and rest into Spirit. . . .

In this place of beauty and relaxation, you have the opportunity to create the perfect mentor for you. . . . Imagine that you see a light on the horizon coming slowly toward you. This is your spiritual Guidance, and it desires to appear in whatever form is most acceptable to you. This mentor or guide is the most powerful, loving and wise being that you can imagine. . . . This being can be human or animal. It can be a man, a woman or an androgynous being. It can be any race that you have an affinity for—Caucasian, American Indian, East Indian, Asian, African, Latino—whatever race gives you a feeling of warmth and safety, which may not be your own race. It can be any age—very young, middle age or very old. You are imagining this so you can make up anyone you want. . . . Imagine the color of this being's hair and the kind of clothing. . . . Now imagine that this spiritual being that you have just created is sitting beside you. Imagine yourself being surrounded with the unconditional love that is emanating from this being of light. Imagine that you can relax and rest as you are being supported and held by this loving being. . . . Ask this being for a name, make up a name you like or listen for a name to pop into your mind. Any name will do. If no name comes to mind, let that be okay. . . . Take a few minutes to be with this loving being of light, knowing that you can go back to this beautiful place anytime you want and speak with this being. . . . Let yourself feel and know that you are not alone, that you are never alone, for this loving being is always with you and has always been with you. . . . This being wants nothing more than to love you and guide you toward your highest good. Relax and know that you are never alone. . . . When this feels complete, open your eyes and come back into the present.

When I work with people from a Christian background, some of them feel afraid of opening to their spiritual Guidance for fear of Satan coming in disguised as light. They have asked me if this can happen when they open to their imaginations and create a guide. Certainly darkness can appear in the guise of light. But since both darkness and light *come only by invitation*, you can be assured that you are drawing only light when you are truly in the intent to learn to love. Your deep desire to love is what protects you from darkness.

This issue came up in one of my workshops in Missouri, and a Christian woman sent me these quotes from the Bible.

Anyone who claims to be in the light but hates his brother is still in the darkness. Whoever loves his brother lives in the light and there is nothing in him to make him stumble. [Emphasis mine.] But whoever hates his brother is in the darkness and walks around in the darkness; he does not know where he is going, because the darkness has blinded him. (1 John 2:9-11)

But you, my friends, are not in the dark, that the day should overtake you like a thief. You are all children of light, children of day. We do not belong to night or darkness, and we must not sleep like the rest, but keep awake and sober. (1 Thessalonians 5:4-6)

By choosing to love rather than hate, by staying in the intent to learn about loving, you stay "awake and sober." When this is the case, you "do not belong to night or darkness."

If you practice dialoguing with the guide you just created—or with whatever or whomever feels loving and comforting to you—asking questions and "imagining" the answers, eventually you will *feel and know* through your own experience that a spiritual being is actually helping and guiding you. You will develop a relationship with this light being, and you will find answers to your questions coming more and more easily. My Teacher has said to me, "We, your spiritual Teachers, are funnels for the vast wisdom and truth that is God, and we help you to access the compassion, love, strength, peace and joy that is God. We come to you even before your birth and are with you always. *You are never alone.* We are always embracing you, holding you within the soft light of love. When you imagine us in any form with an intention to learn about becoming a more loving human being, you access the comfort, power, love, compassion, peace, joy and wisdom that is here for you."

Imagining a being of light—or light itself—surrounding you with love can energize your being and bring you great comfort. Being connected with Spirit is like being connected with an infinite source of power. It is the difference between trying to light your way with a small flashlight and rundown batteries, or with a huge lamp plugged into an industrial-strength generator. Our wounded child-adult is exhausted from running on batteries. We have only to plug into the infinite source that is God to energize our beings.

Trust the Process, the Answers Will Come

The universe is filled with the energy of love and truth. It is filled with all the information there is and it has the answers to all our questions. Just because you cannot see this energy, does not mean it is not there. When you turn on your TV, a picture shows up, even though you cannot see the waves coming through the air. We are like TVs. We are receivers and our intent to learn about loving is the "on" button. When we ask a particular question, we tune in to a particular channel.

In your dialogue with your Guidance, you might ask:

- What is the truth about this belief that is causing me pain?
- What will happen if I give up control of this situation?
- What actions can I take that will show me my belief is false?
- What does my Inner Child need right now to feel safe and loved?
- What would loving action be in this situation?

There are numerous examples of dialogues with spiritual Guidance in some of the chapters to follow.

Often when I work with people, they say, "I don't know how to take care of my Inner Child. I don't know how to be a loving Adult." It's true. Many of us *don't* know how because we haven't had anyone do it for us. We haven't had any role-modeling. The good news is that you do not have to know how to do it, you just need to be willing to ask. That's why Step Four includes asking your spiritual Guidance what loving action you should take.

Asking your guide, God or your Higher Self questions about the truth of your beliefs and about what is loving behavior toward your Inner Child will eventually result in answers, although sometimes they do not come immediately.

They may pop into your head when you least expect it. They may come to you in a dream or when talking to a friend, in meditation or when you are in the shower. They may come verbally or in pictures. You may open a book and find your answer, or meet someone who says the exact thing you need to hear. But whatever form your answers come in, know that they will light the way for your next step.

When you sincerely ask the questions, "What is the truth about this belief?" and "What is the loving action in this situation?" you open the channel for this information to come through you. We have long been told to "ask and you shall receive." Try it. It really does work.

What the Dialogue Process Looks Like

Before we go on to discuss Step Five, I am going to give you a brief example of a man working with Steps Three and Four so you can see what the process looks like in action. There are many more examples of dialogues in the chapters to follow.[2] Although the purpose of this book is to teach you how to do the Six Steps on your own, many of the examples of the process that I am going to explain show me acting as a facilitator. I am including these examples because I think that when you have a chance to observe my role in these dialogues, you will best learn how to do them for yourself.

Hans

Hans is sitting in my office. It is his third session with me. A successful businessman in his late thirties, he was brought up in a rigid religious household and continues to practice that religion. He has a strong belief in God but little personal experience of God.

Hans knows that an emotional wall protects him from getting hurt. He has just realized that having the wall means that his heart isn't open to loving, and this is why his wife, Tonya, wants to leave him.

"I want to open my heart. I want her to stay. I love her. But I'm scared to take down this wall."

"What do you think you could do to make it safe, Hans?"

"I don't know. Can't you do something?"

"Hans, I am doing everything I know to make it safe for you right now, but you're not open. You want me to do it for you, and I can't. Even if I could, wouldn't I be making you dependent upon me instead of helping you learn to do this for yourself?"

Hans gets angry at me. He yells that this is what he pays me for. Then he starts to cry in deep, wracking sobs.

"Oh God, please help me," he pleads. The sobs continue. When no help comes, Hans' sobs are stifled by anger. He shouts, "God, what the hell am I supposed to do? I am asking you. Now give me the answers!"

"Hans, you can't hear God's answers until you are ready to risk opening your heart. God can't help you any more than I can until you decide you want to learn about loving."

"No!" he screams. "That won't work! God is too busy for me! God has better things to do than talk with me. I'm not important enough for him to take his time with me. If I open my heart, then I will really know that God isn't here for me, and that's too scary! Besides, I'm not what God wants me to be. I'd have to be a different person. I'd have to give up me, give up my freedom, give up being who I am and be what God wants me to be. God doesn't love me the way I am!"

In a subsequent session a few weeks later, Hans was finally able to visualize a spiritual mentor. He created a guide he called Horatio. Hans discovered that Horatio was never too busy for him. As he opened to Horatio's unconditional love, Hans gradually healed his own false beliefs about God. With Horatio's consistent guidance, he was able to see his own inner light.

Here's an excerpt from an early dialogue that Hans had with Horatio. It should give you an idea of what it's like to work with a spiritual guide. Later in the book, you will read many, many more examples of dialogues and learn how to have them with your own guide.

Hans: Margie, I'm afraid to ask Horatio a question. What if he isn't really there? What if I have just made him up, and I get no answer? What if he is too busy for me?

Margie: A wounded part of you—a little child within you—is really afraid that Horatio doesn't exist or is too busy for you. Can you imagine having compassion for this part of you, the part of you that is so scared? Can you imagine comforting this wounded child?

Hans: Yes. I can feel how scared he is. I feel sad that he is so scared.

Margie: Do you feel willing to take a risk for this frightened part of you?

Hans: Yes, I do.

Margie: Then take the risk of asking Horatio what your wounded child needs to start to feel safer. But before asking, tell this little wounded child that even if no one answers, you will comfort him and let him know that you care about him.

Hans: Okay. Little Hans, I will be here to comfort you if Horatio isn't really real. . . . *[Takes a deep breath.]* Horatio, what do I need to do to help this little wounded child feel safer?

Margie: Now, Hans, just open to seeing or hearing or feeling the answer. Notice whatever pops into your mind.

Hans: Well, I just got an image of holding this scared little boy. But I think I am just making this up.

Margie: Have you ever had this thought before?

Hans: No.

Margie: Then let's assume that Horatio gave you this image. If you imagine holding your wounded child, what do you feel?

Hans: I feel . . . good. Kind of filled inside.

Margie: Safer?

Hans: Yes!

Margie: Now ask Horatio what you do that makes your child feel so unsafe.

Hans: [*Asks and listens for the answer.*] Another picture just came to mind. I see myself sitting and waiting for Tonya to hold me.

Margie: Now, ask this child how he feels when you make your wife responsible for his feelings of safety and comfort. Ask him how he feels when you give him away to Tonya.

Hans: Little Hans, how do you feel when I give you to Tonya for comfort?

Child Hans: I feel scared that she is going to go away and leave me alone, and I feel mad at you for leaving me. I don't think you like me. You never hold me like this.

Hans: I can really feel how scared and alone he feels when he's waiting for Tonya to hold him. That's why Horatio told me to hold him! That's really what makes him feel safe!

Margie: So, do you think you just made up these images, or do you think Horatio is really here helping you?

Hans: Margie, I really don't think I could come up with this myself. I'm not totally convinced Horatio really exists, but I feel so much better right now and not so afraid of asking him questions. Something or someone seems to be answering them!

By being willing to take the risk of asking questions of Horatio and imaging the answers, Hans stopped relying on me to make it safe enough to open his heart, and he learned how to do it for himself. Also, through repeated contact with Horatio, Hans eventually had a direct experience of God.

This enabled him to move beyond having a belief in God to knowing God. He talks with Horatio regularly now and keeps his heart open to loving. Tonya no longer wants to end their marriage.

Step Five

Take the loving action learned in Step Four—put God into action.

Healing is about moving out of your false belief system and into living in truth. While bringing through the truth from your spiritual Guidance (Step Four) is essential in healing your false beliefs, it is not enough. Nor is it enough to gain understanding and release your old pain and fear. *Unless you, as a loving Adult, take new loving action on your Inner Child's behalf, nothing really changes, nothing heals.* For example, if your daughter came to you and told you she was scared by your yelling, and you listened and understood but made no attempt to change your behavior, your child would not *feel* heard. She would not feel loved. Likewise, if your Inner Child is hungry for love, attention, safe boundaries, the end of an intolerable situation at work, a fit and healthy body or just plain fun, and you listen and understand but take no action, your Inner Child will continue to feel unloved, unlovable, alone and unfulfilled. And your wounded self will continue to protect against these painful feelings with your various addictions.

You can tell yourself the truth all day, you can stare into the mirror and affirm over and over that you are a beautiful, wonderful child of God, but if you do not treat yourself as a beautiful, wonderful child of God, your Inner Child will not believe your affirmations. Words mean very little without action. A loving Adult takes action on behalf of the Inner Child.

Paradoxically, the way most of us begin doing Step Five is by failing to take loving action. And that's okay. Our opportunity to begin taking loving action comes when we choose to *observe* rather than *condemn* ourselves, to be compassionate with ourselves, for example, when we slip up and indulge in addictive behavior. This is part of Step Five because nonjudgmentally observing yourself choosing the intent to protect and control rather than love is in itself a loving action.

You cannot make new choices until you watch yourself making your current choices. As I said in the discussion about resistance in chapter 4, you will never know that you can *choose* to learn about love until you observe yourself *choosing* to try to control. You cannot choose to love your wounded self until you notice your wounded self. If you are not willing to nonjudgmentally notice yourself acting out the needs of your wounded self, you cannot make new choices.

Taking loving action means learning to love both the core Self and the wounded self. It means releasing judgment and accepting the angry, hurt, shamed and frightened parts of yourself with love and compassion, understanding that your wounded self has been doing the best it can to take care of you and help you feel safe. Loving action means understanding and having compassion for all the parts of yourself that you have hated or judged as inadequate, unlovable and unworthy. *You heal your false beliefs when you learn to be loving to your wounded self.*

God does not hate, resist or judge. As long you hate even

one person on the planet—*including yourself*—you will not move into unconditional love. Becoming one with God means you need to express and release your anger in the anger process in Step Two, or as part of your dialogue process in Step Three, so that you can move beyond your own judgments and resistance to loving. A good place to start is with your parents. You can express and release your anger and judgments towards them so you can love the part of you that *is* them—your own wounded self.

Clients have often asked me, "Are you saying we need to love our parents or caregivers who were abusive to us? Why would we want to do that?" Loving them does not mean you need to like them or condone what they did to you if they were abusive, any more than you have to like your *own* unloving behavior. But if you hate, resent or resist loving your parents, you will continue to hate, resent or resist loving your own wounded self, who is exactly like them. Until you can see your parents as wounded children, you will have trouble having compassion for both yourself and them.

Here are some examples of loving actions you might take with the help of your spiritual Guidance. Some of them are small things you can do in the course of a conversation, say, with a friend.

• Set appropriate limits within yourself. For example, if health and/or addiction is an issue for you, you might need to set a limit for yourself against smoking, drinking, taking drugs or overeating. Remember, you will not be able to follow through on this limit—or any loving action—without God's help.

- Set limits against someone violating you. This could range from something as minor as not staying on the phone with an overly talkative friend when you want to hang up, to something major, like telling a colleague at work that you will not tolerate them stealing your ideas anymore.

- Leave a relationship when someone is abusing themselves or you and they consistently refuse to open to learning about their abusive behavior.

- Speak your truth in a situation even when the truth is painful for another to hear.

- Risk being yourself and owning your personal power even if your partner finds it threatening.

- Leave a lucrative job that you hate.

- Express your true Self by offering your gifts to the planet.

- Surrender to the will of God by inviting the love, compassion and action of God into your being *even if you don't believe in God* (or you don't believe that God is there for you personally).

Frequently, taking loving action on your own behalf means being willing to risk losing something: a relationship, a job, power over others or even a sense of control over yourself. It boils down to this: Are you willing to go on losing yourself through your addictions in order to protect yourself and maintain "control," or are you willing to risk losing someone or something to gain your true Self—your freedom, your soul's mission, your dignity, self-respect, integrity, personal power, passion and connection to God? Are you willing to lose your sense of self to avoid pain, or are you willing to face pain in order to have your true Self and evolve your soul?

There is no right answer to these questions. You are not bad or wrong if you are unwilling to face the pain of loss and loneliness that you believe will arise if you take loving action. What is important is to accept that your present pain is the result of your protective actions and that loss of Self and will not go away until you are willing to risk feeling the pain of loss and loneliness when you let go of "control." And you need to accept that you will not experience the light and grace of God until you are willing to take these risks.

If you find that you cannot take loving action because too much fear or anxiety comes up when you think about taking the action, then you need to learn an energy release technique, such as Thought Field Therapy (TFT), or Comprehensive Energy Psychotherapy (CEP) to de-escalate the feelings. Feelings and beliefs that are deeply programmed into the body can be released through this technique, thus allowing you to take loving action without triggering overwhelming fear or anxiety.[3]

Step Six

Evaluate the effectiveness of your action.

Once you have taken loving action—setting inner and outer limits, speaking your truth, taking care of yourself physically and emotionally—you will need to evaluate whether the action is working for you. First ask yourself what you are feeling. Do you feel happier, less alone, more connected with God? Is your core shame diminishing? Do you feel freer and less afraid? Are you less interested in pursuing your substance or process addictions? Next ask yourself what other evidence there is that you are healing your wounded self and accessing your core Self. Here are just a few of the signs that show that healing is taking place:

- Increase in personal power
- Improved self-esteem
- Increased gratitude and generosity
- Playfulness, spontaneity and creativity
- Compassion for self and others
- A deep sense of knowing
- Truthfulness and trust
- More joy and laughter
- Feeling one with Spirit and others

If the answers to your self-evaluation show you that heal-ing is *not* occurring, go back to Step Four and ask your spiri-tual Guidance to help you discover another loving action. For example, perhaps your Inner Child needs even more time with you, more time in prayer, or needs you to get help with the process. Perhaps he or she needs to be held by someone who can bring through unconditional love to him or her and help heal the wound of not having been held this way as a child. Or, your Inner Child may need you to spend more time having fun with others or may need more time alone to pur-sue passions or hobbies.

Learning to do what really satisfies the needs of your Inner

Child is an essential aspect of effective loving action. Until your inner emptiness is filled in satisfying ways, your wounded self will continue protecting you from the pain of this emptiness with addictive behavior, which only leads you to more emptiness and further alienation from God. So Step Six takes you back, in a sense, to Step One, because to do it properly, you need to tune in to your feelings, both physical and emotional.

Here are some questions that you (in the role of loving Adult) can ask your Inner Child. Be sure to listen carefully to the answers.

- Are you feeling loved by me?
- Do you feel you can trust me to be there for you and to resist when the urge to act out addictively comes up?
- Do you feel you can trust me to not harm others with my anger?
- Do you feel you can trust me to set good limits with others? Or are you still afraid I will give in to them or allow them to violate you?
- Are you feeling safe inside, or are you still feeling alone and afraid?
- Am I defining you or am I still allowing others to define you?
- Do you feel a deep sense of worth that cannot be shaken by others' disapproval, or are you still afraid of rejection?

When you evaluate your actions, you cannot just look at how you feel *in the moment*. Acting out addictively, such as overeating or taking out your anger on someone, generally feels good in the moment—that's how it got to be an addiction. Often, when you take a loving action, such as cutting out sugar or chocolate or caffeine, stopping drinking, taking drugs or smoking, not acting out sexually, no longer taking responsibility for another's feelings, or no longer dumping your anger on others, you feel awful in the moment. Your wounded child-adult feels frightened at having a crutch taken away, or feels deprived of something that gives him or her momentary pleasure, or feels terrified of rejection and aloneness. Your addictions worked to make you feel better for the moment, so when you stop them, you will likely go through a period of feeling much worse. You may go through both physical and emotional withdrawal. Often, what works for you in the short term undermines you in the long term, while what works in the long term may not feel good in the short term.

Even though loving action may not always feel *good* in the moment, if it is truly in your highest good, it will feel *right*. You will experience a sense of inner rightness when you act in a way that is in harmony with your soul. There is a sense of lightness, freedom and power that comes from taking good care of yourself, even when it feels difficult, frightening or painful at first.

When you check in with your Inner Child to evaluate your actions, you must be sure you are talking to your core Self and not your wounded self. Your wounded child-adult will often tell you that you are making a mistake when you give up a cherished addiction. Your child-adult has many rationalizations for wanting to keep the addictions, especially as you start to feel the emotional or physical withdrawal symptoms. You might hear something like this:

- Life is too short to give up these pleasures. What's the point? Why not just enjoy life while I can? So what if I cut a few years off my life? It's worth it.

- Oh, this is not working. Maybe this isn't the right day to start eating differently. I *really* want that doughnut. I'll start eating well tomorrow. One more day of eating junk won't hurt me.

- Life just isn't worth living without cigarettes. I love smoking so much. Not everybody who smokes gets lung cancer, so why go through this hell? Anyway, the stress of not smoking is worse for me than the cigarettes.

- The anxiety and guilt I feel when I don't caretake my husband is too hard, and he hates it. I'll probably end up alone if I keep this up.

If you fall for these rationalizations and give in to the wounded child-adult, you will be giving your Inner Child a pacifier rather than the real thing. You will force him or her to be satisfied with the illusion of nurturing rather than the true sense of joy and well-being that comes from the loving Adult bringing through God's love in the form of loving action.

Here's the bottom line: If you look inside to evaluate your loving action, and you find that you are still feeling genuinely, not momentarily, depressed, frightened, hurt, angry or powerless, then you need to go back to dialoguing with your spiritual Guidance (Step Four) to see what else you need to do regarding a particular situation. This process may go on for days, weeks or sometimes even months (with very difficult issues) before you discover the loving action that really works for you regarding a particular situation.

Let's look now at an example. Natalie is moving through all six steps of Inner Bonding.

Natalie

Natalie came to see me because she felt stuck with grief and rage over the breakup of her relationship. She had recently ended a two-year romance with Alan after discovering that he was involved with another woman and had been lying to her about it. She was having trouble concentrating at work because she was obsessing about him. This was not the first time Alan had been unfaithful to her, and Natalie knew she needed to move on, but she couldn't seem to stop thinking about him.

In our first session I helped her create a spiritual guide, whom she named Analee. The following dialogue occurred a few weeks after we started to work together. By that time, Natalie was fairly comfortable with the Six-Step Process and had been dialoguing on her own with Analee.

Natalie: Margie, I am still so furious at Alan. How could he do this? He said he loved me and wanted to marry me and have children with me. How could he lie to me like this? How could he throw away everything we had?

Margie: Natalie, I'd like to do an anger process with you that I find is very helpful to people in moving the anger through. First imagine that Alan is sitting here in this chair *[a chair directly across from her]*. Then allow your wounded child-adult to tell him in detail everything you are angry at him about. You can yell and scream, you can hit the chair with this foam bat, you can say whatever you want to him, but be very detailed. Say *everything* you wish you could say to his face. Now, start by welcoming your angry child-adult and giving her permission to do this. This aspect of your wounded self is the adolescent, the one who wants a man to take care of her, the one obsessing about Alan. She is the one in charge, the one acting as the adult.

Natalie: *[Holding her teddy bear and imagining her angry child-adult.]* Hello, Natalie. I want you to know that it's okay to get angry. I want you to let it all out. You can say whatever you want to say to Alan. *[Step Two: Using the three-step anger process as a bridge to open the heart.]*

Wounded-adolescent Natalie: Damn you, Alan! What is the matter with you? How could you be such a jerk! You promised me the last time that you wouldn't lie anymore and that you really didn't want anyone but me. How could you have said those things to me when you didn't mean them? How could you have talked about getting married and having children and then go off with someone else? We even talked about what we would name our children. *[Sobbing.]* I thought you had changed. You told me you had. I want you to change. I want you to come back to me and tell me this isn't true, that you really haven't been with someone else all this time. Damn you! You're not even fighting for me! Why aren't you getting some help? Why don't you want to straighten yourself out so we can be together? Why don't you care about how much you are hurting me? How can you just let me go without even trying to change things? I thought I was important to you. *[Natalie continues in this vein for several minutes, sobbing and yelling until her anger runs down.]*

Margie: Natalie, who does this remind you of from your childhood? Who betrayed you when you were a little girl?

Natalie: Oh God! My dad. You know I was four when my parents divorced. My dad would tell me he was going to take me great places, and then he wouldn't show up when he was supposed to pick me up. I'd sit at the window for hours, waiting for him. Sometimes he would finally come and sometimes he wouldn't, but almost always he had a woman with him. I never felt important to him.

Margie: Imagine that your dad is in the chair and let your wounded little child get angry at him.

Wounded-child Natalie: Your women were always more important to you than I was! How could you let a little girl sit and wait like that? How could you lie to me like that? You never really cared about me. I was nothing more than something to show off to your women. I always had to look so pretty for you. The only time you ever bought me anything was if you wanted me to dress a certain way for you or for your friends. You never wanted to get to know me. You never talked to me. I was just a thing to you, not a person. You used me, you used me! I hate you! *[Sobbing and yelling, Natalie again goes on for a while until her feelings subside.]*

Margie: Now imagine that your own adult is in that chair—the wounded adult part of you that we've talked about *[in a previous session]*, the aspect of yourself that has also betrayed you by keeping you in a relationship with a man who had lied to you before. This wounded child-adult part is the adolescent that is obsessing about Alan and wanting him back. Let your hurt little girl be angry at the wounded adult who has not taken care of you and has let you be in this position. *[Here is where the anger process succeeds in moving her into Step Three.]*

Wounded-child Natalie: You don't take good care of me. You lied to me. You told me he had changed when he hadn't. You never listen to me. I knew the truth, I could feel it, but you never listen to my feelings. You're just like Dad—you never listen to me. You don't want to know me and what I feel about things. I feel like I'm still waiting at that window. Don't I deserve more? You tell me you love me, but I don't believe you. If you loved me you wouldn't keep thinking about someone who doesn't love me, who doesn't feel that I am important to him. I want you to let him go and find me someone who is honest and loving. I want you to listen to my feelings. I want *you* to stop looking for a daddy to take care of me. I want *you* to be the daddy I never had. I want *you* to let me know I am important to *you*. You're the one who loves him, not me! I think he's a jerk, but you don't listen to me. I never felt loved by him, not from the beginning. Stop ignoring me! I want you to care about what I want!

Natalie: Wow! I do ignore her. I knew from the beginning that something was wrong with him, but I didn't listen to myself. I thought if I was loving enough to him, everything would be all right. I thought I could make him love me so much that he would never think of another woman. Then, after the first time he lied about another woman, I thought if I got angry enough and made him feel guilty he would never do it again.

Margie: Yes, you have some false beliefs about being able to control how another person chooses to be. Ask your guide, Analee, about this belief *[Step Four]*. Ask her whether it's possible to use love or anger to make another person change.

Natalie: Analee, I've always thought that if I loved someone enough they would love me back, or if I showed them they were wrong they would change. Could you tell me the truth about this? *[Listening inward.]* She is telling me, "People change only when they want to. You can't make them change. Some people don't want to change, no matter how much you love them and want them to." So . . . Alan doesn't want to change and I haven't accepted this.

Margie: That's right. He apparently is not unhappy with how he is. He probably feels that his way of being is working for him, so there is no reason to change.

Natalie: He was always blaming me for our distance, and I thought if I changed enough then he would change.

Margie: Part of not taking care of your Inner Child is being with someone who blames you for his behavior and feelings. As long as you keep picking men like your father and trying to get them to love you, you will end up unhappy. If you want a loving man, you need to pick a man who is already loving. You can't make him so, and trying to only creates pain for your Inner Child. Your Child will never feel important as long as you pick unloving men and then try to control them into loving you.

Natalie: I see that. My obsessing about Alan is hurting her, too. I think I'm ready to really let him go *[Step Five: Taking the loving action]*.

Margie: The wounded adolescent who wants control needs your love and attention in order to feel safe enough to let go of the control. Imagine that your adolescent is sitting with you right now. What can you tell her about your commitment to her? *[Step Five]*

Natalie: I love you. You have really been hurt and you just wanted love, and I haven't been loving you. Underneath all that anger you are a sweet, loving, wonderful little girl, and you deserve to be with a man who loves you. I'm going to listen to you from now on. I'm going to stay tuned into you and not make you be with another man like Alan. When you start obsessing about Alan and wishing he would change and come back, I'm going to give you the love you need. I'm going to spend time with you getting to know you before looking for another relationship. . . . Ah! That feels good! *[Step Six: Evaluating the effectiveness of the loving action.]*

Margie: Your wounded adolescent has been addicted to trying to get a man like your father to love you. Your loving Adult needs to continue to bring through the truth from Analee about how impossible this is, while loving the part of you that wants control. Only by staying connected to little Natalie and to Analee will you be able to break this addiction. Your trust in God will strengthen you through this process, and you will no longer need a man to fill you. Eventually you will feel God's love filling you, and then you can look for a man with whom to share this love.

Natalie: I really don't want to go through this again. I'm tired of it. I'm going to dialogue with these parts of me and with Analee every night. I want to feel God in my heart. I'm tired of feeling empty and trying to get Alan to fill that.

Margie: Good! Don't forget that this process is ongoing. To stay tuned in, you need do it every day for the rest of your life. After a while, it will become natural to you. When your deepest desire is to be a loving human being, first with yourself and then with others, you will practice this. If your deepest desire continues to be to get love from others, this practice will go by the wayside.

Natalie: I really do want to be loving. I'm going to do this.

Natalie had been stuck in her relationships her whole adult life, believing that her best feelings came from getting love from others. Until she saw the truth—that her best feelings really come from being loving to herself and sharing love with others—she was not motivated to learn to be a loving Adult.

Practicing All Six Steps

When you have been doing the Six Steps of Inner Bonding for a while, and you are bringing through the love and taking the action to give your Inner Child what he or she really needs, you will find that more and more frequently you feel a wonderful lightness of being, a sense of fullness in your heart, and joy that bubbles up from within your soul. This is grace, a great gift of God. Fear gradually diminishes and is replaced by peace and joy in the process of learning. The gnawing aloneness within that led to addictive behavior no longer exists when you stay in contact with your Inner Child and meet his or her deep need for love through connection with your spiritual Guidance. You will often feel a sense of aliveness, wholeness and integration. Imagine a figure eight, the infinity sign, that starts from God, crosses through your heart and circles down into your solar plexus in a never-ending flow of love.

Gradually the experience of separation from Self and others that so pained you will diminish, and you will feel a sense of oneness with yourself and others. You will find yourself unwilling to behave in any way that hurts yourself or others; you will discover your integrity. You will experience a deep trust in yourself and God. And you will discover that you no longer have to strive to believe in God, for now you *know* God.

No longer will you experience others in terms of "us" and "them." There is no judgment, no enemy. No one is left out, no one is less than you or more than you. No one is judged as "saved" or "not saved." All are "saved" without distinction by becoming one with love, one with God, no matter what spiritual path they choose. You will come to understand that all ways of learning about love are one way, all paths intended to unite with God lead to God.

These feelings of unity are available to all of us when we open to learning with our Child and God and are willing to take loving action on our Child's behalf.

However, you will not consistently practice these steps until you accept responsibility for your own feelings and needs—until you adopt your Inner Child. Many people resist the idea of personal responsibility, believing that it is too much work and too confining. Both of these objections are false beliefs. In truth, it is far less work to open to learning and let God guide and empower you than to have to do everything yourself. Your wounded child-adult may feel overwhelmed at the thought of taking care of the Inner Child, but it is not the child-adult's job. It is the loving Adult's job, and, far from being overwhelming, it is a joy and a sacred privilege to bring through the love and strength of God to that Child. In truth, personal responsibility is not confining, it is *freeing*. Additionally, you will not consistently practice these steps as long as you hang on to the false belief that your happiness comes from being loved and taken care of by another. As long as you remain attached to the fantasy that someone will come along and love you the way you were never loved as a child, and that this will heal and fulfill you and create your safety and security, you will spend your energy seeking this. Only when you embrace the truth—that *only you in connection with God can heal you, fulfill you and provide your safety and security*—will you commit to the process.

When you operate as a loving Adult you never have to wait for someone to fill your emptiness. You never have to feel alone. You have the complete freedom to fill yourself with love and peace whenever you want. You never have to wait for someone to come along to take loving action for you. You have the complete freedom to take that action for yourself. As children, we did not have this freedom. We needed others to fill us and take action for us. When they didn't, we may have become locked into thinking that we needed others to do this for us or that doing it ourselves was too much work, failing to see that taking responsibility for ourselves is a most delicious privilege and freedom.

Practicing Inner Bonding opens the door to a deep experience of God and the sure knowledge that you do not have to give yourself up, or give up your personal freedom, to be loved by God.

The following chart is a detailed summary of the Inner Bonding process that you can refer to when you are doing the process.

The Six Steps of Inner Bonding

Step 1
Choose to be MINDFUL of your feelings, ATTENDING to your feelings with the WILLINGNESS to feel your pain, learn about and take responsibility for how you may be causing your pain, and take responsibility for creating your peace and joy. Utilize somatic therapies to access feelings.

Step 2
Choose the INTENT TO LEARN with Spirit/God about loving yourself, which opens the heart and creates the loving Adult. Invite love and compassion into your heart. Utilize any meditative/spiritual practices or anything else that helps you to surrender and open the heart to connection with spiritual Guidance—such as being held or doing the anger process.

Step 3
Choose to WELCOME and LEARN with the wounded self and core Self.

• EMBRACE and DIALOGUE with the many aspects and feelings of the wounded self:

Victim, Defender, Fixer, Blamer, Critic, Martyr, Pleaser, Caretaker, Taker, Predator, Avoider, Resister, Obsessor, Perfectionist, Addict

Explore with love, compassion and curiosity the feelings, behaviors, false beliefs and memories of these wounded selves.

—Possible feelings to welcome, embrace and explore:

Fearful	Terrified	Trapped	Alone	Guilty/Shamed	Inadequate	Hurt	Disrespected
Anxious	Panicked	Desire to kill	Empty/Numb	Unworthy	Unimportant	Needy	Excluded
Insecure	Angry	Helpless	Depressed	Unlovable	Damaged	Jealous	Disappointed
							Abandoned

• Ask: "How am I behaving and/or thinking that is causing these feelings?"

—Possible behaviors to welcome, embrace and explore:

With self and/or others:	Denying	Obsessing	Defending	Procrastinating
Criticizing, shaming, judging, lying,	Pulling	Pleasing	Resisting	Attached to outcome
angry, blaming, violent, violating,	Lecturing	Complaining	Caretaking	Acting out addictively
withholding, having expectations				

Making others responsible for defining my worth and lovability

—Possible false beliefs, underlying the above behavior and resulting pain, to embrace and explore:

I am a victim. People and events cause my feelings and behavior.	I am alone. God has abandoned me or doesn't exist.
I am flawed, bad, inadequate, unimportant, unworthy, unlovable.	I'm responsible for others' feelings.
I can and must control outcomes, people, feelings.	Resisting control is essential to my integrity.
I am selfish if I take care of myself.	I won't survive if someone I love disconnects from me.
Others' approval and disapproval define my worth.	I can't handle pain.

• EMBRACE, DIALOGUE with and LEARN ABOUT the core Self, the essence:

					Forms of intelligence:		
Intrinsic goodness	Desires	Gifts	Sadness	What brings joy?			
Intrinsic worth	Passions	Talents	Loneliness	What fulfills the heart?	Linear	Spatial	Spiritual
Intrinsic lovability	Calling	Creativity	Sorrow	What fulfills the soul?	Creative	Physical	Intuitive
Intrinsic competence			Grief		Relational	Practical	Abstract
							Emotional

Step 4

Utilizing imagery, DIALOGUE with SPIRITUAL GUIDANCE/HIGHER POWER.

- Ask for truth about the beliefs uncovered in Step 3 and bring it to the wounded self.
- Ask for the loving action toward the wounded self and the core Self.

Step 5

TAKE the LOVING ACTION(S) learned in Step 4. Examples:

Set loving boundaries within self and with others.	Practice mindfulness.
Care for the body, the house of the soul.	Choose the intent to learn each moment with self and others.
Pursue the calling of the soul.	Practice these Six Steps throughout the day.
Create balance between work and play.	Make amends.
Spend time holding your wounded self and getting held.	Define own worth and lovability daily.
Help others, do service, give to others.	Reach out for help when help is needed.

Step 6

EVALUATE THE ACTION(S). What are you feeling and experiencing? If healing is not occurring, go back to Step 4 to discover another loving action.

Evidence of healing of the wounded self and release of the core Self:

Personal power	Integration	Wisdom	Compassionate	Aliveness	Intimacy
Self-esteem	Authenticity	Knowing	Loving	Passion	Conflict resolution
Peace/Serenity	Transparency	Intuition	Understanding	Creativity	Respectful
Joy/Laughter	Playfulness	Vision	Gentle/Kind	Manifestation	Truthful
Gratitude	Spontaneity	Oneness with Spirit	Trusting	Generosity	Honoring of self/others
Freedom	Connection	Oneness with others	Have integrity		

EIGHT

Dialogues with the Dark Side

Our wounded self is our dark or shadow side, not because it is bad but because it is cut off from the light of God. It lives in the darkness of fear and the heaviness of false beliefs instead of in the light of love and truth. Moving toward "enlightenment" is moving into the light of truth. When we heal our fears and false beliefs, our energy lightens. We may even hear from others, "You seem so much lighter!"

Doorways to Darkness

Just as the light of God enters our hearts when we choose to open to love, the darkness enters when we choose to close our hearts and act from anger, fear, shame, judgment or hurt. This was the point in Luke's battle with his father, Darth Vader in *Return of the Jedi*, the last of the original Star Wars series. In this movie, the emperor, who was the epitome of darkness, was trying to get Luke to join the dark side.

He knew if he could just get Luke angry enough or frightened enough, he would want to kill his father, and then the emperor would own Luke as he had owned Luke's father. The emperor knew that anger and fear were the doorways to darkness.

Our anger, fear, shame, judgment and hurt are the cracks in our energy field through which the darkness enters. The darkness can also enter when we cloud our energy with drugs, alcohol, nicotine or sugar. Do you recall the trial in San Francisco that employed the infamous "Twinkie defense"? About twenty years ago, the mayor and a city supervisor were shot down inside City Hall and their killer got a short sentence because of his "diminished capacity" due to having eaten a diet of only junk food.

In one of my dialogues with my Teacher, she challenged me about darkness. She said, "Margie, you have worked for many years to be physically healthy. Not only that, you have striven to be immune to illness. Likewise, for many years you have sought to become a more loving person. Now your task is to become *immune to darkness*." I was blown away. Becoming immune to darkness means *never* acting out of my wounded self's feelings of fear, anger, shame, judgment or hurt but *always* moving into an intent to learn about these feelings as soon as they come up. I can tell you, it's quite a challenge! I don't know if I will ever accomplish this, but it certainly is a worthy goal.

Through purifying ourselves on the physical and emotional levels by eating well and doing our healing work, each of us can reach a place where our frequency is high enough that we can do this, we can hear our spiritual Guidance *all the time*. Being in conscious connection (and dialogue) with both our Inner Child and our spiritual Guidance at all times is one of

the goals of Inner Bonding. By doing the dialogue processes—
Steps Three and Four of Inner Bonding—we begin to heal the
cracks in our energy field through which the darkness enters,
and we shine the light of truth into the wounded self's fears
and false beliefs.

As I said earlier, when we feel hurt, angry, judgmental,
shamed, blaming, depressed or frightened, our dialogues are
with the wounded aspect of our Inner Child. These painful
feelings come from our own unloving behavior toward ourselves. However, when you have been operating most of the
time as a wounded child-adult, you cannot suddenly become
a loving Adult in order to do the dialogue process. So, often,
your early dialogues may be between one aspect of your
wounded child-adult (for example, the part that chooses to
indulge in binge eating), and another aspect of it (the part
that is furious at being overweight). Since dialoguing between
two aspects of your wounded child-adult won't get you anywhere, you might conclude that Inner Bonding doesn't work.

Here's what's really not working: We cannot bring light to
darkness with darkness. In other words, we can't heal our darkness by being furious at it. We can transform darkness into
light only by learning about and loving the darkness. We heal
darkness only with light—the light of love. Our challenge is to
love the part of us that we judge as bad, unlovable or unworthy, and it's a challenge that calls for the loving Adult.

But how can we have a dialogue between our wounded child-
adult and our loving Adult when we haven't yet developed a
loving Adult? Here is where your imagination comes into
play. You need to imagine that the dialogue is between your
wounded child-adult and the spiritual Guidance that you

imaged, whether it be God, Jesus, Buddha, a personal Master Teacher, a guardian angel, a divine light, or the highest part of yourself. You ask your wounded child-adult questions and offer comfort and help, not from your own thoughts, but from what you would *imagine* your loving, wise and powerful spiritual Guidance would say and do. (You will see two examples of how this works in the dialogues later in this chapter.) Or, if you know a person whom you really feel is loving, wise and powerful, you imagine that person in dialogue with your Inner Child. Either one is a good stand-in for your loving Adult.

Actress Susan Sarandon's character, in the movie *Dead Man Walking*, is a wonderful role model for loving behavior. She plays Sister Helen Prejean, a nun who has been asked by a murderer on death row to help him avoid execution. The murderer, played by Sean Penn, is a despicable human being. Not only did he rape and murder in cold blood, he is a racist and he continues to avoid responsibility with his blame, lies and manipulations. Almost no one in the nun's life supports her efforts on his behalf. They accuse her, blame her, shun her, yet never once does she lose her connection with God. She tells the murderer that he is a son of God and therefore greater than his worst acts. While never condoning his acts, she never condemns him as a person. She lovingly confronts him with himself. Although she does not like him, she loves him. She becomes the face of God for him, and through her love, which is God, he opens his heart and is redeemed. Penn's character is very dark, the worst of the wounded child-adult, while Sarandon's is very light, the best of the loving Adult.

Given that you might not have role models of loving behavior in your daily life, you can use your spiritual Guidance as your role model to emulate and assimilate. Eventually, when you do this long enough, you begin to take on the qualities of your Guidance. This is how you develop your loving Adult. It takes practice. You have to learn to concentrate on this imaginative process and to trust what you hear.

When clients of mine first start to do this, I generally hear them say, "How do I know this is real? It feels like I'm just making this up, that it's *just* my imagination." Many of us have been brought up to believe that when we create—whether it be poetry, a painting, a song, a musical score, a book, a screenplay, a theory—we bring these things forth from our own minds. We may believe that we actually have the capacity to be creative all by ourselves. The truth is that creativity flows when we are open to God, and use the gift of our imaginations.

I no longer believe that my theories, my writing, my paintings or even the words that flow from me when I am working with someone or leading a workshop come from my own individual mind. I experience my mind more as a receiver of divine information, which I can then transmit through my writing, speaking and painting. Just as love, compassion, truth, peace and joy are not feelings we generate from within our own small selves but are gifts from God, so too are our imagination and the creativity that flows from it. We all have the capacity to learn to access the source of wisdom and creativity.

It has taken me time and practice to trust the information that comes through me. I have learned over the years that when I do not trust my spiritual Guidance, bad things happen. This really hit home for me in the summer of 1995 when I was leading an Inner Bonding five-day intensive in

Missouri. It was the fourth day of the intensive and I was pouring some tea from a pitcher during one of our breaks. I heard my Teacher say, "Do not drink that, it is contaminated." I decided I was being paranoid and drank it anyway. The next morning I woke up with a terrible sore throat—the first time I had been sick in years—and so did a number of other people, all of whom had drunk the tea. Even with all the years I had been dialoguing with and listening to my Teacher, I still lacked trust and needed another lesson in humility: That my individual mind, unplugged from spiritual Guidance, doesn't know much.

So it takes a lot of practice, yet practicing seems to be difficult for many people. If you were determined to become accomplished at a particular skill, for example playing a musical instrument, you would think nothing of practicing every day. In fact, you would know that you needed to practice daily in order to become skilled and then continue practicing daily to maintain your skill. Becoming skilled at Inner Bonding is no different. You will become skilled only by daily practice, and you will continue to reap the benefits only by daily practice. It is only through daily practice that you will learn to consistently hear and trust both God and your true Self. The problem is that the wounded child-adult won't practice, so unless you pray daily to God for help in shifting your deepest desire from getting love to being loving, you will not have enough of a loving Adult to override the child-adult and make the decision to practice.

Many of my clients, coming in for help because they are suffering, find that they start to feel better within days of starting to practice Inner Bonding. Then, as soon as they feel better, they stop practicing and go right back to feeling badly. Sometimes they then conclude that Inner Bonding doesn't work. This is like saying that if you have a young son and you give him love one day but ignore him for the next few days, he should continue to feel happy because of the one day you did give him love. This doesn't work with your Inner Child any more than it does with real children. Just as babies need you to be constantly tuned in to them, your Inner Child needs you to be constantly aware of your feelings and needs. Becoming this aware and maintaining this awareness takes daily practice.

The good news is that practice really pays off. Clients of mine who have been practicing Inner Bonding for an extended period of time (it varies for each person) find that eventually they do it all the time. They naturally stay tuned in to their Inner Child and their spiritual Guidance, and they naturally dialogue with them whenever they feel anything other than peace and joy inside. They find themselves doing it in the shower, while preparing meals, doing chores, waiting in line at the market or stuck in traffic. After much practice, they are delighted to find that they no longer allow themselves to feel badly for any length of time. They are progressing rapidly toward wholeness and oneness with God.

Dialoguing with the Darkness

Here are several examples of dialogues where people are struggling to move into the light of love and take loving action.

Jennifer

Jennifer, whom I introduced in chapter two, came to see me for Inner Bonding work because she was unhappy with some of her relationships, especially her relationships with her husband Mark, her best friend and her mother. She was often very angry, even enraged, at seemingly minor incidents, and she seemed to have no control over her rage. While her relationship with her two sons seemed pretty good, Jennifer noticed that as they grew older she was occasionally angry with them, too. She blamed those around her for her anger. If only other people would be more caring, she told me, she wouldn't get so angry.

As Jennifer and I explored her history, she told me that when she was around two years old, she had fallen off an outside flight of stairs and fractured her skull on the concrete below. For a while she hovered near death and had to remain in the hospital for a long time. During the most critical period, she had been strapped to her bed and her parents weren't allowed to see her. Jennifer was told not to cry, that crying would make her worse. She spent terrible weeks alone and terrified, feeling completely abandoned. She unconsciously decided that no one cared about her. Then she sank into her core shame: The reason no one cared about her was because she was bad. By the time she got out of the hospital, these beliefs were deeply imbedded in her wounded self.

Uncovering the root of Jennifer's painful feelings took time, but even gaining understanding of all this did not reduce her sudden outbursts of rage. Awareness itself is rarely enough to alter behavior. As long as Jennifer still believed she was bad, that people didn't care about her and that it was other people's responsibility to change so she would feel safe, her wounded child-adult's behavior would persist. She would continue trying to control getting the love she craved by getting angry and blaming others for her feelings of abandonment. As long as Jennifer did not have a loving Adult caring for her Inner Child, she would continue to feel abandoned, no matter how loving others were. There would always be something that would touch her deep, childhood abandonment wound until her Inner Child no longer felt abandoned by her loving Adult.

While Jennifer had not yet developed a solid loving Adult, she did have excellent access to her spiritual Teacher, Teresa. Below is a composite dialogue between her Teacher, her loving Adult and her wounded child-adult, facilitated during a number of sessions. In this dialogue, Jennifer uses a doll to represent her child-adult.

Child-adult Jenny: [crying and angry] I'm so angry at Mark. He just doesn't care about me. He never wants to spend time with me and he criticizes me all the time. And he doesn't help me when I really need it. We had company over Sunday and he got so involved with the kids and our guests, he didn't even notice when I needed help with things. [Blaming, feeling like a victim. She is not yet in Step One.]

Margie: It sounds like you felt really abandoned again.

Child-adult Jenny: That's right. He always does this to me, and I'm sick of it. I didn't get married to be treated like this.

[She has no intent to learn. Her anger and her blaming serve to protect her from the feelings of aloneness and loneliness that she fears.]

Margie: Jennifer, would you be willing to go a little deeper and see what is under this anger? Are you willing to pray to God and then ask Teresa for help right now? *[Asking her to move into Steps One and Two.]*

She is reluctant to give up her anger and blaming. She is addicted to it, and once she starts, it is hard for her to stop. She finally winds down when I refuse to participate in her blaming. She closes her eyes and takes some deep breaths. Then she speaks with quiet sincerity.

Child-adult Jenny: Okay . . . God, please help me open my heart. Please help me want to learn. Teresa, please help me right now. I really need your help.

After a few minutes, Jennifer calms down and is able to access her Teacher. As her heart opens, she is moved to tears—not from feeling abandoned or victimized but from the love that enters her heart. She now essentially becomes Teresa, speaking as Teresa, allowing the words to come through her.

Teresa *[speaking through Jennifer]*: Jennifer, I am here and I love you. You are not alone.

Margie: Jennifer, please imagine that your core little child is with Teresa and so is your three-year-old child-adult. Ask Teresa first to show you who your core Self is. See if you can see her through Teresa's eyes rather than through your mother's eyes and see why Teresa loves you. *[This is part of Step Four. Steps Three and Four can be done in reverse order. And often you go back and forth between Steps Three and Four.]*

Jennifer: Okay. Teresa, please tell me who I really am as my core Child. *[Jennifer smiles as she sees an image in her mind's eye.]* Oh! She is showing me a beautiful shining little girl, so innocent, so loving, so smart!

Margie: Is there anything bad about this little girl?

Jennifer: Oh no! There is nothing bad about her at all!

Margie: Does she deserve to be loved by you?

Jennifer: Yes!

Margie: Now ask Teresa to show you your wounded child.

Jennifer: Oh, I see her. She is so frightened. She feels so alone. *[Starts to cry again.]*

Margie: Jennifer, can you welcome her and embrace her and ask her why she gets so angry? *[Step Three]*

Jennifer *[In a soft and compassionate tone of voice]*: Jenny, why do you get so angry? *[Jennifer now allows herself to drop down into her Inner Child and speaks from the wounded part of her that is so angry.]*

Child-adult Jenny: It's not my fault. Mark makes me so angry!

Margie: Ask her what she hopes for by getting angry at Mark. *[She asks the question of Jenny.]*

Child-adult Jenny: I hope he will see that he is hurting me and change.

Margie: So you hope your anger will have control over Mark? You hope he will change and take away your pain?

Child-adult Jenny: Yeah, I guess so.

Margie: Is it working?

Jennifer: No, not at all. He is moving further away from me. I'm scared he's going to leave me.

Margie: Jennifer, where did you learn to use anger to control? Who used anger in your family to control?

Jennifer: Both of my parents, but especially my mother. She was always yelling at us and at my father. God! When I was a kid I vowed never to be like my mother and here I am, just like her.

Margie: Did her anger work to control you?

Jennifer: Yes. I was always trying to please her. Until I was a teenager and then I rebelled.

Margie: So now you believe that because it worked to control you when you were little, you can use it to control others?

Jennifer: Yes, I see that. I do think I can get people to stop hurting me with my anger. I see that it is not working. But I feel so awful when people are not caring about me. I don't know what to do.

Margie: You feel awful when you *believe* people are not caring about you, and then your child-adult tries to protect you from this *perceived* threat of abandonment. What is really happening is that *you* are not caring about you. You are abandoning your Inner Child and then projecting this onto others, thinking that they are abandoning you. Imagine that you as a loving Adult are with your wounded child and with Teresa. Can you go over and put your arms around your wounded child? [Step Five]

Jennifer: Yes, I can hold her. She's so frightened. She feels so alone. . . . Oh, I see her in the hospital bed! She wants her mommy. She doesn't understand why her mommy isn't with her.

Margie: Now go over to the hospital bed and pick her up and hold her. Let her know that you and Teresa are here with her, that she is not alone anymore. . . . Jennifer, is she bad? Is she alone in that hospital bed because she is bad?

Jennifer: No. She isn't bad. Well, I don't know. Maybe she is bad for falling off the stairs. She wasn't supposed to be playing there so maybe this happened because she was bad.

Margie: Ask Teresa if this happened because she is bad. [Step Four]

Jennifer: Teresa, did all this happen to me because I am bad? Was I bad for playing on the stairs?

Teresa [speaking through Jennifer]: My dear, you are that sweet innocent child I showed you. That is who you really are. You were not bad for playing on the stairs—you were just being a naturally curious child. You did not fall because you were bad. You were not left alone in the hospital because you were bad. It had nothing to do with you being bad. Sometimes bad things happen to people, but it doesn't mean *they* are bad. It's just part of life.

Margie: Jennifer, you have a very frightened little girl inside who thinks she is bad and needs love in order to

know she is good and that she is not alone. She keeps trying to get that love from others and gets furious when she
thinks they are not giving it to her. Her rage is covering the
awful fear and aloneness, stemming from your hospital
experience, that come up when you can't get someone to
love you and when you are not loving yourself. What your
Child really needs is for you to go in that hospital room in
your imagination and pick her up and hold her, every time
you feel angry. She needs your love and compassion—not
your judgment—when she is angry, blaming and judgmental.

Jennifer: I think I can do that. I feel so much better right
now.

Margie: Now, ask Teresa if Mark loves you. *[Step Four]*

Jennifer: Teresa, I really want to know if Mark loves me or
not. . . . Oh, I see. Oh, poor guy! *[Finally able to have some
compassion for Mark. Compassion is impossible when the
child-adult is in charge of the person's feelings and behavior.]*
He really loves me. He hurts when I get so angry. He's
pulling away from me but not because he doesn't love me.
He just doesn't know what else to do.

Margie: Do you love him?

Jennifer: I do. He is a wonderful man. But it probably doesn't
look like it when I'm blaming him and yelling at him.

Margie: You feel love and compassion for Mark right now,
but as soon as you feel alone and frightened, your compassion leaves and you just feel angry. It will be hard for you to
maintain your compassion for Mark until you develop compassion for the wounded child within you. Would you be

willing to imagine your wounded little child in that hospital bed, every time you feel angry, and go and pick her up before you start to rage? This will be a challenge, since you are so addicted to the anger and it happens so fast. Maybe you could try just holding your doll for about ten minutes every day, imagining it is you as a frightened little child. [Step Five]

Jennifer: I really want to do that. I feel happy inside holding her. I'm going to practice that and see what happens.

One of the characteristics of the wounded child-adult, which we see in this dialogue, is narcissism—wanting others to be responsible for your feelings and needs and having no compassion for theirs. A child-adult, operating from narcissistic rage that originated in an abandonment wound, does not care about the effects of that rage on others. In the moment, he or she cares only about getting someone to take away the pain.

As Jennifer worked with Inner Bonding, she saw that as a wounded child-adult, she was always trying to get love from Mark and others and had never wanted to give love, either to herself or others. In the same vicious circle we talked about earlier, Jennifer's controlling behavior perpetuated her core shame belief that she was bad. Once she shifted her intent from trying to control to wanting to learn and love, she started liking herself. Each time she was able to offer love to her wounded child-adult, healing occurred. Each time she offered love to Mark, her mother, her friends and her children, she felt joy, which further healed her core shame.

It is very helpful when dialoguing with an abandoned part of yourself to think of specific times when you felt alone and afraid. For Jennifer, this was the time she was in the hospital. For you, it may have been an afternoon on the playground or one night lying in bed. Imagine yourself feeling very alone and afraid in that specific situation, then imagine that you as a loving Adult walk in and pick up, hold and comfort your Child. You will find this extremely healing.

Matthew

Matthew had been consulting with me for quite some time and had made a lot of progress in his relationships with his co-workers and his wife, but he still felt empty and alone much of the time. He couldn't seem to get himself to do much dialoguing. He felt stuck.

Matthew was brought up in a fundamentalist religion with many erroneous concepts about God. He believed in God, but he rarely prayed. Through a number of explorations in our sessions together, it became apparent that Matthew's fears about God and his anger at God were keeping him stuck. The following is an excerpt from one of his sessions exploring his wounded child-adult's feelings and beliefs about God. Matthew was already in Step One when we started this exploration. He had also already created, through his imagination, a guardian angel he called Hector.

Margie: Matthew, I'd like you to imagine that Hector is here, surrounding you with love . . . and ask him to help you explore your wounded child-adult's beliefs about God. [*Step*

Two; Matthew does this.] Now, welcome and embrace your child-adult and ask him to tell you what God is to him and why he doesn't want you to connect with God. *[Step Three]*

Matthew: Okay. *[Holding a doll, speaking to it as if the doll is his child-adult.]* Matt, please tell me about how you see God and why you don't want to connect with Him. *[He turns the doll around so it faces me, then hugs it to his solar plexus and sinks down into himself, letting himself feel like the little child he once was.]*

Child-adult Matt: God is a big man with a white beard in the sky. He sees everything you do, and when you do something bad he punishes you. He can get really, really mad.

Margie: God sounds just like your father.

Matthew: That's right! That's how my child-adult sees God! An angry, punishing, righteous and judgmental father.

Margie: Well, I can see why you don't want to connect with God. Move back into your child-adult and talk about what connecting with God feels like to him.

Child-adult Matt: It hurts. God will make me do things I don't want to do—I can't be me. It's too much work; God wants too much from me. He wants me to suffer. You have to suffer if you connect with God because God wants us to. And I'll end up alone. God will separate me from everyone.

Margie: Was your father like this, too?

Matthew: Yes. I couldn't be me with my father. It always felt like he wanted me to suffer, that suffering meant you were good. And one of the ways he punished me was making me be alone a lot, telling me that God wanted me to contemplate my sins.

Margie: It sounds like you are angry at God the Father.

Child-adult Matt: Yeah, but I can't be angry at God. He will punish me if I am angry at him. I am supposed to love God.

Margie: Like you were supposed to love your father? And not get angry at him?

Matthew: Yes. Margie, I know in my head that all this isn't true, but this is what I feel inside. I don't know how to change these feelings. I know they aren't accurate, but they *feel* true.

Margie: These beliefs will not change through your own mind. The truth needs to come to your child-adult from a higher source of truth; it needs to come *through* you, not *from* you. [Step Four] And after it does, you will need to act on this information. [Step Five] So, let's move into Step Four. Imagine that Matt has just said all this to your guardian angel. What does Hector say about what God is?

Matthew moves into connection with Hector by imagining him.

Hector [speaking through Matthew]: God is Spirit—the Spirit of kindness and gentleness. God is nothing like your father. You can even be angry at God, and God will understand. God helps you to feel a part of everyone. God takes away your feelings of aloneness and helps you share love with others. *[Matthew starts to cry.]* Being disconnected from God is what's causing you to feel so alone and empty.

Matthew *[sobbing]*: I know this is true, but my child-adult doesn't believe it. What do I do?

Margie: *[gently]*: Respond to Hector from your child-adult.

Child-adult Matt: If God is so kind, why did he let my father be so mean to me?

Margie: Now answer as Hector.

Hector: Your father's heart was closed to the kindness of God. But God has always been here helping you, as he did through your dog, who had the same name as I do.

Matthew: My dog Hector! Oh, I never made the connection. *[Smiles.]* He was a huge old golden retriever. I loved him so! He was always there when I felt so alone.

Margie: So, because God could not come through your father, he came to you through the big loving heart of your dog.

[Matthew pauses and thinks over what he's been learning.]

Matthew: Okay, I can see that my fear of God is really just my fear of my father. That makes sense. *[Smiles again.]* When I think about Hector—my dog Hector—I can feel my heart open. It feels so good.

Margie: That good feeling is God within your heart. Maybe God gave us dogs so we can directly experience love. They certainly bring through more love than many people do. How are you feeling now? Do you feel more open now to praying and connecting with God?

Matthew: Yes, I really want to. *[laughing.]* I think I can feel closer to God if I think of Him as my dog instead of my father!

Margie: Good idea! Maybe that will also change your concept of yourself. One of my clients prays, "God, please let me be the person my dog believes me to be!"

Jeremy

Jeremy came to see me because he had just been diagnosed with heart disease and his doctor had insisted that he quit smoking. He had tried through the years to quit but had never been able to. Now his life was threatened, yet he was still unable to quit and was quite distressed over this.

Jeremy came from a very lonely background. His father died when he was around three years old and his mother had to work. He was left with baby-sitters who didn't have much time for him. Once he started school when he was six, he was left alone each day after school while his mother was at work. He had a hard time making friends at school and spent much of his time feeling very alone. He got into trouble as an adolescent, but he went on to college and did well. In college he started to drink, smoke and eat poorly. When he came to see me he had cleaned up his diet and stopped drinking in an attempt to control his heart disease, but he was still smoking. Jeremy's wife, Carolyn, loved him very much, yet he continued to feel alone.

The following dialogue is a composite of some of the work we did. Jeremy was already in Step One when he came in to see me, and in the work we did before the conversation that follows, he had imaged a spiritual guide named Joseph.

Margie: Jeremy, take a moment to connect with Joseph, asking him for help in learning about your wounded child-adult. *[Step Two—he does this.]* Now, coming from your love and curiosity for the part of you that is so addicted to cigarettes, ask him why it is so important to him to smoke. *[Step Three]*

Jeremy: Little Jeremy, why do you smoke? Why is it more important to smoke than be healthy?

Child-adult Jeremy: Smoking is the only thing that calms me, makes me feel less alone. While I'm smoking, I feel like I am with my best friend. I can always rely on this friend to be there for me. I can turn to it whenever I want. I feel too anxious and alone when I don't smoke. Nothing makes me feel as good as a cigarette.

Margie: So smoking is the way you have learned to take care of your aloneness—the way that alone little boy handles his feelings?

Jeremy: Yes. The stress I feel when I don't smoke is awful. That can't be good for my heart either.

Margie: That's right, it isn't, but it sounds like you believe that either you smoke or you feel stress.

Jeremy: Yes, that is the way it has been.

Margie: I'd like you to ask Joseph what you are doing that causes little Jeremy to feel so alone and stressed. *[Step Four]*

Jeremy: Joseph, how do I cause my Child to feel so alone and stressed? . . . Joseph is showing me that I ignore my Child most of the time. I don't listen to him, take time with him.

Margie: That sounds like what happened to you when you were a child.

Jeremy: That's right! My mother didn't listen to me. Or spend time with me. I just got left alone all the time. I hated it.

Margie: But now you leave your Inner Child alone a lot.

Jeremy: I guess I do.

Margie: And you depend on Carolyn to fill that aloneness, don't you?

Jeremy: Well, she always tells me I'm trying to control her. I do want her with me all the time. I hate it when she goes out and leaves me alone.

Margie: So you try to use her in the same way you use the cigarettes—to take away the feelings of aloneness?

Jeremy: I guess so.

Margie: What could you do about this?

Jeremy: I don't know.

Margie: Ask Joseph.

Jeremy: Okay. . . . He's saying, "Your Child's aloneness needs to be healed by loving him. Only love feels better than a cigarette."

Margie: How does your child-adult feel about that?

Jeremy: Actually, I can hear him right now. He is saying to me, "This will not work. This is bullshit! As soon as we can get out of here, let's just chill out for a few minutes and have a smoke. This is making us feel tense and tension is not good for us. So let's just calm down with a cigarette."

Margie: Now imagine that you are with Joseph. What would Joseph say to this?

Jeremy: Joseph is saying, "Little Jeremy, I love you very much. You are a very wonderful, bright and caring little boy. I love you too much to let you harm yourself with smoking. I know you believe that it helps you, but it is hurting you. It could kill you. I love you very much, and I will not allow you to harm yourself in this way."

Margie: Now respond as your child-adult.

Child-adult Jeremy: I don't care if it kills me. I'd rather be dead than feel this way. Life isn't worth living if I can't feel good some of the time. Anyway, a few cigarettes won't hurt me.

Margie: Now answer as your own loving Adult, pretending you are talking with a child you adore.

Jeremy: I am here for you little Jeremy. I won't leave you alone any more like Mom did. You are not alone. I am here. Joseph is here. God is here. And Carolyn really loves you and is very worried about you. It deeply upsets her that we continue to smoke. A few cigarettes *will* harm you, and I will no longer allow that. I know I haven't treated you well and that you don't know what a wonderful little boy you are. I will start to spend time with you and learn more about who you are. That will help you to feel less alone. I see that you smoke because of feeling so alone for so long and I will no longer leave you alone.

Margie: I would like you to agree to attend Nicotine Anonymous. You need some support with this and you need to strengthen your connection with God.

Jeremy: Okay. *[When he takes this action and the one suggested below, he will be doing Step Five.]*

Margie: Also, you need to commit to dialoguing every day with your Child, especially when you want to smoke. Instead of turning to the cigarette to fill the emptiness, you need to consciously turn to Joseph and God. Instead of smoking, ask Joseph what you can give to your Inner Child and to Carolyn. Start to think more about what you can give to yourself and to others. You also need to start being conscious of the voice of your child-adult, luring you toward the cigarette. Now ask Joseph what you can give to Carolyn.

Jeremy: Joseph, what can I give to Carolyn? What would be loving to her? . . . Joseph is saying to stop and pick up some flowers for her. She loves flowers, and I hardly ever buy them for her. She would really love that! She'll be so surprised!

Margie: How do you feel now? *[Step Six: Evaluating the effectiveness of the loving action.]*

Jeremy: Much better! I feel good.

Margie: Jeremy, as soon as you asked how you could love Carolyn, your heart opened and God entered your heart. This is why you feel good. Do you need to smoke right now?

Jeremy: No. I can't wait to see Carolyn's face when I give her flowers!

Jeremy didn't give up cigarettes for good that day. In fact, he struggled with this issue for a number of months. But with the help of Inner Bonding and his Twelve-Step group, he was able to strengthen his connection with God and develop a more powerful loving Adult. His Adult was then able to stop smoking, not through willpower, but through filling his emptiness with the love that is God—love for his Inner Child and love for Carolyn.

Willpower is what the wounded child-adult tries to use to control things, whether it be alcohol, drugs, food, smoking, coffee, anger, TV, gambling, spending and so on. When you strengthen your connection with God and learn to love your Inner Child and others, you no longer operate from the controlling child-adult. You tap into the infinite strength and power of love to help you take good care of yourself and be caring to others. True willpower means using your will to open to the love and strength of your Higher Power.

Many people spend their lives in denial about their shadow side, their wounded self. Not only are they unwilling to explore this aspect of themselves, they do not even admit that it exists or that it is a problem. In disowning their darkness, the darkness is allowed to grow unchecked, and often results in unloving, violating or even violent behavior towards self and others. Until you are willing to move into the intent to learn about your own darkness—about the *good reasons* you have for your beliefs that keep you stuck—without judging or shaming yourself for your woundedness—you will stay stuck in denial and suffer all of the consequences of denial—alone-ness, hurt, depression, fear and anxiety. Until you are willing to love your dark side instead of shaming yourself for it, you will continue to suffer.

The wounded child contains all the memories of your past experiences and all the false beliefs that you developed as a result of these experiences. When you have done the dialogu-ing of Steps Three and Four for a number of months, the wounded child will let you in on these memories, and the con-nection with your spiritual Guidance will enable you to heal the past spiritual abuse—the physical, emotional and/or sexual abuse that created your disconnection from God. Through this process you will discover that God loves you unconditionally. You will know through your own *direct experience* that you do not have to give yourself up to be loved by God.

NINE

Experiencing Self and God Through Vessels of Love

One day I was discussing with Erika the fact that some of the people I was working with were stuck in the wounded self, especially in anger and blame, or in resistance, withdrawal and numbness. All of them understood the concepts of choice and intent. All truly desired to be loving and connected with God. But they couldn't seem to stay open to learning about loving. Some couldn't even pray for openness. As soon as their fear came up, their wounded child-adult was instantly in charge, and they turned to their usual controlling, addictive behavior.

This happens with everyone when they first start practicing Inner Bonding because it takes time to learn to recognize when the moment of choice is at hand and to act on it by making a new choice. But the more people practice the intent to learn, the more they see that they have choices when fear comes up. Most of the people I work with who devote themselves to practicing Inner Bonding slowly gain this awareness and are able to make new choices.

But there are always those who can't seem to make a new choice even after lots of practice, who keep reverting to their wounded self as soon as their fear is touched off. I wondered why and asked Erika what she thought.

"They can't self-nurture until they get that nurturing from someone else," she replied. "They need mothering. They don't know they are loved by God until someone brings God's love through to them. They don't know that God is there for them until they experience Divine Love through someone else. They will stay stuck until they get the nurturing they need."

She was right. Some people, because of certain traumas they suffered as small children, can't know their lovability and worth until they experience it through another. They can't access God directly, especially when they are scared, until they *feel* that God loves them. They need to receive God through another before they can receive God directly. I call people who can do this for others "vessels of love."

Mothering

Mothering is the experience of unconditional love that we all should have received from our parents from the moment of our birth. Mothering happens when we are touched or held with no agenda—that is, the other person has no outcome attached to the holding and nurturing they are giving us. They do it purely from the desire to love. Mothering lets us receive love without having to do anything to get it and without owing anything for it. Mothering gives us the experience of God that lets us know we are lovable and not alone in the universe.

Mothering comes from the loving Adult. The loving Adult must be both mother and father to the Child within. The mother aspect of ourselves—the feminine, the yin—is the part that chooses the intent to learn when we are upset and brings through love to our wounded child. The father aspect—the masculine, the yang—is the part of each of us that takes loving action for us in the world. We each have the capacity to mother and father ourselves and others.

As we heal, we become more and more capable of being instruments of God's love. As we clear out the fears and false beliefs that block our loving, we become clear channels through which Divine Love can flow. We can then serve God by being vessels of love, offering this unconditional love to others, sometimes through mothering or fathering them.

Babies receive this love by being held and touched when Divine Love is coming through their parents. If you missed out on this as a child, it may be necessary for you to have the experience of being held or touched with love as an adult. I always hold or touch my clients when they are in deep pain. Sometimes they need to curl up like a baby in my lap; other times they just need me to hold their hand or touch their shoulder. I have found that most people receive much-needed comfort when they are held or touched. I strongly disagree with the traditional psychotherapeutic injunction not to touch clients, just as I strongly disagree with the rule that teachers should not hug their students. Unfortunately, thera-pists and teachers fear being sued and often hold back giving the healing touch that the client or child needs. Sometimes the only time a child gets the message that they are lovable is when a kind and caring teacher hugs them. How very sad that teachers are not allowed to give in this way.

The laws against holding and touching have come about because some people have abused touch, allowing their wounded self with a sexual agenda to do the touching. As professionals and/or parents it is incumbent upon us to do our own inner work so that we *always* come from our loving Adult when offering comfort and touch to others. Unfortunately, too many therapists and educators, as well as clergy, operate from their wounded selves.

When I originally discussed this with Erika, I had been in the habit of holding or touching my clients when they were sad or frightened, but I hadn't thought to hold them when they were angry and blaming, or resistant, withdrawn and numbed out. Now I saw that this was exactly what some of them needed.

Mothering can help people who really do have an intent to learn about their own intrinsic lovability. Holding an angry or withdrawn person who does not have the desire to take responsibility for themselves, however, will only foster their dependence. If their anger or withdrawal is a tactic (conscious or unconscious) to get someone else to take responsibility for them, it is inappropriate to hold them.

Since that discussion with Erika, I have put this into practice with wonderful results. I have encouraged people to recognize their need for mothering and to seek it from friends and mates. Sometimes this is very challenging. It is often difficult for women to ask for mothering from women and for men to ask for it from men. Equally difficult may be to get it from the opposite sex without sex becoming a part of it, or from the same sex in gay relationships for the identical reason.

Occasionally people turn to gay relationships because they erroneously conclude that because they want to be held by someone of their own sex, it must mean they are gay. Sometimes they sexualize their need for mothering, believing that the only way they can get held is to have sex.

Sex is not mothering and does not have the healing quality that mothering has. *Mothering never has sexuality attached to it.* While sex with a loving Adult is a way to bring through God's love, two people cannot reach this kind of expression until both have done their inner work and truly know their own lovability. Sexuality does not heal the wounded child's core shame. Rather, it can perpetuate it.

Do you remember Jennifer, who felt so out of control with her anger and blame? She is a good example of someone who needed mothering in order to know she was lovable enough to connect directly with God. Jennifer was stuck in an inner system that kept rewounding her Inner Child. Because of the core shame that became deeply embedded when she was alone in the hospital for weeks as a small child, Jennifer believed she was unlovable. Whenever she thought someone was uncaring toward her, she got angry, thus abandoning her Inner Child (by blaming someone else for her feelings instead of taking responsibility for them) and perpetuating her belief that she was unlovable. She could not feel lovable while she was behaving so unlovingly. So each time Jennifer became angry and blaming, she rewounded her Inner Child.

Jennifer often came into her sessions already angry at me. While she was driving to my office, she projected her own self-judgments onto me and by the time she arrived, she was convinced that I really didn't like her. She would then find something that I would do—maybe I didn't smile brightly enough or I was a minute late—that verified for her that I didn't care about her and that I was judging her. She would start off the session defensive and closed. If I pointed this out, she would say I was attacking and blaming her. This let me know that Jennifer was operating from her wounded child-adult, because it is a hallmark of the child-adult that it always hears information as an attack (the loving Adult hears it as a gift). There would be no convincing her that by offering her information, I was being caring. Being stuck in her child-adult with no intent to learn at that moment and convinced that I was judging her, all Jennifer could do was get angry and blame me for how she felt.

After my conversation with Erika about mothering, I interrupted this cycle by going over to Jennifer and holding her, bringing through God's unconditional love and compassion to her. The first time I did this, it stunned her. Her mind couldn't understand why I would want to hold her if I thought she was a bad person. But Jennifer could not hold on to her anger while she was receiving love through my touch. Her skin took in the message of unconditional love, even when her mind couldn't grasp it. Since the Inner Child communicates through the body, her Child received the communication directly, bypassing the mind. I made sure I touched Jennifer's skin—her arm or hand or cheek—and stroked her hair so that her Inner Child could directly feel God's love coming through me to her.

When her Child *felt* that I wasn't judging her and that I felt loving toward her, even when she was angry, Jennifer's belief in her own unlovability started melting away. It was miraculous to experience the progress she made once she received some mothering. She didn't need a lot of it. Jennifer received mothering from me a few times in individual sessions, then joined a women's group and received mothering from some of the women in the group. She was soon able to give it as well as receive it. As Jennifer shifted out of her belief that she was unlovable, she became less reactive when her abandonment issues were triggered. She soon reached the point where she was more consistently able to bring through God's love to her Inner Child when she did start feeling alone and unwanted. She was no longer stuck in the vicious circle of feeling rejected (due to her own core shame), then acting out in anger, thereby confirming her own unlovability.

If Jennifer's true intent had been to get someone to fix her instead of to take responsibility for her own feelings, my mothering would not have helped her to heal. Instead, it would have perpetuated her addiction to having others fill her up. I have found that when someone has a true intent to learn to love themselves, mothering begins to help immediately. Holding people who want to heal themselves is an energizing experience for me, while holding those who have no intent to learn is very draining. They are a bottomless pit of neediness and holding them only enables them to continue in their addiction to getting others to take responsibility for them.

Giving to Get

Holding someone will not be healing if the person *doing* the holding is giving to get, that is, if the holder has an agenda attached to the holding, such as to get love back, to be seen as a loving person, to get sex or to manipulate the other person into not being angry. The person being held will not feel that he or she is receiving Divine Love. Instead, he or she will feel used in some way. This is especially dangerous if the person who needs to be held has sexual abuse in his or her background. Children who have been sexually abused end up feeling objectified, that is, instead of feeling worthwhile in their own right, they feel like objects that are used for other people's benefit. Later on, as adults, if they are offered comforting by someone with an agenda—especially if the agenda is to get sex—the holding will feel invasive and awful instead of loving and comforting.

This can become confusing in a marriage when a husband puts his arm around his upset or crying wife ostensibly to comfort her, but secretly hoping this closeness will lead to sex. If she pushes him away, he may become hurt or angry, accusing her of being cold and rejecting his help. She may not even know why his touch feels so bad, and so she may take his accusations as true, thus confirming her core shame. Only when couples understand the concept of intent can they begin to make sense out of these interactions. Our intent cannot be concealed. It is always manifested through the energy that we unconsciously transmit to the other person. We can act nice, but if our intent is to get something in exchange for what we are giving, the energy will feel bad to the other person. Others will feel pulled at instead of loved.

Understanding the intent behind your action is the only way to untangle the complex interactions that follow. It can really get to be a mess if an angry or crying person is trying to get love to fill up his or her emptiness, and the person's mate responds with the kind of holding that comes from the wounded child-adult, which also is trying to get love. Then they are two empty, codependent people, each making the other responsible for filling himself or herself up, and both getting hurt or angry when they don't get what they want. Couples who have not done their individual healing work are often stuck in this dynamic. They may eventually separate or divorce, each blaming the other for the marital problems, only to find themselves in similar situations in future relationships.

The tangled mess of codependent interactions becomes clear when both people embrace a desire to learn about their intent regarding each other. As both people do their inner work, each is more frequently able to maintain an intent to learn. Then they become true instruments of God's love, capable of helping each other heal.

Fathering

Fathering is taking loving action for our Inner Child, as well as for others when they are unable to take action for themselves. While our mother aspect does the first four steps of Inner Bonding, our father aspect takes loving action in the world (Step Five). All truly loving action that you take for yourself is also loving action for others, since taking loving action brings through God's love. People who are needy may not feel loved by the loving actions you take for yourself, but people who do take responsibility for themselves will applaud them. Likewise, all loving action taken for others is also loving toward yourself.

Any action that brings through Divine Love to yourself or others is loving action and therefore enhances your self-esteem. *Just as giving and receiving mothering lets you know you are lovable, giving and receiving fathering lets you know you are worthy.*

During my five-day intensives, I sometimes work with men and women who have been physically and sexually abused by a parent. In many cases, the other parent either did nothing to protect the child or actually participated in or encouraged the abuse. Allowing the wounded child to express his or her hurt and rage is a crucial part of the person's healing, but equally important is for them to express themselves as an outraged loving Adult, letting the abusive parent and everyone else know that they will never again allow anyone to abuse their Inner Child. Sometimes the person is so afraid of their own anger—fearing that by expressing it they will become like their abuser and hurt others—that they cannot express that outrage. When this is the case, they need someone to do it for them. Here is an example of how fathering helped both the giver and receiver.

Kimberly was a teacher in her late twenties, plump and dark-haired with enormous green eyes. She was timid and quiet, with a very sweet and loving nature that rarely got expressed. Kimberly had memories of being repeatedly sexually abused by her father, who was also a rageaholic. She was terrified of her own anger and allowed others to walk all over her. The only way she knew to protect her Inner Child from being taken over and controlled by others was to not be in relationships at all. She had no loving Adult to set appropriate limits. All her wounded child-adult knew how to do was withdraw.

As a result, Kimberly was very lonely, but she preferred that to giving herself up to others. She had left her marriage because she had lost her sense of self. She had become a care-taker and was completely controlled by her husband, because she feared his anger and ridicule. Since Kimberly was new to Inner Bonding and had not yet done the work necessary to create a loving Adult capable of setting boundaries, her Inner Child still felt fearful and unprotected.

Max, who was also in this intensive, was a man I had worked with for some time. Max was in his early forties, a tough, wiry engineer. He, too, had uncovered extensive physical and sexual abuse at the hands of his father. However, his father was also the only one who had ever showed him any caring and affection. His mother was cold, hard and brutal, while his father occasionally showed some tenderness. Because Max had hung on to this tenderness as his only link to love, it was extremely difficult for him to express any anger toward his father, even though his father was now dead. Instead, Max himself had become a violent man, taking his anger out on other men in hundreds of fights.

Max feared that if he got angry at his father, he would lose his feeling of love for him. If I ever encouraged him to express his outrage at his father for hurting him, his anger turned on me. Max was stuck in his healing process with his rage, which is why he decided to come to the intensive. He was unable to express his love and creativity because he was so afraid of his anger and pain—and as we saw earlier, our joy and our pain are both carried by our Inner Child. If we can't access one, we can't access the other.

The time I want to tell you about came up while Kimberly

was working on herself. The air was tense with her unex-
pressed anger at her father. I asked Kimberly if she would like
someone else to express her anger for her. She said yes, she
would love that. She turned to Max and asked him. Max
grinned, then got up, picked up a plastic bat and proceeded to
yell at, threaten and pound on a pillow that represented
Kimberly's father. Kimberly loved it. Finally someone was
standing up for her and protecting her. Max had taken the
role of the loving father, taking action on her behalf.

In doing this for Kimberly, Max opened the door to the
possibility of being a loving Adult for his own Inner Child.
The next time Max worked, he was finally able to express his
outrage toward his father for hurting him so much. He saw
that he could do this and still maintain his love for his father.
It was a huge breakthrough for Max, enabling him to move
out of his stuck place and begin moving on with his life. He
began expressing his creativity through painting, something
his Inner Child had longed for most of his life, but which he
had been unable to do. Through reaching out and fathering
Kimberly, Max found the father within himself—the father
who could finally take loving action for his own Child.

Six months later, Kimberly attended another intensive.
This time she was able to stand up for herself with her father,
hitting a pillow with the bat and yelling at him for hurting her
so badly. Much to Kimberly's surprise, she discovered that after
standing up for her Child, her food addiction began to subside.
She had struggled with her weight for years, but as soon as her
Inner Child knew that there was a loving Adult within to
stand up for her, she no longer needed the weight to feel safe.

God, being Spirit, wishes for each of us to become instruments of love and compassion. God does not have physical eyes, hands or arms through which to express love. We are each here to learn to be a unique expression of Divine Love. None of us can heal alone. We need each other to reflect God's love for us—through energy, words or touch. Imagine what a wonderful world we would have if each of us embraced the purpose of becoming instruments of Divine Love and accepted each new challenge as an opportunity to further evolve our souls.

I have found that no matter how many blocks to loving I heal, God always presents me with new challenges regarding giving and receiving love. I used to feel upset when difficult situations came my way, but now I find that I actually invite these challenges into my life. They are what hones us, and when we choose to walk a spiritual path, we experience this honing for the rest of our lives. *This is what we are here for.* This is why we were born. Challenges present themselves whenever we have relationships with others—friends, mates, parents, teachers, therapists, physicians, neighbors, co-workers, employers and so on. We can use each of these situations to challenge ourselves to learn to bring God's love through to ourselves and to others.

As you do your own inner work, you will find that more and more often you can reach out for help rather than to get fixed, and you can reach out to help rather than to fix. Being able to give and receive love is very satisfying and healing to both people involved.

The Importance of Receiving

When you connect with both your Inner Child and your spiritual Guidance, your heart is open and you are available to give and receive love. When your wounded child-adult is in charge, your heart is closed to both giving and receiving. The wounded child-adult only knows how to give with an agenda attached and how to take instead of receive.

Not receiving love is as unloving as not giving love. When we do not receive others' love, we rob them of the joy of giving to us. When your heart is closed and you are unavailable to receive, you rob God of the opportunity to give you the love, compassion, truth and power that is God. True giving is one of the ways we express the love we receive from God. Not being received by another feels sad and lonely. When two or more people have open hearts, we create a circle of love, which is the highest experience of life. We each bring God's love through to ourselves and send it out to others. We connect with God, ourselves and others. When two or more people are able to do this, there is joy, there is love—there is God.

Parents sometimes do not receive their children's love, giving them the message that their love is meaningless. One of my clients remembers being devastated as a toddler when her love wasn't received. She had offered her father a crayon because she loved him and wanted to give him something that was of value to her, and he brushed her off with a shaming comment: "I don't want *that.*" When what you offer your parents appears to have no value to them, you may go into core shame, concluding that *you* have no value. When a parent receives what a child tries to give, the parent is also giving *to* the child. Receiving children's gifts tells the children that their lovingness has value, that *they* have value.

Giving and receiving occur simultaneously—when you give, you receive the experience of your worth, and when you receive, you experience your lovability. When you mother or father someone or are being mothered or fathered yourself, both of you give and receive. When you cannot receive, you cannot give.

Slater was stuck. He had been working with Inner Bonding for about two years and had uncovered memories of intense shaming and criticism by his father. His mother had been weak and needy and had never provided any safety for her quiet, withdrawn son. Slater deeply desired to connect with God, but whenever he tried, all he experienced was criticism. He tried to imagine a Teacher, but his Teacher would turn into his father criticizing him. Without a connection to God, he could not create a loving Adult to heal his wounded child, and he couldn't connect with God because of the images of verbal abuse.

Slater had never had an experience of receiving unconditional love. He did not believe this existed. As lonely as he was, Slater did not want to be in a relationship because he did not want to take responsibility for another's feelings or suffer rejection if he didn't comply with the other person's desires. Yet he could not break through his block and receive the unconditional love that is God until he could receive it from another person. The whole situation felt hopeless to him.

In one of our sessions, I asked Slater to let me be an emissary of God and just bring love through to him. He closed his eyes as I stroked his arm, imagining myself to be a vessel bringing through the love and light of God. After fifteen minutes or so of this, he opened his tear-filled eyes and said, "That is the first time I have ever felt love." After this, Slater was able to begin experiencing Divine Love for himself. Compassion for his wounded child filled his being and this compassion extended to his family and friends. For the first time in his life he was able to give and receive love.

People sometimes ask, "What does God want from me?" I tell them that God does not want to take anything from you nor will God ever reject you. All God wants is for you to *receive* Divine Love and act upon it by becoming an emissary of that love.

Caring and Caretaking

It is important to understand the huge difference between caring and caretaking. You are caretaking when you give to someone out of fear, obligation or guilt. You are caretaking when you have an agenda attached. For example, you may want to be seen as good and loving, or you may want to be loved back or avoid anger. You are also caretaking when you do for another what they need to do for themselves. Giving that harms you—physically, emotionally, financially—is caretaking. Caretaking is draining. You are not bringing through God's love. You are giving in the hopes of getting something back. When you don't get it, you feel drained and resentful.

You are caring when, out of your love, empathy and compassion, you do for others what they cannot do for themselves, with no strings attached. You are caring when you take care of babies, children, the elderly, the disabled and the ill (provided they are not using their illness as a way out of personal responsibility). You are caring when you are mothering, bringing through God's love to others who cannot yet do this for themselves. You are caring when you are fathering, taking action for others when they cannot take action for themselves.

You are caring when you give something to another as a gift with no strings attached. You may give money or time that comes from your heart and brings you joy to give. You might make a lovely dinner for someone, even though that person is fully capable of making dinner, because it gives you joy to give to him or her in this way. There are many little things you might choose to do for others because it makes their life easier, not because you expect anything in return, but because it gives you joy to do so. This is caring. This is love. This is being an instrument of God.

Caretaking is giving from the wounded child-adult—giving to get, or giving out of fear, obligation or guilt. Caring is giving from the loving Adult, being an emissary of God.

Taking and Receiving

You are taking when you have expectations about what another person "should" be giving you. You are taking when you expect others to do for you what you can and need to do for yourself. You are taking when you try to control what others choose to give. You are taking when you do not take responsibility for your own health and well-being and expect others to give themselves up for you—to take care of you physically, emotionally, financially, sexually or spiritually. Anytime you expect someone to sacrifice themselves for you, you are taking. You cannot be giving when your intent is to take. This is the true definition of selfish—wanting only to take from other people, wanting others to sacrifice themselves for you and giving to them only with the intent to get something in return.

You are receiving when you accept help when you need it. You are receiving when you allow others to mother or father you, to bring through Divine Love to you. You are receiving when you lovingly take in what is offered from the heart—compliments, appreciation, validation, gifts. It is the loving Adult who allows the Inner Child to receive. It is the wounded child-adult who blocks out receiving, who just wants to take and have control over what is given.

There is no sense of obligation when you are caring and receiving—only when you are caretaking and taking. Feeling a sense of obligation can alert you to the fact that the other person is caretaking rather than caring. When there are strings attached to giving, you will probably feel obligated. When someone gives to you from the heart and obviously receives joy in the giving, you will not feel obligated. When someone is caretaking, an invisible scorecard is kept and eventually the caretaker will get angry if you do not even the score by giving him or her something back. Many people automatically keep this invisible scorecard and, in addition to feeling that you owe them something when they caretake you, they feel that they owe you something when they take from you. This scorecard ruins many relationships.

In a session with Connie, one of my clients, we explored her difficulty reaching out for help when she needed it and receiving help when someone offered it to her. Connie had been on a committed spiritual path for many years, yet the peace she sought eluded her. As we explored the beliefs of Connie's wounded child-adult, she discovered an old and deep false belief: "Receiving from others puts you into your ego; it diminishes your spirituality because it makes you rely on others instead of relying on God. Receiving from others also makes you vulnerable to being controlled, because now you owe them." Connie had not realized that the love she could receive from others would be, in fact, God's love, which is a free gift with no strings attached.

Taking and caretaking come from the wounded self. Receiving and caring come from the loving Adult. The wounded self in all of us is narcissistic. It is driven by fear and its most important priority is to protect us. This creates a lack of empathy and caring for others. We become centered on ourselves, unable to give from the heart or to receive love. It is a very lonely and isolated state.

The wounded child-adult in us may fear being controlled by others if we open to our natural empathy for others. You may have grown up with an empathic parent who allowed himself or herself to be controlled by his or her mate. From seeing this, you may have concluded that empathy makes you vulnerable to being controlled. (The real culprit here is a lack of appropriate boundaries.) Or, if you have a mate whom you are able to control through his or her empathy, you may fear that the same will happen to you if you open to your natural empathy. When you fear being controlled if you are empathic, you may act empathic from your wounded self as a form of control, rather than giving true empathy from your loving Adult. For example, you know your mate wants your empathy, so you act empathic to get something—maybe even empathy—back. This eventually creates much distrust within your partner, who learns that your empathy is not heartfelt, has strings attached and is not something he or she can count on.

When trying to feel safe by protecting against being rejected or controlled is more important than creating true safety by loving yourself and others, you are in your wounded child-adult. Mothering and fathering will not help you when this is your intent. It will only help when your true desire is to become a loving human being to yourself and to others.

Through practicing Inner Bonding, you can learn to tell the difference between your own and others' wounded child-adult state and loving-Adult state. This important information lets you know whether it is appropriate to give mothering or fathering. Giving mothering and fathering can be great gifts to both the giver and the receiver when the other person is truly receiving.

SECTION III

Putting God into Action

It is not enough to understand and release your old pain and fear. It is not enough to recognize and reject your false beliefs and learn truth from God. Unless we take new, loving actions based on this truth, *nothing changes*. This section expands upon the two final steps of the Six-Step Process: Step Five, which is taking the loving action inspired by God, and Step Six, evaluating the effectiveness of that action.

TEN

Creating a Healthy House for the Soul

Your body is a sacred temple that houses your soul while it does the work of evolving in lovingness. That's why caring for your body is one of the most important ways that your loving Adult puts God in motion in your life. You need a clear and healthy body to keep your frequency high enough to hear your spiritual Guidance.

The body is also one of the vehicles through which God and our soul communicate with us, by giving us feelings from which we can learn. A loving Adult takes the loving action of keeping the body physically and emotionally healthy, clear, open, serene, free of toxicity and fit so that you can clearly experience your feelings.

Do you see taking care of your body as a burden or as a sacred privilege? Do you even think about taking care of your body? Or do you take your body for granted, thinking it will continue to serve you without any special care? We live in a time where our environment does not support us well regarding caring for our bodies. Our air, water and food are often contaminated. Electricity bombards us through all our kitchen appliances, TVs, computers and power lines. Many of us have jobs where we are sedentary. The stresses in our society are numerous, and stress—both physical and emotional—erodes the immune system. To have a healthy body, we need to pay attention to it and embrace the sacred privilege of taking care of it. Using the Six-Step Process, this can be a joy, not a chore.

When you do not know that your body is a temple that houses the precious being of your Inner Child, then you may abuse it as you seek to numb your pain and find momentary pleasure. Weight and health issues abound in our society, which would not be true if we were loving Adults who experienced caring for our bodies as a sacred privilege. As a loving Adult you would set loving inner boundaries: You would get enough exercise, you would set appropriate limits regarding what you put into your body, and you would create a healthy balance between work and play so as not to be in constant stress. You would not devote yourself to working all the time, which gives your Child no time to play, create or relax, nor would you ignore your responsibilities. You would learn how to create inner safety in relationships by not taking others' behavior personally and by setting loving boundaries with others. You would take action to provide financial security for yourself so you would not be overly stressed about money, and you would set appropriate limits on what you spend so as not to overextend yourself and create more stress.

Self-care concerns the boundaries—the limits—we place or do not place on ourselves. As a loving Adult, you set inner boundaries that empower you, that create an inner sense of safety and enhance your self-esteem—the same limits you would set if you were taking loving care of an actual child. Loving parents do not indulge their children by allowing self-destructive behavior such as eating junk food, smoking cigarettes, using drugs and alcohol, or getting little sleep, nor do they create such rigid limits that the child has no choice or flexibility.

Inner Bonding provides a process for learning to love, honor and respect your Inner Child so that you naturally and with joy provide the very best for him or her. Eating well, exercising and eliminating stress become your natural way of being: not something you have to force yourself to do, but something you do from love. Your focus is entirely on the health of your body, not, for example, on the number of pounds you weigh or the measurement of your hips. The self-discipline to accomplish this comes through you from God when you accept the powerlessness of your child-adult to control your eating and your lifestyle, and open to Divine Love coming through you.

Let's say your anxiety is building, which usually leads you to binge. Your wounded child-adult wants to eat everything in sight, especially the two pints of ice cream in the freezer and the muffins you bought on the way home. This time, however, you remember your decision not to live like this anymore. Instead of eating, you move into the Six-Step Process. You choose to feel your anxiety and take responsibility for it. You state your intention to learn from the anxiety, which opens your heart. Then you dialogue with your Inner Child. Your dialogue may start like this:

"Little one, I love you and I know you are feeling very anxious and want to eat, but I'm not going to continue to stuff you. I want to know what you need from me. I want to know what I'm doing or not doing that is creating your anxiety. I want to nurture you and fill you with my love, not just with food. Your health and well-being are important to me, and I'm no longer going to let you harm yourself with bingeing. What do you really need from me?"

You listen to what your anxiety is trying to tell you, dialoguing with your wounded child-adult and your spiritual Guidance, until you understand your feelings and behavior, and what loving action you need to take. Finally, you take that action and evaluate whether it was effective.

You will find, as you move deeper into Inner Bonding, that the more you see, feel, value and cherish your precious Inner Child, the more motivated you are to behave in ways that create health, safety and an inner sense of integrity. In addition, the more you choose to take loving care of your Inner Child by creating a healthy house for your soul, the more loved and cherished your Child feels. It's another one of those win-win propositions.

Guidelines for Self-Care

Sometimes we have gotten so off track in caring for ourselves, we need help recognizing what healthy actions are. Below is a guide for being a loving Adult to your Inner Child by caring for your body physically and emotionally. It includes information about what's appropriate in terms of food, substances, sex, money, work, time and feelings.

There are two important caveats about this guide, however. First, it has come from my personal Teacher as guidance for me. That means *it is not definitive*. If some of the recommendations do not feel right to you, cast them aside and dialogue with your own spiritual Guidance to discover what will enhance your sense of health, safety, self-esteem and inner integrity.

Second, do not read these guidelines and feel that you have to start following every one of them right away! If you view my Teacher's suggestions that way, you will feel overwhelmed and be tempted to turn to your addictions to soothe your upset feelings. Instead, regard the actions listed below as *information* about what loving self-care may look like. If you have not taken much loving care of yourself in your life, you may find some things that surprise you.

Food

The loving Adult:

- Tunes into the body's signals, feeding you when you are hungry and stopping when you are full, neither overfeeds nor underfeeds you.

- Puts healthy food in your body. Places limits on the amount of junk food, sugar, caffeine and chemicals (such as preservatives, artificial sweeteners and other food additives) that you consume, allowing these only occasionally. If you have a severe reaction to substances like sugar or MSG, your loving Adult makes sure that you never eat them. In cases like this, strict boundaries are enforced.

- Makes sure you get a balanced diet with plenty of fiber, fresh fruits and vegetables, proteins and grains, and essential fatty acids. If you are not sure what foods contain fiber, protein and fatty acids, take a look at a nutrition book and learn about them.

- Makes sure you get to eat foods you like (except for those that are self-destructive), so you do not feel deprived.

- Reads about health and nutrition so you can make healthy choices and not leave this important area up to others.[1]

- Moves into Inner Bonding if the child-adult wants to eat too much or too little, wants to purge, or craves unhealthy foods. Explores the feelings and false beliefs that are triggering the addictive behavior and takes loving action to fill the Inner Child's needs in healthy ways.

Weight and Grooming

The loving Adult:

- Decides what weight is normal and healthy *for you as an individual* and makes sure that you maintain that weight through proper diet and exercise. The loving Adult does not allow the wounded child-adult to make this decision, since the child-adult's view is often very distorted, as in the case of anorexia.

- Does not comply with or resist others' views on how to dress or how to wear your hair, but rather makes these decisions based on what makes you feel best.

Smoking

Just as a loving parent would not give a child cigarettes, so a loving inner Adult does not buy cigarettes for the Inner Child. If the child-adult is addicted to cigarettes, the loving Adult does whatever is necessary, through Inner Bonding, to break the addiction and heal the cause of it. Addiction to nicotine is one of the hardest to break, and it is often related to deep levels of loneliness and grief and a profound need for nurturing.

Cigarettes are both physically and emotionally addictive. They become a person's best friend, something that person can turn to when feeling lonely or stressed and there is no loving Adult to handle these feelings. A nicotine addiction can also develop as an unconscious effort to self-medicate due to a troubling brain allergy or a hormone imbalance. Brain allergies result when the brain is hypersensitive to a toxin, causing severe physical and emotional responses. Some people have a brain allergy to nicotine, which causes an intense desire for the very substance they are allergic to; this also triggers extreme anxiety or even violence when they don't get it. Likewise, hormone imbalances that cause anxiety are often soothed with nicotine. Nicotine can also serve as a chemical antidepressant. A loving Adult understands these issues and does not judge the wounded child-adult who has a hard time giving up cigarettes. Instead, the Adult continues to learn with compassion about what the Child really needs and develops a solid connection with God so that the addiction can eventually fall away. In addition, the loving Adult does the research necessary to discover how to best handle the physical addiction to smoking. A loving Adult also prays for release from this and other addictions and asks others for help as well. This applies to all substance abuse.

Drugs

The loving Adult:

- Does not allow the Inner Child to consume any recreational or psychoactive drugs on a regular basis.

- Explores and heals through Inner Bonding whenever drugs are desired addictively.

- Does not use prescription drugs to avoid taking responsibility for and exploring feelings of anxiety and depression. Prescription drugs can sometimes provide much-needed relief and a window of opportunity to do inner work. However, they become a Band-Aid instead of a support when they are used *instead* of inner work, rather than *in addition* to it. Many people find themselves no longer needing their medication for anxiety or depression after practicing Inner Bonding for a year or two.

- Reads books on nutrition such as *Potatoes, Not Prozac*[2] to learn to balance the body chemistry nutritionally so that the need for prescription drugs recedes.

Alcohol

The loving Adult:

- Drinks no alcohol if you are addicted to it. Explores and heals the addiction through Inner Bonding and Twelve-Step programs.

- May allow occasional light drinking when no alcoholism is involved and you are not driving. A loving Adult never drives when you are under the influence of any amount of alcohol or drugs, nor rides with someone who is.

- Does not ever allow you to be put in a situation where alcohol or drugs can compromise your health, safety or emotional well-being.

- Does not use alcohol as a social crutch, to deal with sex, to unwind when you haven't been taking care of yourself or in any other addictive way.

Exercise

The loving Adult:

- Makes sure you get enough exercise.

- Finds forms of exercise that are enjoyable for you. It's very important to do exercise you really like, otherwise you will probably drop it.

- Does not place rigid demands on you to the point of exhaustion, underweight and stress. Does not exercise addictively. Over-exercising can often cause as many problems as under-exercising. A loving Adult finds a healthy balance that can be maintained over a lifetime.

I have discovered that I love to walk because I talk to my Inner Child and my Teacher while I walk. I get to exercise and, at the same time, connect with myself and God. I talk out loud during my walks—I'm not sure what my neighbors think, but I love it! I also carry a tape recorder with me because some of my best ideas come while I'm walking and dialoguing. I seem to hear my Teacher best when I am moving and out in nature. Much of what is in this book came from my Teacher talking with me while I was on my walks.

Activities

The loving Adult:

- Makes sure you wear a seatbelt when in a car.
- Makes sure you wear a helmet and protective clothing when riding a motorcycle, and makes sure that you drive safely or ride with someone who drives safely.
- Makes sure you wear a helmet when biking, and a helmet and protective padding when in-line skating.
- Makes sure you wear protective clothing when participating in work or hobbies that could injure your eyes, skin or internal organs.
- Requires that you either are competent or have a competent person with you when participating in hobbies, sports or activities that could be life-threatening. These include flying, gliding, boating, race-car driving, rock climbing, backpacking, sky diving, paragliding, hanggliding and so on. However, the loving Adult does not refrain from trying these activities if this is what your Inner Child desires. A loving Adult does not prevent the Inner Child from taking risks but does everything possible to minimize the risk.

Money

The loving Adult:

- Sets appropriate inner limits to make sure you are financially secure, while allowing you to enjoy the fruits of your labors.

- Does not allow you to addictively use spending and the accumulation of clothes and toys to fill your emptiness, take away your pain or give you a feeling of worth, even if you are wealthy. Rather, the loving Adult uses Inner Bonding to help you fill your emptiness and define your worth.

- Does not engage in social financial competitiveness. Does not make purchases for image, status symbols or social standing.

- Never allows you to addictively get into debt over the accumulation of clothes or toys, or over expensive activities such as vacations, dining, gambling or beautifying.

- Allows debt under specific circumstances, such as buying a house, starting a business, attending school or getting other training that can lead to personal growth and security.

- Does not give away or lend money that you cannot afford or buy expensive gifts that you cannot afford.

- Does not give away your personal power and choice regarding money—or anything else—to a leader or guru.

- Lets your Inner Child know that when you have extra money, you deserve to spend it on things that give you joy and pleasure—clothing, vacations, activities, gifts for those you love, tithing and donations to charity.

- Provides fiscal planning and establishes consistent savings patterns when possible.

Sex

The loving Adult:

- Always uses a condom or makes sure partner wears one in all situations other than with a long-term, monogamous sexual partner.

- Does not allow the child-adult to use sex addictively. Explores and heals the causes of the desire to act out in sexually addictive ways and seeks help for sexual addiction.

- Allows appropriate masturbation. If the masturbation is addictive, that is, if it is being used to bolster worth, fill emptiness, or avoid intimacy and rejection, then the loving Adult uses Inner Bonding and seeks help to explore and heal the source of the addiction.

- Does not allow the child-adult to act out addictively through exhibitionism, voyeurism or sexual violence of any kind. The loving Adult recognizes the need for healing when these desires are present and moves into Inner Bonding and seeks therapeutic help.

- Never objectifies other people sexually or uses sex to harm or have power over another human being. Does not engage in sadomasochism or bondage.

- Makes no sexual demands on partners. Allows sex to emerge from love rather than neediness.

- Does not impose others' rules on your sexuality. Allows you sexual freedom within emotionally and physically safe limits.

- Listens to the core Self and spiritual Guidance about decisions concerning birth control and abortion, rather than following someone else's value system.

Time and Work

The loving Adult:

- Does not procrastinate. The loving Adult does what has to be done in time to avoid negative consequences.

- Puts forth the best effort at work. Desires to do things well.

- Does not use work or busyness addictively to avoid facing pain.

- Creates a balance between work, personal growth, play and time to do nothing.

- Makes sure that both work and free time are fulfilling.

- Gets enough sleep, but does not allow the child-adult to sleep away the time.

Feelings

The loving Adult:

- Is always in the intent to learn about the Inner Child's feelings.

- Allows the Inner Child to release upsetting feelings in appropriate ways—crying when sad, screaming and pounding when angry—without dumping these feelings on others or blaming and/or physically harming others.

- Allows the Inner Child free expression of joy and excitement.

- Does not allow the wounded child-adult to wallow in self-pity, worry, obsessive or negative thinking.

- Continues to practice thinking the kind of thoughts that create peace, love, safety and joy within.

Healing Addictions

When people come into traditional psychotherapy to deal with their various addictions, they often find that they make no progress whatsoever. Twelve-Step programs have proven more helpful for substance abuse and process addictions because they rely on a Higher Power to give people the strength to abstain. But even Twelve-Step programs do not go far enough. They do not show you how to develop a loving Adult to heal the *underlying cause* of the pain that has led to your addiction. In a sense, the program itself becomes the loving Adult, and people find themselves dependent on the program to maintain their abstinence. While I highly recommend Twelve-Step programs for the wonderful support they give, I also recommend that individuals practice Inner Bonding so that at some point they no longer need to rely on a program or therapy, but can rely on their spiritual Guidance and their loving Adult instead.

One client consulted with me after having been in Overeaters Anonymous for three years. Barbara was very slender and maintained her weight by following a rigid food plan. Her Inner Child was unhappy with the rigidity but her wounded child-adult would binge as soon as she went off her food plan. She had no loving Adult capable of eating in a less rigid and more natural way. Highly motivated, Barbara took to practicing Inner Bonding with a deep determination to succeed. It took her about a year of doing Inner Bonding regularly before her loving Adult was solid enough and connected enough to her Higher Power to allow her to safely stop her rigid diet. Barbara now eats normally.

Adam came to see me after he decided to quit smoking pot. He had been addicted for ten years and had made the firm decision to quit but was really struggling with it. He had never been able to follow through on this decision before. This time, however, he started practicing Inner Bonding so that when the pain came up—the pain he had suppressed with marijuana for ten years—he was able to deal with it in a new way. By opening to his pain with an intent to learn and bringing through the love and truth of his spiritual Guidance, Adam finally did quit smoking marijuana. In addition, he discovered a new depth and passion within him that eventually led to an entirely new and satisfying career.

The following are examples of dialogues to help you understand how to practice the Six Steps of Inner Bonding to develop your loving Adult and create a healthy house for your soul.

* * * *

Caitlyn was driving home at six o'clock in the evening and all she could think about was picking up a quart of chocolate ice cream. She knew that if she bought it, she would eat it. She had promised herself for the millionth time that she would not do this again, but she seemed to have no control as she pulled into the parking lot of the market. She had a huge sense of inner agitation and conflict as one part of her, her wounded child-adult, desperately wanted the ice cream and another part, her core Self, was screaming "No! Don't do this to me again!"

This was Caitlyn's moment of choice. She could choose the intent to protect and try to soothe her underlying agitation with ice cream, or she could move into Inner Bonding and find out what her Child *really* needed to feel safe and comforted. She turned off the engine, took a deep breath and chose the intent to learn. Then she addressed the part of her that wanted the ice cream.

Caitlyn: I can feel your agitation. Why do you want ice cream?

Inner Child: I like it. It tastes good. It feels good inside.

Caitlyn: Yes, it does—for the moment. But you always feel bad later because you hate being fat, and the sugar makes you feel bad. I love you and I don't want you to feel bad.

Inner Child [*angry*]: You don't love me. You never pay any attention to me. At least ice cream feels good for the moment. It's better than nothing.

Caitlyn: Tell me about feeling unloved by me.

Inner Child [*angry*]: You never talk to me. You never listen to me. You don't pay any attention to me. You never stand up for me. Just today at work, when Jim criticized me, I felt shamed and alone. Where were you?

Caitlyn: So when Jim criticized you and I didn't say anything, you felt alone?

Inner Child: Yeah, just like I did with Mom. She always let Dad criticize me and she never stood up for me. I wasn't important to her and I'm not important to you. So just go get me my ice cream.

Caitlyn [*gently*]: No, not this time. I don't want to ignore your feelings and just pacify you with food. I want to learn to love you. Tell me more about how you feel.

Inner Child: How I feel is pissed at you! You're such a wimp! I hate you! You let everyone treat me the way Dad did. And you criticize me the way Dad did. I never do anything good enough for you. I know you hate me.

Caitlyn: I understand why you feel this way. I have been treating you the way Mom and Dad treated you and I don't blame you for being angry. You must be very hurt inside. I can feel that you are in a lot of pain.

Inner Child: [*Starts to sob.*]

Caitlyn: It's okay to cry. I'm here. I'm not going away. I want to understand your pain.

Inner Child [*sobbing*]: I feel so alone. I have to do everything myself. Most of the time I just feel overwhelmed. It's too much for me. I don't know what to do when people criticize me. I always feel like everything is on me. I feel so afraid and alone and empty. I need you but you are never around. I have always felt alone. Mom and Dad were never there for me. At home no one is there for me. I just feel alone. I never feel like I'm good enough. (*The false belief behind the feelings.*)

Caitlyn: My dear sweet little one, I am so sorry that I have not been loving with you and that I haven't let you know what a precious Child you are. I can see why you are always wanting to eat. I want you to know that I am going to learn how to love you rather than stuff down your feelings with food. You are a wonderful Child, but I know you won't know this until I pay more attention to you and learn to stand up for you. How are you feeling now?

Inner Child: I feel a little better. I like it when you talk with me. I don't feel so alone.

At this point in the dialogue, Caitlyn's craving for ice cream started to ebb and she was able to drive home without agitation.

Often eating disorders and smoking are symptoms of an underlying mothering issue. The Inner Child did not receive adequate nurturing and uses the food and/or cigarettes to fill the emptiness. Many clients tell me that cigarettes comfort them when they are feeling alone. Do you remember Jeremy, the smoker with heart disease, in chapter 8? Through dialoguing with his Inner Child, he discovered that he was smoking in order to fill up the loneliness he had carried since childhood, when he was left alone a lot by his mother.

Sometimes smoking or eating provides physical as well as emotional comfort. Madeline did the following dialogue in my office.

Madeline: I'm struggling again to get control over my eating. I can't seem to regain the control I had last year. Everything is going so well—my work is great and I'm getting more time to play—so I can't figure out why food is still such a big issue for me.

Margie: Madeline, when was the last time you did not have to struggle with your weight and eating?

Madeline: I was fine until I broke up with Todd. In fact, I was at my thinnest the day I broke up with him. Right after that I started eating again.

Margie: Maybe food is the only comfort your wounded self has when you are lonely and have no physical contact with anyone. Let's ask your Inner Child about that.

Inner Child: Yeah! Food is hugs!

Madeline: That's right! It is! I haven't had hugs in ages. I mean *real* hugs, the kind you have when you lie naked in bed with someone you love.

Margie: So maybe you need to accept that you will use food for physical comfort until you either learn to connect with your spiritual Guidance and give it to yourself or find another lover to give it to you.

Madeline: I don't want to accept that. I hate being over-weight . . . but I guess I eat because I hate not being nur-tured even more than I hate being overweight. Food does make me feel nurtured.

Margie: Do you ever hold and hug your doll next to your skin while bringing love through from your spiritual Guidance?

Madeline: No.

Margie: Try that. People have told me it brings them the physical feeling of comfort along with the spiritual comfort that their spiritual Guidance provides.

Again, this client is dealing with a mothering issue. Madeline was not held often as a child and she still needs that. When she has no one in her life to hold her, she turns to food for the feeling of physical comfort she craves. Until Madeline learns to self-nurture and to ask for nurturing from others, she will continue to turn to food for comfort.

Food is a difficult addiction to deal with because, unlike other substance addictions such as nicotine and alcohol, you cannot be totally abstinent. A second powerful reason is that it works so well to (temporarily) fill the feelings of emptiness that come from not being loved. Food, especially chocolate and bakery items, feel, very comforting to the body, so it feels as if you are loving and nurturing your Inner Child when you eat them. In fact, it may be the only form of nurturing you have. You will not give it up until your need for love and nur-turing is filled by being a loving Adult to your Inner Child.

Weight often serves as a buffer to keep the Inner Child

safe when the Adult does not set loving boundaries. In fact, substance abuse in general is often how the wounded child-adult handles his or her fear when there is no loving Adult to set boundaries.

Margo had been an alcoholic for seventeen years when she consulted with me. She had tried everything, including Alcoholics Anonymous, to stop drinking but nothing had worked. Instead of addressing the drinking directly, Margo and I worked on her boundary issues: She let everyone in her life— her husband, her son and her business partner—overrun and control her. Using Inner Bonding, Margo diligently started to learn to set loving boundaries. About two months into the process, she came in all smiles and announced that she hadn't had a drink in a week, nor had she wanted one. It turned out that her desire to drink had come from her Inner Child feeling so abandoned when Margo let people run over her. As long as she took care of herself, speaking up for herself and setting appropriate boundaries, she had no desire to drink.

People often have a great deal of difficulty making the choice to dialogue when an addiction is involved. It seems so much easier and more satisfying in the moment to go shopping, have sex, turn on the TV or grab for food, alcohol, drugs, cigarettes or coffee than to take the time to find out what their Inner Child really needs from them. Many of my clients put dialoguing off for quite a while before finally deciding to try it. With addictions, the wounded child-adult is so much in control that it takes a well-developed loving Adult to start the process of dealing with these addictions. This is why Margo and I first worked on her setting boundaries, an action that the loving Adult takes.

The Vital Importance of Boundaries

Creating a healthy house for your soul is about creating an environment of safety for your Inner Child. Your Child feels safe when your loving Adult sets responsible inner and outer boundaries and recognizes the intrinsic worth of the core Self so that you can handle rejection by not taking it personally.

During an Inner Bonding group session, Eunice did the following dialogue with her Inner Child:

Eunice [*speaking to her Inner Child*]: I know we are both tired of being so overweight, yet we just can't seem to do anything about it. There must be a good reason that we keep this weight on.

Child-adult Eunice: I don't like being fat, but I'm afraid to be thin.

Eunice: Why are you afraid?

Child-adult Eunice: Because when I'm thin, Jack [her husband] is always after me for sex. And I don't like sex with him.

Eunice: Can you tell me more about why you don't like sex with Jack?

Child-adult Eunice: He is not nice to me. He criticizes me all the time. He yells at me a lot. He withdraws from me a lot. I don't feel loved by him. He wants to have sex with me for his own needs, not because he loves me. I feel used by him. He wants me to dress up in sexy things and act in weird ways that I don't like. He wants me to watch porno movies with him and fantasize yucky things with him. I hate it. When I'm fat, he stays away from me.

Margie: It sounds like when you are thin, your Adult does not protect you from being used by Jack.

Child-adult Eunice: That's right! She gives in to him all the time and makes me do yucky things I hate to do. I don't feel safe when I'm thin.

Eunice: She's right. I don't know how to say no to Jack. I've been taught that it's a wife's job to satisfy her husband and that if I say no I'm being selfish and being a bad wife. But I don't have to deal with this much when I'm fat, because then Jack is not attracted to me.

Margie: Are there other areas in your marriage where you give yourself up to Jack?

Eunice: Oh yes. I do it all the time. Many times I don't do things I want to do because he wants me to do something with him. I let him decide how we handle our money and where we go on our vacations. Sometimes I even let him overrule me on what to do on my own birthday.

Margie: So your Inner Child is certainly not going to trust you to take care of her by setting boundaries about sex until you start taking care of her in other areas, is she?

Eunice: I guess not.

Margie: So it seems pointless to keep trying to lose weight until your Child trusts you to protect her by setting loving boundaries against being used sexually. Are you willing to start taking care of her and setting limits in some other areas?

Eunice: Yes, I am. I'm tired of feeling like this. Sometimes I think I'd rather be alone than be married to Jack, that it would be easier and feel better.

Margie: Well, that is an option. But if you ever want a relationship, you will still have to deal with taking care of your Inner Child. Any relationship will challenge you in this area. If you just leave, you miss an opportunity to grow into a more loving Adult. This marriage is challenging you to show up for yourself. Who knows how Jack would be if you set loving boundaries and treated yourself with respect? He might even start to respect you. And if he doesn't, you can always leave then. But why not take a chance on setting boundaries for yourself with Jack and see what happens? You might be surprised.

Eunice: Okay. It feels scary, but I'm willing to try.

Margie: What are you most scared of?

Eunice: I guess of Jack thinking I am a bad, selfish person.

Margie: Do you believe you are bad and selfish?

Eunice: I don't know. I've been told that so much that I'm afraid of it.

Margie: So one of the things you need to do as a loving Adult is embark on the journey of discovering the beauty of your core Self, of who you really are, instead of letting others label you "bad" or "selfish" or whatever. Are you willing to take on that job?

Eunice: Yes.

Margie: Let's start right now by moving into Step Four.

Eunice, put your focus into your heart and move into an intent to learn with your spiritual Guidance. [*Eunice closes her eyes, sits in silence for a moment, then nods.*] Ask your Guidance for the truth about who your Inner Child really is, about whether or not you are bad or selfish if you set loving boundaries for yourself. Ask your Guidance to speak through you to your Inner Child, telling her the truth about who she is.

Eunice: Okay. [*She breathes into her heart, silently asking for the truth. Then she opens her eyes and looks directly at the doll that represents her Inner Child.*] Little one, you are a treasure. You are a good, kind, loving little girl. You would never deliberately hurt anyone. You have such a loving heart, you just want everyone to be happy. You are not at all a selfish person. You never have been. It is Jack who is being selfish by expecting you to take care of him instead of taking care of his own feelings. He expects you to make him feel like he's lovable and worthwhile by doing what he wants, especially sexually, but that is not your job. It is loving to say no to him and give him the opportunity to learn to take care of his own Inner Child.

Margie: Now ask your Child how she feels.

Eunice: How do you feel right now?

Inner Child: I like that you said that to me, but I'm not sure that you mean it. I will know you mean it when you start to say no to him and listen to me instead.

Eunice: Okay. I'm willing to do this. I have felt so desperate about this that I've sometimes felt like killing myself. I wouldn't really do it, but I have felt like it. I guess that's how unhappy my Child is about this situation of my not standing up for her. I'm really going to do this.

It took a great deal of courage for Eunice to face this issue because it related to childhood issues of rejection. But as she slowly started standing up for her Inner Child, she was gradually able to create a truly healthy house for her soul, inside and out.

Boundaries that we set within ourselves are also important issues in self-care. Below is a brief dialogue between Joanna and her Inner Child. Joanna would very much like to get out of debt, but finds herself shopping and spending even when she doesn't really need anything.

Joanna: What are you needing from me when you want to shop and buy things?

Inner Child: Attention, I guess. And reassurance, too.

Joanna [*speaking to her spiritual Teacher*]: My Child says that when she wants to buy things, what she really wants is attention and reassurance from me. What does it look like to give her this?

Teacher: Spend some time each day holding your bear, rocking her in the rocking chair, caressing her, and telling her how wonderful she is, reassuring her that she is a very lovable little girl and that you are here for her. Pin a picture of yourself as a child onto the bear and concentrate on seeing the beauty within you as a child. As you begin to see your beauty, feel the loving energy from me coming through you into her. Also, seek out friends who can hold you with unconditional love. In this way, you can begin to heal your Child's need for attention and reassurance.

Joanna: And this will help my spending addiction?

Teacher: It will take some time, but real love feels far better than buying things, so if you are consistent, eventually your Child will prefer the nurturing to shopping. But you must give her this *every day* and especially when she wants to shop. As soon as she starts to feel a lack of nurturing energy from you, she will feel alone and will want to take away the feeling of aloneness by buying things. It takes attention and consciousness to reach for your bear instead, but if you do it, it will work.

Joanna was blown away by the experience of having so much wise information come directly through her. This is not unusual. My clients often tell me they are astounded at the information they are able to access.

The following dialogue was written down by Stephanie, a twenty-eight-year-old stunt artist who needs to stay in good shape for her work. On the morning of this dialogue, she did not want to get out of bed and exercise. Sometimes Stephanie shows up for her Inner Child and sometimes she doesn't. When she feels afraid and lonely, she tends to get lethargic and cry instead of taking care of herself. Stephanie is in contact with a spiritual Teacher named Nimo.

Stephanie: Good morning, little Stephanie. Can you tell me why you don't feel like exercising today?

Inner Child: I'm scared.

Stephanie: Can you tell me why you feel scared?

Inner Child: Because I feel alone and I want someone to hold me. I want you to love me. I'm very scared.

Stephanie: I love you very much and I will protect you. Would you like me to hold you?

Inner Child: Yes. *[Stephanie holds her doll.]* Will you always love me? *[Starts crying.]*

Stephanie: Why are you crying?

Inner Child: Because you don't do this enough, and I don't trust that you will.

Stephanie: Nimo, how do I make her feel loved and safe?

Nimo: Hold her, tell her you love her. She is a beautiful, perfect baby girl. Pour all your love into her. Trust this process.

Stephanie: Okay. . . . She still feels scared and still wants to cry.

Nimo: Let her grieve over the love that you've been unable to give her.

Stephanie: Okay.

Nimo: These are tears of a rainbow. Don't let them frighten you. Be proud of yourself. You are very lovable and I love you and will always be by your side. You are never alone. Feel my warmth around you.

Stephanie: I feel it. *[Crying and smiling.]*

Nimo: Do something fun with your Child today. She wants to know you love her. Praise her and reward her for her willingness to share her pain with you. If you get scared, call on me.

Stephanie: Thank you, Nimo.

Nimo: You're welcome, my child.

Stephanie: Little Stephanie, how about we do something fun today for exercise?

Inner Child: Yes. Yes.

Stephanie: How would you like to do yoga?

Inner Child: Yes! I like yoga because it's fun and I feel good afterwards. Can we sing and dance today also? I want to laugh, too.

Stephanie: Okay, we'll sing in the car and take our singing class on Friday. We'll dance in the living room tonight, and I'll make you laugh all day. Today we'll play, but we must also make time to run so we can be strong and healthy.

Inner Child: Okay.

Stephanie: Are you ready to get up?

Inner Child: Yes!

Stephanie: Okay. I love you.

Inner Child: I love you, too.

Samuel sought my help because he started smoking pot again after getting married recently. He had not smoked in a long time. He was deeply in love with his wife and felt very loved by her. They had a satisfying and active sex life and had talked about having children in the future. Their communication was excellent; they had fun together and shared many common interests. He was totally perplexed as to why he was suddenly smoking pot again. The only other time he had struggled with this was when he had lived with a woman for a year. He had thought that his pot problem then was caused by the problems they had in their relationship. But those problems did not exist in his marriage, and yet he was smoking. Below is a condensed version of a dialogue Samuel had in an Inner Bonding session with me:

Loving Adult: Why are you smoking pot? I'm sure there's a good reason. Is there some way I'm not taking care of you? I really want to know what the problem is.

Child-adult: I feel anxious a lot. I'm smoking because I feel anxious and tense.

Loving Adult: But what are you anxious about?

Child-adult: I just want to make sure Ariel [his wife] is happy. She seems so happy when I'm with her, so I try to be with her a lot, and then I don't have time to do other things I want to do—or have to do. And I never have any time alone anymore.

Loving Adult: Well, would you feel better if we spent more time alone?

Child-adult: I don't know. I'm afraid that then Ariel would not be happy and that scares me.

Margie: Are you saying that you feel responsible for Ariel's happiness?

Child-adult: Yes. Aren't we together to make each other happy?

Margie: Samuel, was that what it was like when you were growing up?

Samuel: Oh, yes. That's how it was. My dad made sure that Mom never felt alone. He was always available for her. Mom would get angry and sullen and withdraw if Dad wasn't there when she wanted him there.

Margie: Is Ariel that way?

Samuel: I'm not sure, but I think so. She's not as bad as Mom, but she does seem sad when I want time alone or I'm busy with other things or other people.

Margie: Have you talked with her about this?

Samuel: No. I guess I didn't realize how anxious it was making me. I guess it just seems natural to try to always be there for her.

Margie: But it sounds like it's making you feel trapped, is that right?

Samuel: Yes! I feel so unfree. I love Ariel, but I hate not being able to do what I want to do.

Margie: It sounds like you are making Ariel's Inner Child more important than you—that you are taking care of her Child instead of taking care of yourself.

Samuel: That's exactly what I'm doing. I guess I've believed that I'm responsible for her Child, just as Dad was responsible for Mom's.

Margie: Do you want that responsibility?

Samuel: No! But what will happen if I don't do it?

Margie: What are you afraid of?

Samuel: That she will feel sad, and then I will feel guilty.

Margie: So you feel guilty when she is sad because you feel responsible for her feelings?

Samuel: Yeah.

Margie: How does the smoking issue come into this?

Samuel: I smoke when I'm anxious and also when I want time alone. I think that smoking gives me an excuse to have some time alone. I've given up some of the things that are important to me, like going to the gym, and I smoke when I feel anxious about this.

Margie: See if you can move into Step Four. Ask your spiritual Guidance what would be the loving behavior toward yourself in this situation.

Loving Adult: The image that is coming to me is that I have to plan time to go to the gym and have time alone— I have to plan it into my day just as I plan time to work and sleep and be with Ariel. If I don't plan it, it won't happen. I think if I did that I would feel a lot better.

Margie: Now ask your Guidance how to deal with your anxiety and guilt if Ariel is sad or upset about your doing this. Also ask how to deal with your false belief that you don't have the right to take care of yourself in this way.

Loving Adult: I have to keep telling my Child that Ariel's feelings are her own responsibility, that my Child's well-being is my responsibility. I have to let Ariel handle her own feelings.

Margie: What will you do if she gets mad at you, or gets sullen like your mother?

Samuel: I don't know. That's what really gets to me.

Margie: This is the hard part, Samuel. But it's important for you to realize that if Ariel really loves you, she will support you doing for yourself whatever makes you happy and she will learn to take care of her own feelings. As long as you are willing to take responsibility for her feelings, *she* doesn't have to. She needs to learn to make herself happy without you always around. Your mother never learned this because your father was always there taking care of her. He enabled her to be needy and addicted to him. He probably convinced himself that he was being loving, but it is never loving to support someone in being unloving to themselves and others. If you don't want Ariel to be addicted to being with you, then you need to be loving to yourself—which is also loving to Ariel because it will give her the opportunity to become more self-sufficient. She will feel much better about herself when she can make herself happy and not have to depend completely on you. Her Inner Child will feel safer and loved by her when she can rely on herself to be there instead of always relying on you. So you need to keep telling yourself that you are being loving to yourself and to Ariel when you take care of yourself. It's important to do this now, before you have children, so you won't be role-modeling codependent and addictive behavior for them.

Samuel: So if I start to exercise again and take time alone for myself and keep telling myself that this is loving to both me and Ariel, maybe I can get through this anxiety without smoking. And when she gets mad or sullen, I need to remind myself of all this—that I am being loving and that I'm not responsible for her feelings and let her work them out or offer to explore them with her. Sounds good to me, but I guess I'll have to try it and see how it works.

Samuel was able to follow through on this, and he reported to me that he was no longer smoking pot. In addition, Ariel never did get angry or sullen. Samuel had projected his mother's behavior onto Ariel, expecting her to be like that when, in fact, she wasn't.

As loving Adults, our job is to learn as much as we can about how to create and maintain our physical and emotional health. It is our job to stay tuned into our bodies and find out what creates our greatest sense of well-being. But we cannot take care of ourselves unless we are well-informed. We cannot leave it up to doctors to lead the way—we must take responsibility for our own health and well-being. We each need to explore the many different theories of nutrition, as well as the connections between the mind, body and spirit, and the healing power of prayer.

To maintain a stress-free inner environment, you need to learn to set loving boundaries in relationships with others. When you allow others to control you with their criticism, anger, sarcasm or withdrawal of love, and when you allow others to shame and blame you for their unhappiness, you are not setting loving boundaries. (We'll discuss how to take care of yourself in relationships in chapters twelve and thirteen). Allowing your Inner Child to be abused in any way will make him or her feel alone and unsafe, and that is when your wounded child-adult will most likely turn to substance and process addictions to numb the fear and fill the emptiness. *Taking loving action means doing what you have to do, without harming yourself or others, to create a sense of safety within.* By dialoguing daily with your Inner Child and your spiritual Guidance, you will discover what this action needs to be.

You can affirm over and over that you are lovable and worthy, but if you ignore your pain and fill your emptiness with your addictions instead of dialoguing with your Child, exploring what you are doing to cause the pain and giving yourself what you really need, then your affirmations are just empty words. If you tell an actual child that she is a precious being and that you love her very much, then ignore her, discount her feelings, sit her in front of the TV or give her a cookie when she comes to you in pain, she will not feel lovable, loved or worthy. Spending time with her laughing and playing, bringing her Divine Love, gazing at her with love and being there when she's in pain will let her know that, in her innermost self, she is lovable and important to you. *The same is true on an inner level.*

I have seen people struggle over and over to lose weight, stop drinking, stop smoking, stop using drugs, stop spending or stop stressing out. And over and over, when they shift from the intent to protect and avoid their feelings into the intent to learn and love themselves, they develop a powerful, loving, spiritually connected Adult who is able to follow through on their decisions easily and naturally.

Intent is the key. As long as your primary desire is to protect yourself against feeling your painful feelings, you will not be able to stop hurting your body, no matter how much willpower you exert. As soon as your primary intent is to be a loving person to yourself and others, you will begin the process of taking responsibility for your pain, connecting with God and healing the wounded self. *Intent is a major key to creating a healthy house for the soul.*

The goal here is to attain—and maintain—a high level of physical and emotional health that gives us the energy to do all the things we want to do and have what we want out of life. When we feel vibrantly energized and healthy (other than when we are physically ill or disabled due to accidents or inherited or environmental factors), we know we are taking appropriate loving action for ourselves. This energy and health translates into a higher frequency that enables us to more easily stay in direct communion with God.

ELEVEN

Defining and Expressing the Soul

The loving actions that we take in Step Five are not only about the health and safety of our body, but also of our soul. Taking loving action for the soul means allowing ourselves to act from the truth of who we are. It means letting our core Selves express all that we are—our gifts, talents, creativity and passions.

As you practice Inner Bonding and take loving action based on the truth of who you are, you gradually liberate yourself from the fears and false beliefs that limit you and open to expressing the gifts God gave you. As the wounded self heals, the core Self is revealed and you are privileged to remember, define and experience who you really are. Rather than having to give ourselves up to be loved by God, we discover that God supports us in being all that we can be. This is why God gave each of us gifts as well as avenues to express these gifts. We express God in us when we share who we really are and the gifts we were given.

Defining Ourselves

How do we define who we really are and discover our gifts? When we operate from the wounded self, we hand over the job of defining our worth to others. We attach our worth to how we look and perform, then we attempt to control getting others' approval through looking and performing "right." Not only is it exhausting to always try to figure out what doing it "right" means, it puts us in a nearly constant state of performance anxiety. Instead of doing things *well* for the satisfaction of it, we try to do them *right* to win approval, which leads to the rampant incompetence that permeates our society. When we are doing things *right* for approval, we tend to do them just enough to get by and get the approval or money we seek. We will do them *well* only when doing them is an expression of our being.

When we define our own worth *internally* through our connection with our spiritual Guidance, we open to the truth of who we really are, and what we do becomes an expression of who we really are instead of an attempt to gain approval.

This is summarized in the following chart:

Self-Worth

EARTHLY PATH OF FEAR

WE DEFINE OUR WORTH:

EXTERNALLY BY APPROVAL
which we need to CONTROL through:

Looks
Must look right

Performance
Must do it right

This creates FEELINGS of: anxiety, fear, panic, depression, guilt, shame, victimization, insecurity, resentment, jealousy, aloneness, hurt, distrust of self and others, WHICH WE PROTECT AGAINST FEELING.

WORTH

CREATES

SPIRITUAL PATH OF LOVE/COURAGE

WE DEFINE OUR WORTH:

INTERNALLY by receiving the truth of who we are through GOD/SPIRIT/DIVINE LOVE

Through practicing Inner Bonding we recognize and embrace our ESSENTIAL GOODNESS, CARING, LOVABILITY, JOY, EMPATHY, COMPASSION, INNER KNOWING

This creates an experience of our INTRINSIC WORTH and personal power, unrelated to looks, performance or external approval.

With others by:

Defending, explaining, demanding, lecturing, anger, judging, blaming, shaming, complaining, caretaking, interrogating, denying, evading, lying, withdrawing

With self by:
Procrastinating
Resisting
Addictions

With self by:
Overworking
Overachieving
Perfectionism

Relationship problems

Paralysis, Blocked creativity

Exhaustion

LOW SELF-ESTEEM

RESULTS

JOYFUL EXPRESSION OF SELF

• Authentic, honest, loving relationships.
• Natural competence—as an expression of passion and purpose—doing things *well* for the joy of it rather than doing them *right* for the approval. *Doing* as an expression of *being*.
  • Creativity, trust of self.
  • Living in peace, joy and gratitude.

The bridge from the left side to the right is practicing the Six Steps of INNER BONDING®

As you can see from the chart, you cannot accurately define yourself without connecting with your spiritual Guidance. *The truth of who you are comes from God,* not from others or your own wounded self. That's why healing begins with establishing a spiritual connection, then bringing that truth down to your Inner Child. As you learn to see yourself through the eyes of God rather than through the eyes of your parents or other caregivers, you gradually remember and define yourself from truth rather than from false beliefs. The more your core Self feels seen and loved by you, the more it will let you access your gifts, for your gifts are in your core Self. Then you can experience the joy and sacred privilege of expressing who you really are.

Here is an exercise you can do daily as part of Step Four of Inner Bonding. In this exercise, you bring through the truth of who you really are. Imagine your spiritual Guidance is here with you right now. Imagine that you as a young child are here as well. Now imagine that you are looking at your Child through the eyes of your spiritual Guidance. What do you see? Do you see your innocence, your beauty, your lovingness, your light? Do you see that you are a perfect individualized expression of the Divine?

Practicing seeing yourself through the eyes of your spiritual Guidance every day will lead you to remember who you are and what your gifts are. As you see your Child through the eyes of your spiritual Guidance, check off the gifts and talents that apply to you. If you truly let your spiritual Guidance read and respond to your list, you may find some surprises.

Checklist of Gifts and Talents

- ❏ Sports—coordinated, athletic
- ❏ Mechanical—can make or fix things
- ❏ Construction—can build things
- ❏ Green thumb—can grow things
- ❏ Clothing—can design patterns and/or sew
- ❏ Cooking, creative cuisine
- ❏ Crafts—weaving, quilting, needlepoint
- ❏ Drawing
- ❏ Painting
- ❏ Ceramics
- ❏ Sculpture
- ❏ Commercial art
- ❏ Landscape design
- ❏ Architecture
- ❏ Furniture design and making
- ❏ Interior design
- ❏ Set design
- ❏ Costume design
- ❏ Jewelry design and making
- ❏ Playing one or more musical instruments
- ❏ Singing
- ❏ Dancing
- ❏ Choreography
- ❏ Writing music, composing
- ❏ Acting
- ❏ Directing
- ❏ Production
- ❏ Screenwriting
- ❏ Writing—fiction
- ❏ Writing—nonfiction
- ❏ Writing—poetry
- ❏ Science—creative research

Checklist of Gifts and Talents *(continued)*

- ❏ Inventing
- ❏ Innovative ideas
- ❏ Advertising
- ❏ Selling
- ❏ Public speaking
- ❏ Teaching
- ❏ Psychological insight
- ❏ Psychic
- ❏ Networking
- ❏ Humor
- ❏ Healing
- ❏ Healing touch
- ❏ Eye-hand coordination
- ❏ Social interaction
- ❏ Leadership
- ❏ Organizing things
- ❏ Business—creating, running and/or fixing
- ❏ Languages
- ❏ Typing
- ❏ Computers—creating new programs
- ❏ Computers—using software
- ❏ Computers—building hardware
- ❏ Raising money
- ❏ Making money
- ❏ Parenting
- ❏ Remembering details (excellent memory)
- ❏ Sharing warmth, love, caring and understanding
- ❏ Inspiring others
- ❏ Helping others
- ❏ Listening
- ❏ Empathy and compassion
- ❏ (Add your own)

_____

_____

_____

_____

Expressing Our Souls

Remember the image from the guided meditation where you imagined love as being the color violet? Let's continue the metaphor. When we participate in an activity, we are either in our wounded self—trying to get bits of violet from people and activities to fill the emptiness within us—or we are in our core Self and our actions are an expression of the violet that overflows from within us. When we offer our gifts from love, we express our souls.

God provides numerous arenas through which we can express our gifts, talents, creativity and passion. These include work, service, parenting, creativity and play, relationships and sexuality. It is our privilege as loving Adults to explore these arenas and discover the most joyous ways of expressing our love and the beauty of our souls.

Work

Each of us comes into this life with special God-given talents. In a loving family these talents are allowed to develop so that we can discover what we came here to contribute. Too often in our society, however, we don't know or use—especially in the workplace—the talents we were given. Our work becomes drudgery, something we have to do before we can relax and have some fun. In many indigenous societies, work is a fully satisfying part of life as each person contributes his or her special talent to the success of the whole. When you discover your talents and express them through some form of work, you will experience work as a joy and a sacred privilege rather than a burden. Your job will become a loving action to express and evolve your soul, rather than just something you have to do to survive or get the love you are seeking.

In *The Continuum Concept*, Jean Liedloff wrote about her experiences living with the South American Yequana Indians.[1] She discovered that the Yequana have no word for "work." They have words for various activities that we consider work, but they do not distinguish work from other ways of spending time. What we call work is something they do because it is an expression of who they are and it fulfills them. Liedloff described a rather unusual situation that occurred in the village while she was living there. One of the men had been taken away as a child and had lived in the city for most of his youth. He came back as a young man and had no desire to work. The rest of the community happily supported him for five years, and no one ever tried to make him work. Then one day he decided he wanted to work and started to lay out his garden. The chief thought it was hilarious that it took this man five years to discover that he wanted to work. Everyone brought up in the community naturally desired to work, and none of them could fathom why anyone would not want to.

Marlo Morgan wrote in *Mutant Message Down Under* about her experiences with a nomadic tribe of Australian aborigines, who call themselves the Real People Tribe and told her they were the first people of the Earth.[2] They took her on a four-month "walkabout" across the blazing desert of Australia while educating her about their spirituality, healing techniques, mental telepathy and relationship to the environment. For these very wise people, work is something they do as an expression of their God-given talents, and the name they eventually choose for themselves reflects this talent, names such as Sewing Master, Great Stone Hunter (a man who had a talent for finding precious gems), Tool Maker, Good Listener, Great Composer, Dream Catcher and Spirit Woman.

In our society, we tend to ignore our special talents and choose our careers according to what will give us a sense of security. Too often, however, what makes us feel safe does not fulfill us spiritually. I work with many people who, after doing what they believed they should do to earn money, change their minds in midlife and seek to discover their gifts. When they experience the joy of sharing their particular talent with the world, they generally find that they can earn enough money to support themselves. Even if they earn significantly less than when they worked at something they disliked, they find that they are far happier.

The false belief that earning a lot of money will bring us peace and joy often leads to anxiety and depression when we achieve our financial goals and discover that we still feel empty, insecure or alone.

Roger worked for many years as an attorney, but he never enjoyed it. He made lots of money, yet when he consulted with me he was suffering from anxiety and depression. He had become an attorney because his father had been an attorney and wanted him to follow in his footsteps. Roger had gone along with what his father wanted for him because he didn't know what else he wanted and now, in midlife, he was miserable. He yearned to discover his passion.

A few months after starting to practice Inner Bonding, Roger remembered that he had really wanted to be a teacher. He had never seriously considered teaching because he felt he couldn't make enough money, but now he was willing to make far less money because he was so unhappy with his present work. Roger went back to school and got his teaching credential and is now a high school social studies teacher. The last time I spoke with him he was radiant! He loved working with adolescents, and he felt he was making a real contribution to their lives. For the first time ever, he felt alive and passionate about his life. His wife decided to take up some of the financial slack by doing something she had always wanted to do: design children's clothing. She started her own mail-order business and is thrilled with it. Their marriage and family life is flourishing because both of them are happy and fulfilled within themselves.

Ricki came to see me because she was so unhappy working as an accountant of a big import business. Yet she had no idea what else she wanted to do. It took about a year of practicing Inner Bonding before her Inner Child told her that she wanted to be a nutritionist. Ricki hadn't wanted to hear her Child because she didn't want to go back to school. Finally she was so unhappy that she decided to listen. She is now back in school enjoying discovering her passion.

While it may not always be possible to change your work immediately to something you love, if you follow your passion, it will often lead you there. And even when you have to earn money in ways that do not express your soul, you can seek volunteer opportunities and hobbies to express who you are. Often these can lead to the work that you will eventually do.

Alfredo worked as a manager of a large supermarket. With his small savings, he decided to start pursuing a hobby that had always fascinated him—restoring old cars. He used all his extra money to buy his first old car and spent many blissful hours restoring it. He was so good at it, that he was able to sell his restored cars for a lot of money. Eventually he was able to quit his job at the market and pursue his passion full time. Ultimately he started a project in a prison teaching inmates to restore cars. Alfredo now loves what he does and receives great satisfaction from helping others.

Your soul has a deep desire for you to express yourself through work, to produce something that is both of value to you and contributes to society in some way. It is your job as a loving Adult to discover what that is and to bring it about.

Service

As we heal from spiritual abuse, connecting with Divine Love and taking loving action for ourselves, our hearts become so filled with love that we feel compelled to help others. We may find ourselves doing various forms of service not because we think we should, but simply because it gives us great joy. Unfortunately, many people who become involved in service organizations act from the motives of their wounded child-adult, who wants to be seen as "good" and win approval. This is not service—it is caretaking, giving to get. True service springs from a full heart, a heart so overflowing with love it spills out to others.

There are many forms of service and we each need to find the way that works best for us. There is no right way. We can serve by helping one person, such as being a Big Brother or Big Sister to a disadvantaged child, or we can be of service by helping whole groups, such as raising funds for environmental projects. We can offer our time building houses for the poor, or we can offer money. We can choose to be of service to people, animals or Mother Earth. Your service may be in being a loving parent to your children, helping a friend in need or being a loving mate who supports the other's highest good in many little ways.

Doing service is a matter of discovering your passion and then offering your time and love. You might have a special interest in protecting the environment, stopping child abuse, helping the homeless or caring for the dying. You might offer service through your creativity, creating beautiful drawings, ceramics or quilts to donate to charitable causes or give as gifts. As you practice Inner Bonding and get to know your Inner Child, he or she will let you in on your passions.

Steve discovered his passion for helping the elderly when his father became ill and was in a convalescent home. A hard-driving businessman, Steve was surprised to find how joyous and fulfilled he felt when he visited his father and brought his humor and compassion to the other elderly at the home. Being with the elderly was so satisfying, Steve decided to cut back on his work and spend more time at the home. He had discovered what makes his heart sing.

Kurt, the president and CEO of a large and successful company, had a similar experience that led him to change his life. While reading the paper one day, he came across an article about a privately run school in South Central Los Angeles for gang members and school dropouts. He was drawn to visit the school and soon found himself becoming involved with some of the kids. Kurt discovered that he felt filled with love and joy when he was at the school helping the kids. Mentoring them became his passion and his service.

Work, too, can be service. When you experience your work as helping people and you love doing it, it is service, whether you are a hairdresser, a teacher, a physician, an auto mechanic, a therapist, an attorney or a bus driver. While you get paid for your time, no one can pay you for the love you put into it. Love is always a gift that comes *through* you.

In fact, *anything* you offer that expresses your love is service—your time, creativity, encouragement or a warm and caring smile to a hassled store clerk. Service is not only expressed in specific works but also in your intention in each and every moment. Have you ever smiled at a stranger or offered a compliment just because you noticed something in him or her that caught your eye? When was the last time you said how much you appreciate someone? When your heart is open to others, service can be as ceaseless as prayer.

The practice of service does not have to be done only on an individual level. It is possible for whole families to participate in service projects. Rather than relaxing around the house and watching TV together, you can participate in a local environmental or social project. Families who do service together generally maintain a higher level of values and unity than those who do not create the time for such activities.

Each of us needs to find the service that excites us, enlivens us and fills our heart with joy as we express God's love through our actions. Giving for the pure joy of giving feeds the soul. We love God by loving the children of God and serving them in any way we can. It is through service that we can truly grow spiritually. Through service, we are confronted with our issues and given the opportunity to practice our lovingness and expand beyond what we think our limits are. The depth of our service is the depth of our devotion to God.

Erika, along with being the co-creator of Inner Bonding, is a chaplain and founder of Hope America Ministries Foundation, which is an extension of Inner Bonding. Erika travels around the country ministering to the poor, the homeless and anyone in need. She finds jobs and housing, gives first aid, provides sleeping bags, food and other supplies to the homeless, and even does weddings and last rites when that is needed. When she calls me on the phone to tell me of the people she helped that day, she is always filled with incredible peace and joy, knowing that she is offering her special gifts of love and compassion where they are most needed.

Parenting

Parenting, like work and other forms of service, can be experienced as a burden or a sacred privilege. When your intent in having children is to get something from them—such as to take away your loneliness, get cared for in your old age or gain an identity as someone's mom or dad—you are acting from your wounded self, and you will experience your children's demands as a burden. This is when child abuse is most likely to happen.

Child abuse is always from an out-of-control child-adult who feels burdened by the demands of the child or wants to control the child in order to avoid feeling powerless. When you have not done your inner work to heal the wounds from your own childhood, you may have deep pain, rage and feelings of powerlessness from your spiritual abuse, especially if it included physical or emotional neglect, or verbal, physical or sexual abuse. You may take these feelings out on your children. You may expect your children to give you what your parents did not and become enraged when you don't get it.

Loving parenting means being there for our children as well as for *ourselves* so that we do not expect them to do it for us. Our children need us to take care of them, but we must find a way to do so without sacrificing our own Inner Child. I was brought up to be a caretaker—to put myself aside and take responsibility for others' feelings. When I became a mother, I moved right into this caretaking behavior with my children, putting my own Child aside in order to take care of their needs. Often this left me exhausted. Parenting—the way I was doing it—definitely felt like a burden rather than a privilege. I was there for my children but not for myself. When I started doing Inner Bonding, I realized that at least half of good parenting is being a role-model for personal responsibility—and I was not providing my kids this role-modeling. As I learned to take responsibility for myself, parenting became a true joy. My children were adolescents when I started to provide this responsible role modeling, but fortunately it is never too late to be a healthy role model for our children.

As you become a loving Adult and discover the beauty of your core Self, you will experience parenting as a great gift. Raising your children becomes a wonderful adventure as you bring through Divine Love to them, then watch their souls evolve and contribute what they came here to contribute. When you are in an intent to learn, your children become your teachers. They challenge you to further heal and evolve your soul.

I work with many parents who would never have sought help were it not for their children challenging them. A good example of this are Cameron and Celeste, parents of Aaron, fifteen, and Bernard, twelve. Cameron and Celeste consulted with me because Aaron told them that he didn't want to live with them anymore unless they received help. He told them he was tired of always seeing his mother anxious and angry and his father withdrawn. Aaron had recently spent some time with another family that was open and loving and that was how he wanted to live. It was not his parents' meanness to him that upset him—it was their meanness to each other.

One of the greatest gifts we can give to our children is our own wholeness. As we explore and discover our core Self and our unique gifts, we give our children permission to do the same. As we learn to see and value ourselves as an individualized expression of God, it is far easier to see and value the uniqueness within each of our children. Often behavior problems in children result from their not being seen for who they really are. Our society tends to pathologize unusual behavior instead of trying to understand it. The drugs we give children for such behaviors as attention deficit disorder are often a way of protecting ourselves from knowing who they really are and what they really need—emotionally, spiritually and nutritionally. Let me give you an example of what I mean.

Elliott was born into a quiet, restrained family that did not easily express feelings. Elliott came bounding into the world filled with intense and creative energy. To his family, this little boy was an alien, and they went about trying to "fix" him. Through anger and silence, they attempted to mold him into their quiet, restrained way of being. Elliott reacted to this unloving behavior by becoming even more intense and getting enraged. He became the "bad boy" of the family, and he acted out his assigned role to the fullest. When, as an adult, Elliott sought my help, he was convinced that he was a bad person and a hopeless rageaholic. He had overcome alcohol and drug abuse, but he was addicted to getting approval and to raging when he didn't get it. His marriage was falling apart as a result.

Through Inner Bonding, Elliott discovered the wonderful, intense, caring and highly creative little boy who had never been acknowledged by his family. He discovered that his "bad boy" had become a protection against the agonizing pain of being so unseen. As he learned to see himself and give himself the approval he had always sought from others, the creative genius within him soared and his intense rage gradually subsided.

As you embrace your individuality and the uniqueness of your soul, you stop trying to fit your children into a mold. You stop seeing them as dysfunctional when they do not fit the norm. You give them permission to discover their passions and how they would most enjoy expressing their gifts and contributing to society. Instead of the emphasis being on getting good grades and getting into good schools, the emphasis is on supporting your children in being all they came here to be. Imagine what your life would have been like if your parents had said to you, "I don't care about your grades. I don't care if you go to college or what college you get into. I don't care how much money you end up making. All I care about is that you discover your gifts and your passions and how you can best offer them to the world."

Now imagine saying that to your children, as well as to your own Inner Child.

Creativity and Play

While not all play is creative, all creativity is play. In fact, creativity is the highest form of play. Creativity is the experience of being inspired by Spirit and bringing that inspiration into some kind of form. In Greek the word *spiritus*, from which the word spirit is derived, means Divine Breath, and this is what inspiration is—opening to Divine Love breathing creativity through you.

Creativity can be manifested through many forms of art, science and invention, as well as through humor, sexuality and healing. If you face a canvas with the intent of creating a painting, but your primary intent is to paint a "good" painting in order to gain approval, earn money or avoid disapproval, you shut off the flow of creativity and painting will not be a joy. It will be a task to complete in order to receive the reward. There is an excellent example of this in *Healing Your Aloneness:*

Hal used to play the piano as a child; as an adult he had wanted to buy one for a long time. The day the piano was delivered he quickly ushered the movers out the door so he could play it right away. Armed with his only piece of sheet music, a Mozart sonata, he attacked the piano. He found that his hands were stiff and the piece was difficult to play. But Hal was going to make this fun no matter how hard it was, or what it took to finish the piece. Within a few moments his body was

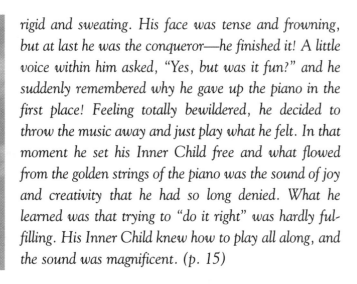

rigid and sweating. His face was tense and frowning, but at last he was the conqueror—he finished it! A little voice within him asked, "Yes, but was it fun?" and he suddenly remembered why he gave up the piano in the first place! Feeling totally bewildered, he decided to throw the music away and just play what he felt. In that moment he set his Inner Child free and what flowed from the golden strings of the piano was the sound of joy and creativity that he had so long denied. What he learned was that trying to "do it right" was hardly fulfilling. His Inner Child knew how to play all along, and the sound was magnificent. (p. 15)

When your intent is to learn and be loving to your Child, then the experience itself is the reward as you receive inspiration and bring it into form.

If you have sex with a set goal in mind—having an orgasm, getting connected with the other, getting affirmed, getting filled and taking away loneliness, relaxing or even having fun—it probably won't be much fun. Instead of being in the moment, which is how you receive inspiration, you are focused on the goal and there is no creativity in the experience. Being sexual with someone in order to learn more about expressing your love is a highly creative experience, a delightful form of play that is immensely satisfying. I will say more about sexuality below.

If you engage in a conversation with someone about a particular topic, whether or not your discussion is creative and experienced as play again depends upon your intent. Even if you are discussing something about which you disagree, the conversation can be a delightful experience of creativity and play when both people are in the intent to learn. But if one or both of you want to be right or fear being run over and controlled by the other, then the discussion will be tense instead of free-flowing. You cut off the flow of inspiration when you move into the intent to protect. Your wounded self will attempt to make points or hold the line against losing rather than learn, and it will be anything but fun and creative.

Unfortunately, most people act from their child-adult when disagreements arise, especially over hot topics such as abortion, religion, politics, money, parenting, sexuality and communication. Even people on a learning path can move into their judgmental and blaming child-adult over the issue of who is "right" and who is "wrong." Some people move into their child-adult during *all* disagreements, always needing to win (or avoid losing) in order to feel safe. Sadly, they miss out on one of the greatest joys in life—learning, discovering and creating something new with others. We will not solve our individual or global problems until we can approach each other with a deep desire to learn.

Learning is a form of play because it is deeply creative and brings a profound sense of joy and satisfaction. The more we heal from spiritual abuse, the more we find ourselves bubbling up with joy and letting it explode into deep belly laughs. Eventually the healing process moves out of the realm of drudgery and into joy. This often happens at my five-day intensives. The first couple of days are usually filled with pain and anger as people release their pent-up tears and rage. This opens the door for exploring and releasing the false beliefs that have kept them locked into their pain and anger. This, in turn, opens up space for truth and love to come in. By the third day, although our work is going even deeper, there is laughter amid the tears. By the end of the intensive, many of the participants leave knowing that the learning process, even though it includes moments of pain and fear, can be a fun and joyful form of play. Several participants have even remarked that the intensive was the best vacation they ever had.

Part of the loving action of the loving Adult is to make sure you have time to play. We all need time to play and we each need to discover what our Inner Child experiences as play. For some, a sport such as tennis, swimming, golf, softball or basketball is play. (People playing sports express their core Selves—the physicality of the body is an expression of God, too—when playing rather than winning is the goal.) Others experience artistic expression—music, art, writing, dance—as play, while still others experience social gatherings as play. Even work can be play when it is a loving and creative process. Whatever play means to you, remember that *the Child in you loves to play* and it is up to you as a loving Adult to make sure you have enough of it in your life.

Sexuality

While I've already mentioned sexuality as a form of play, it is much more than this, and it is integrally tied to relationship, which we will discuss in the next chapter.

God gave us the gift of sexuality not only to perpetuate our species, but to express our love through our bodies. However, too often sexuality is not experienced as a sacred privilege, a gift to be cherished, but as an addiction, a way to fill the emptiness, numb the fear or satiate the need for power of the wounded child-adult. Sex without intimacy comes from the child-adult rather than the loving Adult and is a momentary fix rather than the Divine play it is meant to be.

This has created a huge problem in our society. If we all operated as loving Adults who desired to express and evolve our souls, incest and rape would not exist. If we operated from the spiritual rather than the earthly perspective, we would never violate others nor willingly allow others to violate us. If evolving our souls towards love was our highest priority, we would never knowingly do *anything* hurtful to another person.

When we embrace the sacred privilege of sexuality, we experience it as creative play, an expression of Spirit. Sexual expression between two people who are truly sharing love is a sweet and passionate experience of grace. Those who allow their wounded child-adult to indulge in the addiction of sexuality may never experience the great gift that has been offered to them.

The Difference Between Connection and Intimacy

Sometimes we confuse connection and/or sexuality with intimacy. Connection with another occurs when we are connected with God and ourselves. When your heart is open, you can connect with anyone else whose heart is open. You can have a momentary connection with the cashier at the gas station, expressing God in that moment through your open heart.

You don't confuse that connection with intimacy (unless you are operating from your wounded child-adult). But when you meet someone with whom you sense a soul connection (the feeling of having known them before), you may mistake that connection with intimacy and feel drawn to have sex with them. Afterward, you wonder why you feel empty.

Intimacy occurs when people create a safe space to deeply share themselves with each other—sharing their fears and passions, their struggles and creativity, their wounded selves and core Selves, their hearts and their souls. Intimacy is being compassionately present for each other in the healing journey. True intimacy involves a mutual commitment to tell the whole truth and be in a learning process with each other. When people are intimate with each other, they are devoted to creating a safe space for each person to be all of who they are.

Intimacy may or may not include sexuality. You can be intimate with your friends, your parents and your children, for example, without being sexual with them. It is only when you are intimate with a mate that sexuality becomes a part of intimacy, a profound, playful, creative and fulfilling expression of God's love.

We cannot be intimate with someone unless there is a sense of equality between us. By equality I mean that we are equal in our knowledge of our core Selves, equal in our level of healing, equal in our degree of personal power. People are drawn together either by their common level of woundedness or their common level of healing. When one person knows his or her own goodness and another does not, they will not have genuine intimacy.

If you are healed enough to know your own goodness, worth and lovableness, and you are with someone who believes he or she is unlovable or unworthy, you cannot be intimate with them. Because this person feels one down to you, he or she may feel threatened by you. This person may seek your approval, give himself or herself up to avoid your rejection, resist you or attempt to diminish you. You will always feel a sense of loneliness when you know your own worth and lovableness and you are with others who do not. You cannot have the ecstasy of play and intimacy without equality. And you cannot *make* others feel equal to you. Their sense of equality has to come from within, from knowing their core Selves through the eyes of God. You can help them with this, but you cannot do it for them. Helping them may be fulfilling, but it is not intimate. Intimacy occurs when two or more people help each other through mutual sharing and learning.

I am sitting with a woman named Letty at one of my five-day intensives. My intent is to be fully present for her with my love and support as she does her inner work. I would love to play with her in the sense of high play—to share love as she learns about her pain and her joy. However, her heart is closed. Her intent is to figure out how to do her inner work "right" so she can get my approval. She does not know that she already has my love. Because of her closed heart, her Child feels alone, and Letty wants to use me to take away her aloneness rather than learn with me. I am aware of *my* loneliness as I work with her because she sees herself as less than me. My feelings of loneliness are valuable to me because they give me information about Letty. They tell me that her heart is closed. Gently, I ask Letty to notice her intent. She realizes that she wants my approval. Grinning, she chooses to learn about this rather than judge it. Now her heart is open. Now we can play! Now Letty can learn about the beliefs of her wounded self and discover more of her core Self. Now we can move toward equality and genuine intimacy.

When we are devoted to the daily practice of defining ourselves internally, through the eyes of our spiritual Guidance, we open the door to expressing the gifts of our soul. Whether we express our souls through work, service, parenting, creativity, play, sexuality or relationship, we discover the joy of being fully who we are. The rewards of doing our inner work and becoming a loving Adult are well worth the time and effort it takes to heal the wounded self.

TWELVE

The Relationship Path to God

Just as we all need time to regenerate our bodies, which we do when we sleep, we all need time to regenerate our souls. There are two primary ways of doing this and *both* are necessary for the soul to feel fulfilled. One way is alone, through prayer and meditation, being with nature, learning and expressing our creativity. The other way to regenerate our souls is in relationship with others who are open to learning and sharing love with us. Shared love, joy and laughter are the highest and most fulfilling experiences in life. And learning how to create this with another person is the most sacred—and the most challenging—path to God.

Being in a relationship stirs up our deepest fears of rejection and abandonment, domination and engulfment, loneliness and helplessness to control others. When these fears are activated, choosing love instead of control is a trial by fire. That's why relationships are God's greatest gift to us for evolving our souls.

319

Most of us enter into relationships in the hopes of receiving the love and sense of security we did not get as children. It is common to pick someone as a partner—or even as a friend, employer or employee—who reminds us of one or both of our parents, and then try to control getting what we did not get in our family of origin. At the root of this behavior is a deep desire—conscious or unconscious—to heal the wounds from our spiritual abuse. With each new relationship, we hope that this time the person will love us or care about us in the way we want.

But as long as we operate from our wounded selves, we will re-create our original scenarios over and over again, both at home and at work. As wounded child-adults, we do not feel whole, so we repeatedly seek others to fill us up. It is as if we are each born with an invisible plug that allows us to connect to a dependable source of love and fill ourselves up. If we do not know how to plug into God—the only truly dependable source of love—then we walk around empty and unplugged, hoping to find someone who will be our source of love. When two wounded people meet and plug into each other, they may call this falling in love. But it is not. It is a codependent relationship where each person makes the other responsible for being his or her dependable source of love. Because this doesn't work, eventually both people will notice they still feel empty and will blame each other for the lack of love they are experiencing. Until each takes responsibility for plugging into God as their individual source of love, they will continue to feel alone and disappointed in each other.

I remember waking up one morning several years back in tears. I didn't know why I was crying, but I was willing to feel my pain and find out. I chose the intent to learn, then I asked my Inner Child why she was so upset. She told me, "Because no one has ever been consistently unconditionally loving to me." When I thought about this, I realized it was true and I felt tremendously sad. Moving into Step Four, I turned to my Teacher and said, "My Child says no one has ever been consistently unconditionally loving to her."

"Of course they haven't," my Teacher replied. "People cannot consistently love *you* unconditionally until they consistently love *themselves* unconditionally, and no one you know has learned to do that yet. Likewise, you cannot consistently love others unconditionally until you consistently love yourself unconditionally, which is something you are still learning. So don't expect this from others. It is your responsibility to give your Child the consistent unconditional love she wants. And you can only do this by receiving it from God, then passing it on to her." I felt so much better hearing this. I had always felt deprived that no one had given me consistent unconditional love. Eventually I learned not to expect it from others, but to open my heart and receive it from God instead.

When I tell this story at my workshops, I am often asked, "If I learn to be a loving Adult and take care of my own feelings and needs, why do I need a relationship?"

When you are a loving Adult taking responsibility for yourself, you seek a relationship, not to be taken care of and completed by someone else, but to share the fullness of your being—the love in your heart—with a partner. You seek someone to evolve with as you each face the opportunities inherent in the relationship path to God. As loving Adults, we seek the challenge of being in a relationship in order to become more loving to ourselves and others rather than to *get* love. Relationships challenge us not only to be one with the Divine within us, but to share that Divine Love with others.

The deepest experience of God occurs when two people are truly loving and intimate with each other, when they share all of themselves and there are no barriers to the flow of love. Two people who come together to share love can help each other heal and evolve. It is codependent if they are trying to do this *for* each other. It is healing if they are doing it *with* each other.

Love means something different to the wounded child-adult than to the loving Adult. In our language we have only one word for love, but Spanish has two, *te quiero*, which means, "I want you for me," and *te amo*, which means "I am love extending to you." *Te quiero* is how the child-adult defines love: "I want from you, therefore I love you." *Te amo*, on the other hand, is the loving Adult's definition of love: a gift from God. The loving Adult operates from Divine Love, love that seeks not to control or get from others, but to bring through the truth, compassion, caring and understanding of God to yourself and others.

The challenge of taking care of ourselves is substantial even when we are not in a relationship. It is not easy to remember to move into an intent to learn, especially when we are stressed. It can be hard to bring in our loving Adult and set limits for ourselves about our substance and process addictions. But a far more complex situation arises when we are in a relationship, especially if we are in conflict or we fear conflict with the other person. Learning to take responsibility for our own feelings without violating the other, and caring about the other without taking responsibility for the other's feelings is an enormous challenge. It is so easy in relationships to feel victimized by the other person.

Feeling Victimized

Many of the people I work with struggle with the issue of feeling victimized in relationships. A good example happened the other day on the phone. A woman named Angela had read one of my books and called to get some help. The conversation went something like this:

"My husband John spends most of his time either at work or doing his hobbies. He never seems to want to spend time with me."

"Angela, are you wanting help with how to take care of yourself or how to get John to change?"

"Well, I just want things to be better."

"How do you respond when John doesn't spend time with you?"

"I get really angry."

"Why do you get angry?"

"Because he's not paying any attention to me."

"But why do you use anger as your way of dealing with this?"

"Well, what am I supposed to do? It's so frustrating. He's like a brick wall."

"Would you be willing to back off from him and just start taking care of yourself, making yourself happy in whatever ways you would if you were not in a relationship?"

"But then we would *never* spend time together. What kind of a relationship is that?"

"Well, it sounds like John is resisting being controlled by you, that he feels controlled by your anger and backs off. If *you* back off and take care of *yourself*, perhaps he would find you more attractive and want to spend time with you."

"I'm not the controlling one," she says. "He is."

I can see that Angela is not in an intent to learn. I decide to offer her one more bit of information, then end the conversation if she chooses to stay closed.

"It sounds to me like you both are trying to control. You are controlling with your anger, and he is controlling with his resistance. You are in a power struggle in which you see yourself as a victim. You can break this struggle by taking care of yourself instead of making him responsible for you."

Angela does not like hearing this.

"Well," she says, her voice tight with anger, "thank you very much." Then she hung up.

Obviously Angela feels victimized by her husband's choices and wanted me to tell her how to get him to change. She has no faith that if she takes care of herself, she will be happier than if she continues to see herself as a victim. Controlling is more important to her than loving.

Whenever you expect another person to be responsible for your feelings or you take responsibility for another's feelings, you set up a codependent system. Sometimes you are on the taking end of that system—trying to make the other person responsible for preventing your aloneness and loneliness. At other times you are on the caretaking end—being responsible for preventing the other's aloneness and loneliness (in the hopes that when they feel loved, they will return the favor by making you feel loved). The "benefit" of this behavior is that trying to control how others feel protects you (temporarily) from your own feelings of aloneness, loneliness and helplessness over others.

Whenever we choose to find our happiness, worth and safety through others, we have to try to control them to give us what we want. Then, when they don't come through for us in the way we want them to, we feel victimized by their choices. There is no way not to feel victimized until we are ready to take responsibility for ourselves.

Don and Joyce are in a continual power struggle over how to handle their children. Joyce tends to be authoritarian, while Don is fairly permissive. When Joyce gets frustrated with Don's parenting, she usually yells at him about his permissiveness. Sometimes she goes on for over an hour and he just sits and listens. When he tries to talk with her, she refuses to listen. Don then feels victimized because he has listened to Joyce but she won't listen to him.

When I asked Don in a session why he sits and listens to Joyce yell at him, he said that he hopes if he listens to her, she will listen to him. I asked him if she ever had listened to him during these conflicts, and he answered, "No."

"Why do you need her to listen to you?" I asked.

"I want to explain to her why I did what I did with the children."

"Why do you need to explain it to her?"

"So she won't be mad at me."

So by explaining, Don hopes to control how Joyce feels about him. He hopes to get her approval instead of her anger. He hopes, by letting himself be yelled at, to control Joyce into listening to him and allowing him to explain himself to her.

When this doesn't work, he feels victimized by Joyce's yelling and blames her for being such an angry, controlling person.

If Don were willing to take responsibility for approving of himself through his connection with God, he would not sit there when Joyce was yelling at him. Instead, he would set a boundary against being yelled at, stating that he will listen to her only when she speaks to him with respect and only when she is open to learning with him. But as long as Don needs Joyce to approve of him so he can feel secure or worthy, he will not set this boundary. Until Don turns to God—instead of Joyce—for confirmation of his security and worth, he will continue to feel victimized by Joyce's unloving behavior.

Loving Actions in Conflict

When a conflict arises in a relationship, there are only two consistently loving actions you can take:

1. Move into the intent to learn with the other person.
2. Set loving boundaries and act on them if necessary.

Intent to Learn with Others

Being in an intent to learn with someone about yourself and them *without judging yourself or them* is far more complex than doing this just with yourself. That's why you will not be able to maintain an intent to learn with another until you have practiced the Six Steps long enough so that when you get stressed, you can still consistently remember to be in an intent to learn with yourself.

Being in an intent to learn with another means four things:

1. You believe that both you and the other person have very good reasons for your feelings and behavior.

2. You are willing to state your total truth and hear the other's total truth.

3. You are willing to feel the pain of your loneliness and your helplessness over the other person rather than protect yourself by trying to control them.

4. You have no investment in the outcome. The only way you will not have an investment in the outcome is if you have done your own Six-Step Process and discovered the loving action you need to take for yourself in the situation. You must know how you are going to take care of yourself if the other person turns out not to be open to learning and resolving the conflict. If you attempt to explore a conflict and are invested in the outcome, then you will try to control. Learning cannot occur in a controlling environment.

Setting Loving Boundaries

Most people have no idea how to set loving boundaries with others. Often, when we first realize that we have the right to set boundaries against any form of infringement or violation, we find ourselves doing so with hostility, acting from our wounded child-adult. We violate others with our anger and blame as we lay down the law and attempt to control them into respecting us and not violating us. In other words, we end up doing the very thing we do not want others to do to us. We act with a modified version of what I call the "gang mentality of the wounded self," which is "If you disrespect me, I will kill you."

When we allow our wounded selves to try to control others—or allow others to control us—we are not taking care of our souls. We cannot put God into motion in our lives while we are trying to control things. In order to behave lovingly in conflict with others, we must be willing to let go of control: of blaming, resisting, complying, having to be right and having to win. This is a tall order. It means letting go of trying to make others open up to learning, understand our point of view, or be different than they are. It means letting go of the outcome of the interaction and just taking care of our own Inner Child. It takes real dedication to love to overcome our wounded child-adult's desire to control.

Being in an intent to learn with others and setting loving boundaries in relationships is not about trying to get others to treat us well. It is about making our own choices about how we are going to take care of ourselves when we are being violated or do not get what we want from the other person. It is about being honest with ourselves about what our personal limits are—what we will tolerate and what we will not—and telling others about them. And it is about taking action, verbally or nonverbally, to maintain the boundaries we have set in ways that do not harm, violate or blame others.

In order to do this, we have to compassionately listen to the desires and feelings of our Inner Child, then act on these desires and feelings from our loving Adult rather than from our wounded child-adult. The child-adult will always blame others for our feelings, while the loving Adult takes responsibility for behaving in a way that respects our own and others' feelings. *Until we are willing to open to learning and speak up for ourselves by setting loving boundaries, we will feel victimized by others' behavior.*

Creating a Safe Environment

Relationships thrive when both people take responsibility for their own sense of safety within, and for their openness and honesty with each other, actions that create a safe space for both to open *with* each other. We all need to feel safe in order to open our hearts, be vulnerable and risk loving. Often we find ourselves relying on our external environment to create this sense of safety—that is, if others accept us, we feel safe. Yet this safety vanishes in a flash the moment someone becomes judgmental, non-accepting or angry. Is our safety really such a fragile thing?

The answer is, yes and no.

There are two kinds of safety: safety within and safety without. And safety within—unlike safety without—can become very reliable.

Safety within is created when we have a consistent loving Adult who stands up for us, speaks our truth, sets loving inner and outer boundaries, helps us to not take rejection personally and takes loving care of our bodies. We experience safety within when we stay connected with God, bringing love and compassion to ourselves and others. We feel safe within when we act on the Guidance we receive from Spirit.

Doing all this will make us feel safe to be spontaneously ourselves, except when we are in an intimate relationship that is very important to us. Then it takes *both people* to cre-ate the safe space to be open and vulnerable. A safe space is created when:

- Each person not only takes full responsibility for his or her own feelings, but also for behaving in a way that does not deliberately violate the other.

- Each person takes responsibility for staying open to learning about themselves and the other person. The intent to learn creates a clear, safe energy. Most of us are very sensitive to energy, even if we don't realize it, and the relationship space feels unsafe when the energy is tense due to the intent to protect.

- Each person sets inner boundaries for their own behavior when their issues are triggered. They do not indulge themselves and act out their fears by yelling, blaming, shaming, threatening, physical violence, smothering, resisting or withdrawing.

- Each person learns to truthfully tell the other (without blame and with an intent to learn about themselves and the other) when they feel afraid, rejected, unheard, unseen, engulfed, disrespected, misunderstood or pulled on, as well as when they feel loved, loving and grateful.

When we indulge ourselves and act out our fears, we dam-age the safety of the relationship. When one or both partners are afraid to speak their truth because the other usually reacts with controlling or resistance, love slowly dies. When we are committed to loving ourselves, we may eventually leave a relationship where we cannot be completely truthful without encountering blame or resistance. It takes both partners to create a safe external environment where love and passion can flourish.

If you begin relationships by trying to create a safe space for others but not yourself; that is, if you take responsibility for their feelings instead of your own, they may become dependent upon you for their sense of safety, and they are likely to get angry and blame you if you later pull back and focus on yourself. Caretakers tend to start relationships this way, then feel burdened by it and pull back. Then they wonder why their partner is upset with them. When you take responsibility for someone else's feelings and sense of safety, you usually end up feeling victimized by their anger.

The Challenge of Loneliness

It can be very difficult to remember to move into the intent to learn and to set loving boundaries with others, especially in the heat of conflict. Many of us had no role models for this type of behavior, and taking these loving actions can set off some of our deepest fears. The biggest challenge in speaking our truth and setting loving boundaries with others is *the fear of feeling our loneliness and helplessness over others' intent.*

When we feel alone (as opposed to lonely), we have the option of opening our hearts and feeling God's presence in our lives. We also have the option of being a loving Adult for our Inner Child so he or she doesn't feel alone inside. But, unlike aloneness, *loneliness is an existential fact of life*, that is, it is a part of our existence on this planet. So is helplessness over others' choices. Most people feel much safer trying to control with anger, withdrawal, compliance or resistance than staying open, setting loving boundaries—and feeling their loneliness and helplessness when others stay closed-hearted.

Is there no way to be here on this planet without feeling lonely at times? Isn't loneliness caused by having our hearts closed? Couldn't we just open our hearts and feel better? It's not that simple. When you open your heart to God's love, you will not feel alone inside, but you may still feel lonely. It's inescapable. There are so many existential realities that cause loneliness.

First, just being in a body is in itself lonely. In the spiritual realm, there is no physical separation between one soul and another. We feel and experience each other directly when we are not in a physical body. Deep within our souls, we all know this, and it motivates us to seek communion—a sense of oneness—with others and with God. We feel lonely because our souls remember how wonderful it was to have true communion. We miss it.

Second, there is the loneliness we feel when we do not have family or close friends with whom to share our love. There are many people in our society who live alone and do not have families. Our modern lifestyle—living in separate houses with little sense of community—can make it hard to meet other people. This type of loneliness does not occur in tribal societies. Similar to this is the deep loneliness and grief of having lost a loved one to death, divorce or some other factor that has ended the relationship.

Finally, there is the loneliness of having your heart open and being with someone whose heart is closed. If this person is only an acquaintance or someone we meet in passing, we may feel a moment of sadness when we experience their wounded and closed energy. But if this person is a parent, child, mate, close friend or someone we work with closely, the loneliness and sadness we feel in response to being shut out by them can be very deep. If you are unwilling to feel the loneliness, you may blind yourself to the fact that his or her heart is closed. Or you may tap-dance around trying to fix it, unconsciously believing that you have caused the other person to close his or her heart. Meanwhile, you feel worse and worse, more and more lonely, until you are driven to soothe your pain with your addictions.

The truth is, your feelings of loneliness can be very helpful. They can give you the important information that either the other person's heart is closed or yours is. You are certainly going to feel lonely when your own heart is closed. And you are going to feel equally lonely when your heart is open to learning and playing but the person you care about is not. When this happens, you have some choices. You can say something with an intent to learn, or you can accept the fact and back off. Either way, you can do something loving for yourself rather than just batter yourself on another's closed heart.

However, if you close your own heart in response to others closing theirs, you will feel alone and stressed. It is easy to feel victimized then and think another person's negative energy is stressing you. But your own closed heart is actually causing your stress and aloneness. The moment you close your heart, all energy—negative and positive—gets stuck in your body, where it can affect your health very seriously. The moment you choose the willingness to feel your loneliness and helplessness over others, open to God so you are not alone in these feelings, and stay in compassion for both yourself and the other person, the negative energy of the stress will move through you to God.

The following poem was written by Erika:

Loneliness is the only pure pain.
    All other pain is born of it.
  It alone
      ultimately fathers every
      conceivable protection against it.

We begin to wither at its mere mention.
    It is the ultimate Separation
      of the soul
      from humanity.

It is what we fear we cannot survive,
For it is the hurt we alone
        Cannot repair.
Loneliness is a fissure of the heart
      that can be bridged only by another.
We inflict it,
    despise it,
        and deny it.

Never realizing
    That in its presence
We are forced to move forward . . .
Loneliness
    is the book
      we refuse to read . . .[1]

The urgency with which we try to avoid loneliness comes from our infant memory, recorded in our bodies, of the terror of being helpless against abandonment or engulfment by others. On a cellular level, it feels as if our very lives are at stake. So the moment our feelings of loneliness and helplessness arise, the wounded self goes into action, intent on protecting us at all costs. As child-adults we will do anything to deny these terrifying feelings or make them go away. This is what we are going up against when we try to remember to stay open to learning and set loving boundaries with others.

While feeling helpless over others is certainly painful, it is no longer life-threatening, because we are no longer children, no longer helpless over ourselves. We are adults who can take loving action and bring Divine Love to the frightened Child within us. It is very important that we remember this because others' choices can set off our infant fear of helplessness and loneliness in a split second. Unless we are willing to feel these painful feelings, we will instantly protect ourselves by becoming controlling. This is what creates power struggles in relationships.

Our fear of setting loving boundaries by speaking our truth and saying no to someone is also rooted in the fear of the terrible loneliness we are afraid to feel if that person rejects us for not doing what they want. When you fear rejection and loneliness, you may give yourself up to the other person rather than risk setting a boundary with them. Or, like Gregory in chapter 4, who frustrated his controlling mother by dawdling whenever he complied with her orders, you may *appear* to give yourself up but secretly engage in passive resistance. Fears of engulfment and the resulting resistant behavior are rooted in the deeper fears of rejection, helplessness and loneliness.

The bottom line is we will not feel free to speak our truth and set loving boundaries until we are willing to open our hearts and feel our loneliness and helplessness. This may sound hard to do, but God is there to help. When we open our hearts, we open to God and we no longer feel alone with these painful feelings. We experience ourselves as innately worthy and lovable and we are guided by God in how to take loving care of our Inner Child.

Existential loneliness and helplessness over others are not feelings that will go away if we change our beliefs—they are core Self feelings, not wounded self feelings. Opening the heart opens us to these feelings. We cannot open to loving without opening to the pain of loneliness. Remember, joy and pain are in the same box. When we do not open, we stay empty, unable to connect with our essence, our core Self, unable to connect with God. When you bring love to your Inner Child instead of choosing to protect in the face of these feelings, the door opens to receiving the spiritual lessons of loneliness. You discover that there are lights within the dark-ness and each light is a new soul lesson.

The Lessons of Loneliness

Your loneliness may be a message that you need to change something specific in your life. You will be motivated to make these changes only when you have the courage to feel your loneliness and see what it tells you. While operating out of your addictions, you are not seeking to truly give and connect with others—you are just trying to take away your loneliness and aloneness. But if you feel your loneliness, it can motivate you to move out of your addictions so you can connect with others and share your love. It can also move you to take loving action—to change your relationships and your lifestyle.

One of the major lessons of loneliness for me has been learning that I no longer have to protect myself against feeling lonely; it is a very manageable feeling when I am in communion with God so that I am not alone in my loneliness. For most of my life, I used my addictions to work, busyness, anger, judging, food and caretaking to protect myself from feeling my loneliness. I couldn't see that these were addictions until I was willing to feel the loneliness that they were covering. I now find that the addictions feel worse than the loneliness. I welcome feelings of loneliness because of the information they give me about myself and others—about whether my heart is open or closed and whether others' are open or closed. Before I was willing to feel my loneliness, I would close my heart in the face of others closing theirs and become irritated or judgmental. Now I am much more likely to be compassionate with myself and others when this happens. Embracing my own loneliness enables me to understand and feel compassion for the fears that drive people to close their hearts.

Perhaps the most significant lesson loneliness can teach us is gratitude. Since loneliness and helplessness are the most difficult feelings to feel, they provide us with the most profound opportunities to evolve our soul, opportunities that we do not have in the spiritual realm. When we embrace them as challenging gifts, we can feel grateful to God for the sacred privilege of being here on this planet. Gratitude opens us to receiving a direct experience of God. When that happens, the door opens to having wonderful loving relationships with others. When we truly embrace, with gratitude, the privilege of evolving our soul, we are able to stay open to learning with others, even in the face of fear. We set loving boundaries rather than attempt to control others. We become who we were meant to be, in all our fullness and glory.

THIRTEEN

Telling the Truth to Those You Love (and Others)

Now that we have looked at why relationships are a vital part of our spiritual path, I want to give you some role models for taking loving action in relationships. The information about what to do to set a loving boundary during conflict with another needs to come from our own spiritual Guidance. This happens when we do Step Four. When we set the loving boundaries, we are doing Step Five.

As with discovering any loving action, what works for us in one situation may not work in the next. New situations always come into our lives to challenge us and help our souls grow. Below are some ideas about loving ways to handle different types of conflict. The suggestions offered here, as with the guidelines for a healthy body in chapter 10, come from my own spiritual Guidance. *They are not definitive.* By opening to your spiritual Guidance and asking, "What is the loving action in this situation?" you will discover what action is right for you.

When you can stay open to learning with others and set loving boundaries, you can keep the energy between you open to loving—open to God. *These two skills are the basis of creating loving and caring relationships, both at home and at work.* While they may sound simple, they take much practice. But when you master these skills, you will have taken a huge leap in the evolution of your soul. Through practicing the Six Steps of Inner Bonding with yourself and practicing these two skills in your relationships, you create a loving Adult who knows how to handle both rejection and engulfment. And the more you practice, the more you will directly experience God's love and wisdom.

A Case Study of Loving Boundaries

Let's start with a common situation that couples encounter, very similar to the case of Samuel and his wife in chapter 10. It's Friday night and Robert wants to read, but his wife, Linda, wants him to watch TV with her. When he says what he wants, Linda gets angry and yells that he never wants to spend time with her.

In this situation, Linda is being a victim, blaming Robert for her feelings of aloneness and loneliness. If Robert gets angry back at her or withdraws, then he is also being a victim, blaming her for his feelings. If he chooses to be a loving Adult, he first tunes in to his Inner Child (Step One), noticing and acknowledging how lonely he feels when Linda gets angry and blaming. He opens to his spiritual Guidance, opening to learning and bringing compassion into his heart (Step Two). He welcomes and embraces his lonely Inner

Child, reassuring him that he is not wrong or bad for wanting to read and that he is not responsible for Linda's unhappiness (Step Three). He accepts that he is helpless over Linda's intent to try to control him with her anger rather than learn about loving herself.

By accepting his loneliness and helplessness over Linda's feelings and behavior, and opening to learning with his spiritual Guidance about loving himself (Step Four), Robert embraces this conflict as an opportunity to evolve his soul, and he thanks God for the privilege of this moment. He is then able to move into compassion with Linda, recognizing that when she yells, she may feel lonely and afraid and she has no loving Adult in that moment to handle these feelings. Then he moves into the intent to learn with her and sets a loving boundary (Step Five). All of this takes only moments if he has spent enough time practicing the Six Steps.

Let's see what this looks like in action.

In a soft, open, compassionate and caring tone of voice, with the true curiosity of the loving Adult and no investment either in getting Linda to be open or in having a certain outcome to the conflict, Robert says, "Honey, I really don't like being yelled at. But there must be a good reason that you are angry at me. Do you want to talk about it?" Knowing that Linda generally responds to touch, he reaches out and takes her hand to help her wounded child feel safe and loved.

Robert knows that his being in an intent to learn does not guarantee that Linda will open. If she does open to learning, they can go on to explore the fear and beliefs under her anger.

Robert: Why do you believe that my not wanting to watch TV means that I don't want to spend time with you?

Linda: It just seems like you always find other things to do rather than be with me. I feel shut out a lot.

Robert: Well, maybe you are right. If that's true, there must be a good reason for it. It would be much easier for me to look at this if you believed I have good reasons for it rather than yelling at me for it. Yet there must be a good reason you yell. Do you know what that's about?

There is much to explore here: the fears and false beliefs behind Linda's yelling, and the fears and false beliefs behind Robert's withdrawal from Linda. Linda can explore her abandonment issues and the ways she tries to control Robert rather than take care of herself. Robert can explore his engulfment issues and the ways he withdraws rather than set loving boundaries. Their intimacy grows when each speaks their truth and is open to learning about themselves with each other.

"What," you might ask, "does Robert do if Linda *doesn't* open to learning with him?"

If she doesn't open and continues to blame him, Robert can set a loving boundary by saying, "I'd like to explore this with you when you are open to it, but I'm not available for being blamed. When you want to explore, let me know." Robert accepts his helplessness over Linda's intent and disengages from the conflict rather than trying to get her to open. Then he acts on the limit he set by leaving the room *without* anger (also Step Five). Once he is alone, he goes through the Six

Steps to make sure his Inner Child is okay, and he explores the issue that Linda brought up—his withdrawal from her.

"But," you might object, "what if after he leaves the room, she won't leave him alone? What if she follows him around, yelling at him and blaming him?"

When that happens, Robert may need to go into a room with a door he can lock, or he may need to leave the house for a while. If he goes into a room and locks the door and Linda continues yelling at him from outside the door, he can play music loudly or wear earphones. Robert cannot actually make Linda stop yelling at him without violating her in the same way she is violating him—yelling at her, threatening her, maybe even hitting her—but he can take himself away from her until she is open to learning. What he can also do, which is very helpful to both of them, is to send her love, visualizing the light of God around her, and pray for her to remember that she has the choice to open her heart.

It is vital for Robert to reassure his Inner Child that Linda's behavior is not personal—that is, it is not about him. It comes from her own wounded self. If he takes her yelling personally, he will revert to his wounded self and will probably end up punishing her if she does finally open. Then the tables will be turned: She will be open while he is closed. They repeat this cycle *ad infinitum* if they keep taking the other's behavior personally.

Part of Robert's job as a loving Adult is to refuse to be a victim, to reassure his Child that Linda's choice to be open or closed has nothing to do with him. He is not causing it, not even by his withdrawal. While his withdrawn behavior certainly affects her—it probably triggers her abandonment issues—how she responds to it is entirely her choice.

When we are being victims, we desperately need others to feel compassion for our pain because we are not feeling compassion for our own pain. We are not being loving Adults. We are trying to get others to be the Adult for us. When someone is pulling on you to be the Adult for them, you need to have compassion for yourself as well as for them. If they are open to exploring their choice to be a victim, then it is loving to stay and help. It is loving to be a vessel of love if you know they really want to learn but are stuck. It is loving to be a loving Adult with them, but not for them. If you know they have no desire to get unstuck—that they just want you to fix them—then it is not loving to stay and "help." You would simply be allowing them to plug into you as their source of love instead of plugging into God *through you*.

Boundary-Setting Opportunities

One Sunday a number of years ago, Erika and I decided to go horseback riding. We had heard about a place in Malibu Canyon where we could rent horses and ride along the beach, so we called and made an appointment. We arrived there on time and an elderly man named Luke greeted us, telling us that he was the owner. Instead of getting our horses ready, however, Luke started talking about himself, telling us in great detail about his war days. He went on and on, completely controlling the time and the conversation. It was like that joke about the name of the Twelve-Step program for people who talk too much: On and On Anon. After a while, I told Luke we wanted to go riding, but he kept right on talking. I didn't know what to do. I kept glancing at Erika and could see that she, too, was bored stiff, yet neither of us said anything. We both felt trapped and immobilized. We didn't want to hurt the man's feelings by saying anything, and we didn't want him to get angry and not let us ride, so we spent a miserable hour listening to him. We did finally get to ride, and it wasn't worth it. The horses were really nags. In fact, one of them was a donkey!

On the way home, Erika and I discussed our feelings about letting ourselves feel trapped by Luke and how upset we were that we hadn't known what to say or do. We each tuned in to our Teachers and asked what we might have done differently. This is a composite of what they said:

> *The reason you had a problem is that you made Luke's Inner Child more important than your own, and you made riding more important than taking care of the boredom and agitation you both felt. You each needed to pay attention to your Inner Child and realize that it was not worth feeling so trapped. If you had been willing to take responsibility for your own feelings and needs instead of taking responsibility for Luke's feelings, you could have spoken your truth and dealt with the consequences. You could have said, "Luke, we would like to ride now," and walked away toward the horses, effectively cutting off the conversation by setting a boundary and taking action. If Luke had become upset with you, you could have told him that either he got the horses ready or you would leave, again setting a boundary and taking action to maintain it. In order to take this loving action for yourselves, you needed to be willing to feel the*

sadness if Luke got angry as well as the sadness and help-lessness of not being able to ride. By allowing yourselves to feel victimized, you tried to control Luke's anger and blame, and your own potential sadness and helplessness.

We asked our Teachers why they did not advise us to move into an intent to learn with Luke, and they explained:

It is not always appropriate to move into an intent to learn. You do not attempt to learn with people whom you know from past experience are sure to stay closed. This would be abusive to yourself, like hitting your head against a wall. Other times, as in the situation with Luke, it is appropriate to just set the boundary and act on it. You move into an intent to learn with others when they are people with whom you want to continue to have a relationship. Since Luke was not someone with whom you wanted to continue a relationship, you just needed to take care of yourselves in a way that did not violate him.

* * * *

It is always painful to be ridiculed by one of our parents. Janelle experiences this with her father, who shames her for her spiritual beliefs, telling her that she is crazy for going to a nonsectarian church instead of following the family religion. He denigrates her in front of others at family gatherings, laughing at her and ridiculing her for her beliefs. She has tried to talk to him about it, but he won't discuss it. He just goes into more shaming. He has no intent to learn about her feelings or her beliefs.

In this situation, it is crucial that Janelle show up as a loving Adult and not allow her Child to be annihilated. As in dealing with all conflicts, Janelle would first need to be in Step One, the willingness to accept her feelings of helplessness over her father's choices and loneliness over his not caring about her. She would need to attend to her Inner Child's loneliness by connecting with her spiritual Guidance in Step Two, so her Child is not alone in the loneliness. Then she would need to accept this as an opportunity to evolve her soul. Janelle could then go through Step Three, talking to her wounded self and exploring her beliefs about her right to take care of herself around her family. Once she accepts that she has the right to take care of herself, she can ask her Guidance in Step Four for the loving action to take.

There are two ways Janelle can set a loving boundary in Step Five. She can confront her father publicly or privately. If Janelle decides to do it publicly, then the next time she is at a family gathering and her father shames her, she can say "Dad, I love you very much, but I'm no longer available to being shamed and ridiculed by you. If you keep this up, I'm going to leave." She might fear doing this because she believes it is her responsibility to protect her father's feelings, but her true responsibility is to take care of her Inner Child.

Her father might get angry in response to Janelle's saying this, or he might go into denial or shame her further, saying she is too sensitive and he is only joking. In this case she would have to follow through on the boundary she set and leave. If her father repeated his behavior at the next family gathering, she could leave again after another public announcement, and she could tell him that she won't attend any more family gatherings until he agrees to no longer shame her. Then she would need to follow through on that.

If Janelle decides to confront her father privately, she could tell him (and all her other family members individually) that she will no longer attend family gatherings until he agrees to stop shaming her about her religious beliefs. If her family values her presence at family gatherings, they will become her allies in dealing with her father, unless they are too afraid of him.

In order to set this boundary, Janelle has to decide, as is so often the case, that she is willing to lose her father or her other family members rather than lose herself. Of course, she always has the option of mentally ignoring him instead of setting a boundary. Her choice depends on what feels truly loving to herself. If she can ignore him without feeling a loss of self, then that would be most loving. But if being shamed feels more abusive or painful to her than the possibility of losing her family, then she would need to set the boundary. In order to set a loving boundary, she needs to be willing to feel and attend to the loneliness and helplessness that she will probably feel if her father refuses to deal with the issue and her family members do not support her. If Janelle does not take loving action on her own behalf, she will continue to feel victimized by her father. If she does take loving action, then she needs to evaluate the action in Step Six, tuning into her feelings to see if she is empowered by the action she chose.

✳ ✳ ✳ ✳

Natalia's best friend, Janice, is angry at her a lot, and when Natalia asks why, Janice says it's because Natalia judges her all the time and she feels shamed by her. Natalia acknowledges this, knowing that she has a tendency to be judgmental, and is open to learning about it, but she does not want to be blamed and judged for being judgmental. She does not want to be told she is responsible for Janice's choice to use her anger as a way to deal with it.

After dialoguing with her Inner Child and reassuring her that she is not responsible for Janice's anger, even when Natalia *is* being judgmental, Natalia would then need to ask her spiritual Guidance how to approach Janice in a loving way—a way that takes care of her own Inner Child without blaming Janice.

There are two explorations that could occur here. One is about Natalia's being judgmental; the other is about Janice's anger. Natalia could say, "Janice, I really care about our friendship, and I want to know when I am being judgmental. I would really appreciate it if you could point it out. But I feel judged when you get angry about it and blame me for your anger. Can you point it out to me without getting angry? I know that you have good reasons for getting angry—just as I have good reasons for being judgmental. [*Remember, both anger and judgmentalness are ways we protect against our pain— usually our loneliness or helplessness over others.*] If you are willing to, we could explore them together."

If Janice continues to be angry and is unavailable to explore, Natalia would need to set a boundary: "Janice, I am not available to talk with you when you are angry at me and want to blame me for your behavior. Let me know when you are done being angry at me." Then she would need to disengage until Janice lets go of her anger. She would need to do this each time Janice gets angry until Janice either stops being angry or Natalia decides that the friendship is on hold until Janice is ready to take responsibility for her own behavior. Meanwhile, Natalia could explore her tendency to judge people on her own.

Renee's husband, Donald, has a habit of coming up behind her and grabbing her breasts. She hates this. It makes her feel like an object. She feels like Donald is acting from his needy wounded child and is trying to take something from her, rather than coming from love and wanting to give to her. She has asked him over and over to stop, yet he keeps doing it.

In order to move into an intent to learn with Donald and set a loving boundary, Renee needs to be willing to feel the loneliness she feels when Donald doesn't care about her feelings. She needs to be in compassion with herself so she can move into compassion with him. Then she can approach the conflict with caring and curiosity—a compassionate intent to learn.

> **Renee:** Honey, there must be a good reason why you keep grabbing my breasts when I've told you I don't like it. I'd like to understand it.
>
> **Donald:** Oh, come on. I'm just doing it in fun. It's not hurting anything. (*He is unwilling to open to learning about himself with her*).
>
> **Renee:** Why don't you hear me when I tell you that I don't like it?

Donald: Well, sometimes you let me do it, so it must not be that bad.

Renee: So because I give in to you sometimes, that makes you not believe me when I say I hate it?

Donald: Yeah. Besides, what's the big deal? *[He is not asking a real question. Instead, he is discounting her feelings in an effort to have what he wants.]*

Renee: Donald, I have very good reasons for hating it, and I would be happy to tell you what they are when you are open to it. *[Accepts her loneliness and helplessness over his intent to protect and does not engage in exploration because she knows that would only leave her feeling even more lonely since Donald is clearly not open to learning right now.]* Meanwhile, I don't want you to do it ever again. *[Sets the boundary.]*

Donald: *[Looks hurt and confused.]*

If Donald is open to exploring his hurt and confusion with Renee, she can assist him in this. If not, she would need to walk away and not take responsibility for his feelings, instead praying for him to open his heart and take responsibility for his own wounded Child. She would not discuss this issue with him again unless he came to her with an intent to learn. When setting a boundary like this, it is not helpful for Renee to tell Donald *why* she doesn't like it when he grabs her breasts *unless he asks with an intent to learn*. If she explains herself to Donald when he is not open to learning, he may shame her for her reasons. She cannot force him to understand her feelings. Therefore, explaining herself when he is not open is hurtful to her own Child.

The next time Donald grabs her breasts, she can immediately turn around, look him in the eye, and say calmly but firmly, "Stop. This feels awful," and walk away. *(Taking action on the boundary.)* If he tries it again, she can respond in the same way. If she keeps respecting herself by setting a loving boundary, he will probably stop doing it and may learn to respect her feelings.

✳ ✳ ✳ ✳

Simon and his live-in lover, Paul, are in the process of furnishing a vacation house. Paul has taken on most of the responsibility for decorating the house and does most of the shopping himself, using Simon's credit card, since Simon is the primary wage-earner. Simon wants Paul to have access to the credit card, since he does grocery shopping and takes care of other errands, but he does not want him abusing it. He is the only wage-earner in the relationship, which he is not happy about, and while he makes a good living, he is fairly frugal. He has made it clear that he wants to be consulted before Paul spends his money on anything costly. Yet Simon comes home one night to find that Paul has purchased a very expensive piece of furniture without consulting him. This is not the first time this has happened.

Simon has only two choices, to accept the piece of furniture or return it. If he accepts it, he must be willing to have Paul continue to buy expensive things without consulting him. If he sets a loving boundary and returns it, he must be willing to incur Paul's anger, disappointment or rejection. It has to be more important to Simon to take good care of himself than it is to protect against the loneliness he will feel if

Paul gets angry at him, rejects him or blames him for his own disappointment. Once Simon has done his own Six-Step Process, he can move into an intent to learn with Paul:

Simon: Paul, there must be a good reason you didn't consult me before buying this. I'd like to understand.

Paul: I was afraid you would say no.

Simon: I might have or I might not have—at least we could have discussed it. Do you believe that I shouldn't have a say in what we spend?

Paul: No, but I really wanted it.

Simon: Well, then we could have talked about it. But this way, I have no say and that feels violating to me. I feel used when you don't respect what is important to me and just spend money without discussing it with me. It looks to me like having the things you want is more important than respecting me. So, since you chose not to consult me, I want this returned. Do you want to handle it or shall I?

If Paul gets angry and blames Simon in any way, then Simon can set a boundary against that by saying, "I'm not available for being blamed by you. I just want you to be a real partner and treat me with respect." Once Simon respects himself by setting an appropriate boundary, he is much more likely to get Paul's respect. And Paul is unlikely to buy expensive things again without talking to Simon about it, knowing that Simon will return them.

Paul might tell Simon that Simon is being selfish and uncaring, but in fact Simon is being loving to himself, and whatever is loving to him is also loving to Paul, even though Paul might not think so. By treating himself with respect, Simon offers Paul an opportunity to become a more caring person. If Simon does nothing and accepts the piece of furniture, he supports Paul's uncaring behavior, which is not loving to either of them. Simon puts God into action in his life when he speaks his truth to Paul and treats himself with respect.

Andrea's husband, Sam, who can be a very sweet person, is also very jealous and has a violent temper. Andrea knows that he often listens in on her phone conversations and snoops through her purse. Many things can touch off Sam's jealousy, at which point he yells, threatens, even hits her and beats her up, sometimes in front of their children. He is always very sorry afterward and promises never to do it again, yet the next time his anxiety, jealousy, fear or insecurity comes up, the same thing happens. Andrea has asked Sam to get help, but he comes up with all sorts of excuses why he can't or won't.

The difficult thing for Andrea to accept is that as long as she is there and available for this abuse, it will continue. Sam does not have the inner resources—a developed loving Adult—to stop this behavior without help. His child-adult knows of no other way (other than to attempt to control Andrea with his violence) to deal with the extreme anxiety and fear that are at the root of his jealousy. Sam's jealousy comes from a very deep insecurity and fear of loss, which come from his deeply ingrained core shame beliefs resulting from his spiritual abuse. These beliefs will not change on their own—Sam doesn't even know he has them.

The only boundary that Andrea can set that will protect her and their children from Sam's physical and emotional abuse is not to be there, to leave until he gets the help he needs. As long as she maintains the *hope* that Sam's behavior will change, she will probably stay. As long as she believes that his behavior is in any way her fault—that she causes it or that she can control it—she will stay.

Others' violent behavior is never "caused" by another. It is caused by their own fears and protective reactions, which are the fears and reactions of the child-adult. Until Andrea is willing to accept her helplessness over Sam's behavior, she will stay and try to manipulate him into changing. Until she is willing to feel the loneliness she experiences in this relationship, and take responsibility for her feelings and safety, she will stay. And as long as she believes she deserves to be treated badly, she will stay. Once Andrea realizes that no one deserves to be abused no matter what, she can find a way to leave.

Sometimes people are unwilling to give up the belief that they deserve to be treated badly because they want to believe they have control. If Andrea believes, "I am *causing* Sam to be violent because I am not good enough, and when I do things right, he will change," she may be unwilling to give this up because it gives her a feeling of control. When she is willing to accept her helplessness over Sam, and open to her spiritual Guidance and ask, "What is the loving action toward myself and my children?" she will begin the process of leaving.

Andrea may need to get some help before she can take this step. It is a very hard step to take for many battered women, because their self-esteem is so low. Without help, it is likely that nothing will change. If Andrea is staying due to financial

reasons, then she needs to seek help through community out-
reach centers regarding job training. If she is staying because
she fears being alone, then she needs to seek counseling to
help her develop her own loving Adult so that she can handle
being alone. It is through developing her own loving Adult
that she will be able to take loving action on her own behalf
and on behalf of her children. A loving Adult never allows
the Inner Child nor actual children to be abused.

If Andrea decides to leave, she should not discuss this with
Sam. She needs to just do it, then call him when she is in a
safe place. Since Sam is a violent person, it is not safe for
Andrea to tell him where she is. She can give him the phone
number of a mutual friend for emergencies and tell him that
she will not see him or communicate with him until he gets
some help—and then only with a counselor present.

Marina works as a freelance bookkeeper for a number of different attorneys. She likes her job, but one of her clients, Tom,
is a very angry man. As soon as Marina comes in each week,
he starts yelling at her about the various bills, asking her in an
accusatory tone about the things he does not understand. He
doesn't listen for her answer. He just orders her to fix the problem. Marina has been afraid to say anything to him for fear he
will get even more angry. Instead, she tries to be "nice," acting
as if it doesn't bother her when inside she feels awful.

In order to set a loving boundary, Marina first needs to
accept her helplessness over Tom's behavior. She cannot
make him be kind and respectful, even by being "nice." Next
she needs to be open to feeling how lonely she feels at being

treated this way, and how alone her Inner Child feels when someone yells at her and her Adult does not take care of her. Finally, she needs to decide if she is willing to lose her job with Tom, which could happen if she sets a boundary with him. If losing this work would cause her hardship, then the best she can do is let her Child know that Tom's behavior is not personal. If she is willing to lose her work with him, then she needs to ask her spiritual Guidance what the loving action is in this situation.

There is never just one loving way to handle a particular situation. Marina could say, "Tom, the way you speak to me feels very disrespectful. I'm not willing to discuss anything with you until you treat me with respect." Then, if he continued attacking her, she would need to act on the boundary and leave the room, refusing to engage with Tom until he was respectful. If she has reached the point where she is totally unwilling to be around this treatment any more and she can afford not to work for Tom, she can say, "Tom, if you continue to treat me this way, I will quit."

Sometimes people violate our boundaries without realizing it and are open to hearing our feelings about it, and sometimes they just don't care. It is very important for all of us to know that in our personal relationships we do not have to be around someone who violates us in some way and has no Adult present with an intent to learn.

When you cannot leave a situation where you are being violated, such as when you are in a car, a work situation or a marriage with children where you are financially dependent, then you need to stay open to learning with your spiritual Guidance about how to best take care of yourself within this difficult situation. For example, if Marina financially depends on Tom, her spiritual Guidance might tell her that the loving action she needs to take is to find another bookkeeping client before setting a boundary with him.

Claudia is hurt and angry because her two close friends did not call her on her birthday. She had let them know that being called was important to her, but still they didn't do it. When she told them she felt hurt, they both got defensive and she ended up feeling even worse.

Claudia has been taught that "sharing her feelings" when she is hurt will be helpful, but she does not understand that her *intention* is also important. If her intention in sharing her feelings is to blame others and make them responsible for her hurt, then sharing her feelings is a way to control. In order to communicate lovingly with her friends instead, she would first need to do her own Six-Step Process, exploring her part in creating the situation and identifying false beliefs that caused her hurt and anger.

Part of the problem is that when Claudia let her friends know what she wanted, it was not a request but a demand. A request has no expectation attached to it, while a demand does. Claudia's hurt and disappointment were a result of her expectation. Had she made a request instead of a demand, she would have been curious about why her friends didn't call. She would have approached them with an intent to learn rather than with anger and blame. She would have wanted to know the good reasons they had for not calling. Perhaps they recognized Claudia's "request" as a demand and resisted her attempt to control them. Perhaps they were upset with her for past situations when she made them responsible for her feelings and so they unconsciously withheld from her. Or maybe they just don't care about things like birthdays and it has nothing to do with Claudia. Whatever their reason, Claudia will not discover it until she is in the intent to learn about herself as well as about them.

Georgia has complained for some time about having too much to do, what with her work and the kids and everything, so David has taken over some household responsibilities, such as some cooking and the laundry. He doesn't mind doing these things, but he does mind Georgia constantly looking over his shoulder, telling him how things "should" be done and criticizing how he does them. It seems he can never do things well enough for her. David has told Georgia he doesn't like her criticizing him and telling him how to do things, yet she keeps on doing it.

First, David needs to be willing to feel his sadness about being criticized and his helplessness over Georgia's choices. He needs to have compassion for himself and his own feelings, bringing Divine Love down to his Child and comforting him. Once David lets go of control over Georgia and is in compassion for himself, he can move into a compassionate intent to learn with her, knowing that she has very good reasons for her behavior.

"Honey, I've told you that I don't like it when you keep telling me how to do things, yet there must be a good reason why you keep doing it. I'd like to understand what that is about."

If Georgia opens to learning, they may be able to resolve the conflict through an exploration of her fears. It is also possible that David is purposely doing things poorly as part of a passive-aggressive resistant response, and this could be explored as well. If Georgia does not open to learning and just blames him for the situation, then David could set a loving boundary. He could say, "I'm not available for your criticism and advice unless I ask for it. I want to be free to make my own mistakes. If I find I need your help, I will ask you." Or, he might say, "If you continue to harass me, then perhaps it would be better if you went back to doing things yourself. You can either do them your way or let me do them my way, but if you decide to do them, I don't want to hear your complaints about having too much to do." If he does set the boundary, he could do his own inner exploration to see if he is resistant to doing things well.

✳ ✳ ✳ ✳

Estelle drinks three or four glasses of wine at dinner every night, then spends the evening spaced out in front of the TV. Sometimes she even drives in the evening after drinking. Her husband, Daniel, has told her many times that he worries about her when she drives, he worries about the effect of drinking on her health, and he would like to spend time with her without the wine and TV. That rarely happens. Daniel finds it difficult to carry on a meaningful conversation with Estelle and feels lonely, bored and frustrated with the relationship.

There are only three possible ways of dealing with a situation like this:

1. He can try to change her, which will probably just result in power struggles and resistance.

2. He can try to accept the situation, which—since it is basically unacceptable—will lead Daniel to feel that he is giving himself up and eventually he will get resentful and angry.

3. He can leave. This is the only viable option for setting a boundary when someone is behaving in a way that is completely unacceptable to you.

One of the things that leads people to stay in unacceptable situations is the hope that the other person will change. This is not realistic, since most people do not change until they are in pain. As long as Daniel stays with Estelle, she will not be in enough pain to motivate her to change. She may not be in enough pain if he does leave. She might have to lose her job or injure herself or another while driving before she considers changing her behavior. Even then she might not. Some people refuse to change when faced with the extreme consequences of illness or death, like the person with emphysema who keeps smoking or the person with heart disease who keeps eating poorly and refuses to exercise.

When people you love are unloving to themselves, it is unloving to support them in their self-destructive behavior. If they eat poorly, drink too much, take drugs or smoke cigarettes, or if they judge themselves harshly, are locked into resistance, are very negative or allow themselves to feel victimized, it is loving to say, "I think this negativity (or this substance or this situation) is very unloving to your body and soul, and I can't support you in being unloving to yourself."

While you cannot stop them from harming themselves, you do not have to support them in doing it.

Often, in order to know how to set a boundary, I write out scenarios of various situations where I have felt my boundaries were violated, and then I practice what I would say next time. I do this for each situation in which I did not respond in a way that made my Inner Child feel loved and safe. I have found that with enough practice writing out various scenarios until I find the words that feel right to me, and with enough rehearsal of these words, I get better and better at moving into the intent to learn and setting loving boundaries in the moment the violation occurs. I also find that learning about what the loving action is in any given situation is a wonderful, creative process of discovery.

I have discovered that when my deepest desire is to love rather than control, and I respond to another's anger, blame or violation of my boundaries by moving into a compassionate intent to learn and setting a loving boundary, I feel terrific. In fact, I feel on top of the world. It has been deeply gratifying to me to know that my feelings are always *my* responsibility because then I can do something about feeling badly—I can practice responding lovingly *no matter what.*

As I mentioned earlier, my Teacher has told me that one of my soul's lessons is to learn to respond lovingly *no matter what,* that there are no conditions under which it is beneficial to respond unlovingly. I would guess that this is a soul lesson for all of us and one of the main reasons we are here on this planet. I find this very challenging. As soon as I am able to keep my heart open in one situation, I am challenged by a new one. This appears to be the way our souls grow when we have opted for spiritual growth. This is the relationship path to God. However, we are never given more than we can handle, and each time I manage to respond lovingly in a new situation, I feel more and more loved, safe and valued.

It is so easy to revert to my wounded child-adult and claim that this time my feelings are not my responsibility. This time it really is the other person's fault. This time the other person has gone too far and no one could expect me to feel okay in *this* situation. But each time I manage to stay connected with love—with God—and take good care of myself, the lesson hits home anew: My feelings and behavior really are my responsibility.

Taking loving action in relationships is not just about setting boundaries when others are violating us. It is also about setting inner limits against violating others. It is the job of the loving Adult to set limits against the wounded child-adult's habitual way of responding to conflict.

Marshall's wife is screaming at him and yelling obscenities. He is enraged and wants to hit her. Instead, his loving Adult recognizes what's happening and talks to his Inner Child: "I know you are very angry and you really want to hit her, but I won't let you do that. It is not okay to hit people." Marshall decides to walk away from his wife and allow his Child to discharge his rage through the anger process. Then he explores his part in creating the present situation. When his feelings are resolved, he comes back and moves into an intent to learn with his wife, asking her why she is so angry. If she is not open, he sets a boundary, letting her know that he will not remain around her if she continues to scream at him. He can pray for her and send her love from his heart but he cannot engage with her in a meaningful way while she is angry.

Most violence is the result of an out-of-control child-adult acting out the rage of not being taken care of by a loving Adult. The seemingly bottomless well of anger dissipates once you practice learning from your anger rather than taking it out on others.

* * * *

Aggie's husband, Allen, blames her for his not having enough time to play golf. Aggie's child-adult wants to defend herself, argue, explain and debate, showing him how poorly he manages his time, proving that it is not her fault. Past experience has shown her that when she does that, however, their interaction escalates into a shouting match where they each bring in all their old past hurts and blame each other for them. They both feel badly after one of these battles, wondering how they had such a huge fight over something fairly minor.

Instead of engaging with Allen, Aggie needs to tell him that she doesn't want to talk about this now, then go off by herself and dialogue with her Inner Child, exploring why she feels the need to prove her innocence. What does this remind her of in her past? Was she unfairly blamed for things by her parents? Is she making Allen responsible for validating her as a caring person who is respectful of his time? Once Aggie understands what triggers her defensiveness, she can dialogue with her spiritual Guidance and bring through the truth to her Child: that Allen is the one responsible for his lack of golfing time. She can bring through God's love and acceptance to her Child, giving her Child the acknowledgment Aggie has been trying to get from Allen. Once she is centered and open, she can go back to Allen and set a loving boundary by telling him she does not want to be blamed for his lack of time. Then she can move into an intent to learn with him by telling him that if he wants to explore the time problem with her, she is available.

Mastering the art of staying open to learning and setting boundaries with love and respect when you are in the middle of a conflict with someone is not easy. It takes real concentration and focus. Every time you notice you are in a situation where you feel violated, you will need to be very conscious about staying in your loving Adult. Your tendency may be to set your boundary with hardness rather than firmness until you have had some practice. But you will find that you get seen, heard and respected far more readily when you can stay soft and open than when you are hard and critical. When you've let things go on for a while without standing up for yourself, it is much more difficult to stay open and not get angry. *When you feel angry at another, it is a signal that you have not been taking care of yourself.*

Whatever the issue you are in conflict with someone about, your challenge is always the same: *to choose love instead of control.* When you take care of your boundaries in the moment, it gets easier and easier to stay open to learning and loving in the midst of conflict. You will not get irritated, hurt or angry when someone is needy, judging or rejecting if you stay in compassion with yourself and with them. Fears of rejection and engulfment fade away when your loving Adult compassionately runs things as an emissary of God. Staying in compassion with yourself and others creates the inner safety that we all desire. If you have compassion only for yourself, you may feel angry and victimized by others. If you have compassion only for others, you may caretake and eventually end up feeling victimized as well. Only compassion for yourself and others leads to your Child feeling safe, worthy and loved.

FOURTEEN

Rewards of the Sacred Journey

Practicing Inner Bonding offers both immediate and long-term rewards. Noticing these rewards, or the absence of them (which indicates the need for further exploration and action), is the final step of Inner Bonding, Step Six: evaluating the results of our actions. This is where we go inward, as in Step One, to see how we are feeling, this time to discover whether what we are doing is working for us. Our feelings of peace and joy, among many other rewards of the sacred journey, let us know that our loving actions are working for us.

With time and practice, we find that our inner growth is no longer something that seems like hard work. At times it even seems like play, a delightful and exhilarating experience of discovery. We feel Spirit, the grace of God, flowing through us, leading us toward wholeness. We find that rather than dreading the pain and difficulties of life, we meet them as opportunities to evolve our souls.

As we use the Six Steps to heal from our spiritual abuse, we have the deeply fulfilling experience of knowing that we are not alone, that God is always with us. Our fear is replaced by faith as we experience grace through growth, and growth through grace. Moving out of fear and into faith is a sure sign that we are taking the appropriate loving actions. Faith is one of the wonderful rewards of the sacred journey.

Faith and Trust

Faith is a deep knowing in our heart that God is always with us and that everything that happens is for the highest good of our souls. Faith is what we feel when we move out of the earthly level and onto the spiritual level, recognizing that all earthly challenges are sacred opportunities to evolve our souls. Having a personal experience of God is what teaches us faith, the faith that is *knowing*, not just believing.

Having faith that God is always with you allows you to let go of control. Until you know God is guiding you every step of the way, your wounded child-adult cannot relax its vigilance.

I love this poem by Patrick Overton about faith:

FAITH

When you walk to the edge of all the light you have
and take the first step into the darkness of the unknown
you must believe that one of two things will happen:
*   There will be something solid to stand upon,*
*   Or, you will be taught how to fly.*[1]

As your faith grows, so does your trust in your spiritual Guidance. Day by day, as you do your inner work, taking loving action based on the guidance you learn to hear in Step Four, you come to trust that guidance. In fact, you come to trust it far more than the guidance of your wounded self. You come to trust "the small still voice within" (as the Quakers call it). Eventually the clamoring and worried voice of your wounded child-adult fades into the background. You find that life becomes much easier, even in the face of difficulties, because you go with the flow, rowing your boat gently downstream instead of battling the current.

As your trust in your spiritual Guidance grows, the trust issues that you have with others gradually recede. You no longer need to depend on others to make you feel safe. You no longer need to put your faith and trust blindly in others—you now have faith and trust in your own loving Adult and in your spiritual Guidance. Your Guidance tells you whether or not others are trustworthy, whether or not others are lying or being truthful. You rarely feel betrayed by others because you rarely put yourself in a position to be betrayed by an untrustworthy person. When you put your trust in your spiritual Guidance rather than in what others tell you, you no longer get pulled into situations that are not in your highest good.

Many of my clients have deep trust issues. If their parents were untrustworthy, they may not trust that I care about them and will not deliberately hurt them. They want a guarantee that I will never let them down. They want me to *prove* that I am trustworthy. I tell them that I cannot prove to them that I am trustworthy, and that I will undoubtedly let them down at times since I am human and cannot live up to all their expectations. I tell them that they will trust that I have their highest good at heart only when they learn to trust themselves. As they learn to trust their own knowing, they will be able to *know* that my intention is to act in their highest good. I tell them they will also learn to trust their own knowing about when someone does not have their highest good in mind. When they have faith and trust in their spiritual Guidance, they can truly take good care of their Inner Child.

Faith is a lot like a savings account. You have to add to it every day so that when a need arises, you have enough faith to see you through. When you practice Inner Bonding, you are building up your faith—making deposits in your faith "savings account"—by putting God into action in your life.

Gratitude for the Sacred Journey

Gratitude is another reward of the sacred journey. When we have faith that we are here on this planet, having these particular experiences, in order to evolve in our lovingness, then we can gratefully embrace them. Being here is truly a sacred privilege, a sacred opportunity. If you could remember your original determination to evolve in this embodiment, you would be in deep gratitude each moment for the challenges and opportunities presented to you. You would not be angry or depressed, even when you are lonely. You would know that learning to accept loneliness and stay loving anyway is a major part of the curriculum on schoolhouse Earth.

Since loneliness does not exist in the spiritual realm, we can learn about handling it lovingly only on Earth. In order to do this we need to stay connected to the spiritual perspective *in each moment.* It is so easy to get addicted to the earthly per-spective. On the earthly level there is much loneliness, and it is easy to get stuck in protecting against it. When we see our loneliness from a spiritual perspective, however, it is just another challenge to stay open-hearted. In any moment we can either be in the loneliness and trying to avoid feeling it, or we can be in gratitude for the opportunity to move into love in the face of loneliness.

We need to learn to live *on* the Earth without being *of* the Earth. The moment we are truly in gratitude for the journey, then the loneliness is only part of the journey. When we are in gratitude we do not judge another person for being reject-ing or needy. Instead, we see that they are giving us an oppor-tunity to move into love and compassion for ourselves and them. As long as we believe they are trying to take something from us or hurt us in any way, we are missing the point of the sacred journey. On the earthly level they may want to take something from us or hurt us, but on the spiritual level they are presenting us with an opportunity to evolve our souls.

Remembering why we are here—which is to evolve our souls in lovingness—helps us stay in faith and gratitude. However, it is not just a matter of remembering *why* we are here, but remembering *that* we are here—that we have been given the gift of being on this planet and evolving our souls. We cannot suffer emotionally and be in gratitude for the privilege of being here at the same time. The moment we are in gratitude, we are not suffering.

God did not give us the privilege of life on this planet so we could suffer. The point of our hardships is not to suffer from them, but to stay loving in the face of them. When we stay loving, we will feel sorrow but not suffering, and there is a big difference between sorrow and suffering. Sorrow is what we feel at the suffering of others. Sorrow is what we feel at the death of a loved one when we are in faith that they have gone home and we will see them again. Sorrow and loneliness are what we feel when we miss someone we love, or when we are in the presence of someone whose heart is closed. Suffering is what we feel when we take a loss—or someone's decision to close his or her heart—personally. Suffering is what the wounded self feels. The loving Adult, in connection with the core Self, feels sorrow.

Often our addiction to the earthly level gets in the way of faith and gratitude. It is an addiction to what we can have and achieve. When we are attached to having and achieving, then we are attached to the outcome of things. When we embrace our journey in this life with gratitude, it does not mean that we stop wanting what we want—fame, fortune, relationship—but it does mean that our happiness is not absolutely dependent on getting it. It means that we embrace the journey and make *how we travel* on the journey more important than any outcome.

Most people resist letting go of their cherished plans and embracing the journey. This always reminds me of the joke:

"Do you know how to make God laugh?"

"How?"

"Make plans!"

In order to progress on our spiritual journey, we must be willing to feel lonely. This doesn't mean we *will* feel lonely, but we have to be *willing* to feel it (which is Step One of Inner Bonding) in order to take the next step, to leave the old behind and have faith that the new will come in. There's a paradox here. Unless we open to the journey and are willing to feel the loneliness, we can't be in joy. Joy results from embracing the journey. Joy results from being in gratitude for the journey and the glory of God.

Embracing the spiritual journey does not mean we will not feel sadness or loneliness. It means that those feelings will become manageable, not something we have to protect against. And what makes them manageable is our connection with Divine Love and our gratitude for the journey. Each moment we are truly loving and grateful, we are peaceful, even in sorrow and loneliness.

True gratitude is much more than everyday thankfulness. It is an experience of deep joy and encompassing love that we feel towards God in response to all we receive, perceive and experience on the earthly level. Part of our challenge is to feel gratitude even for the experiences that are difficult—illness, setbacks, losses. These experiences, while often tragic on the earthly level, give us opportunities to become our most loving selves and evolve our souls. In order to find the Divine lesson in a painful situation, we may need to spend some time contemplating and searching for the lesson—as we do in Step Four when we ask, "What would love do here?" The very act of seeking the loving action soothes the gnawing pain of loss and helps us see the same circumstance with new eyes. We discover there are blessings to be found in most things, even illness and loss. For example, a serious illness could move us to reevaluate the priorities in our life, to appreciate the beauty around us or to bring loved ones closer.

It is easy to feel grateful for everyday pleasures. The joy our children bring, the softness of a puppy's fur, a crimson sunset or the simple kindness of a stranger can remind us to say "Thank God" in our head. Deep gratitude for the privilege of being on the planet, however, is almost a physical wave of warmth, a feeling of oneness that deepens our commitment to and communion with God. Gratitude is easy to overlook and even easier to forget. Part of embracing the sacred journey is being dedicated to gratitude—searching for it, experiencing it and expressing it in all that we do, each and every day. Gratitude is essential to building a solid and lasting faith.

Embracing our journey with gratitude means being devoted to becoming all we are meant to be, expressing all the gifts God gave us. This is what will bring joy—to make *this* our purpose, our desire, rather than anything earthly. We need only one goal: to be a pure loving expression of God. The question to ask is, "How can I express God in action through me most fully in this moment?"

To live in the journey each moment, to be the light, to be the love, and to be evolving in that light and love each moment is the point. To stay lovingly connected with God, with ourselves and with others in the face of our loneliness and our helplessness over others is the challenge of the journey.

Integration

Integration is another reward of the sacred journey. Separating our various aspects—our core Self, our wounded self and our loving Adult—and connecting with our spiritual Guidance is what leads to integration and wholeness. It may seem like a contradiction to say that separation leads to wholeness, but it is only through healing the separate aspects of our soul that these aspects can integrate into a healed, whole soul.

If we had not experienced spiritual abuse, we would not have to go through this healing process. If individuals begin their inner work before becoming parents, educators, therapists and other professionals who work with children, they could raise children who are naturally more whole, loving and spiritually connected. We can each do our part in changing the world into a loving and peaceful place by doing our own inner work. We will never change the world by trying to change others. Only by our own deep commitment to our own healing process will we become integrated and whole, beacons in the darkness to light the way to love.

You will find after a few years of practicing Inner Bonding that you no longer need to consider the separate aspects of your Self, even in your dialoguing. Your feelings and thoughts will work in harmony. You will find that you can be conscious of your inner experience, your higher experience and your experience of the world all at the same time. This is consciousness—another reward of practicing Inner Bonding.

Forgiveness

We are often told to forgive others because forgiveness brings you closer to God. Sometimes we are even told to force ourselves to forgive. Yet this is never necessary. Forgiveness is a natural result of developing a loving Adult and healing our core shame. As long as we are still rewounding ourselves with our own unloving behavior toward ourselves, our wounded child will feel angry at those who hurt us in the past and present. Once you learn to love your own wounded child, heal your shame, free your core Self, maintain an intent to learn and set loving boundaries, you will find that you are no longer angry at anyone. When you no longer feel alone because you know that God walks with you, there is no reason to be angry. You move into compassion and forgiveness, recognizing that whoever harmed you is suffering from his or her own fears, false beliefs and disconnection from God. You learn to see beneath the hard shell of others' wounded selves and address the core spark of love within them, no matter how unloving they were—or are—to you. When you have a loving Adult who is able to stay consistently connected to God, you no longer move into your own wounded self in reaction to their wounded self. You become immune to darkness. This is an enlightened state—one that we can move toward each day. I don't know if I will ever reach this enlightened state, but to me, getting there is not the point. The point is being devoted to the journey.

Forgiving and loving yourself leads to forgiving and loving others. Forgiving and loving others leads to forgiving and loving yourself. It's another one of those victorious circles. But do not ever force yourself to forgive others. Your anger at them indicates that you are not yet taking care of yourself. If you force yourself to forgive others before learning how to take care of yourself, you can actually make healing harder for yourself. Forcing forgiveness cuts you off from your feelings of anger and blame. Since your anger and blame let you know that you are not taking care of yourself, you do not want to cut these feelings off. Allow forgiveness to be the natural consequence of loving yourself.

Grace, Peace, Joy

When we embrace the sacred privilege of taking loving action for the purpose of healing and evolving our souls, we experience God's grace. Grace is the feeling of profound peace and well-being that comes when we surrender our individual will to God's will. It is a joyous lightness of being and a feeling of oneness with all of life. A sense of oneness is essential to our well-being. The sense of oneness that is grace creates within us feelings of safety, belonging, community, acceptance, love, power, hope, purpose and peace. It is the result of inviting God into our hearts and healing all that has kept us separate from God. Perhaps our most sacred privilege is this direct communion with God. It is our most powerful, most replenishing and most gratifying state.

The first time I experienced grace I didn't know what to call it. I was standing at my kitchen sink doing the dishes, a task I am not fond of, when out of nowhere a wave of lightness came over my being. Suddenly I loved the soap bubbles, the warmth of the water, the sunlight coming through the window and the birds singing outside. In fact, at that moment I loved *everything*. I felt a sense of oneness with everything and I heard myself singing, in spite of the fact that I can't carry a tune. The song was a childhood nursery rhyme: *Mares eat oats, and does eat oats, and little lambs eat ivy. A kid will eat ivy, too. Wouldn't you?* (As a child I thought the words were: *Mersie dotes and dosie dotes and little lamsie divy. A kiddelie divy too, wouldn't you?*) I felt joyful to the core of my being and I burst out laughing in the middle of my song at how off-key I sounded and how funny the words were! Nothing had ever felt so wonderful. The feeling lasted for about four hours, then gradually faded, but I knew I wanted more of it. Of course, I wanted control over it, and only later, when I talked with Erika and discovered that what I had experienced was called grace, did I learn that it is a great gift, the natural outcome of surrendering to God and opening my heart to love.

"Grace," says Erika, "is a place where the soul rests, where God and soul touch as the soul expands."

To me the experience of grace is the very best feeling in the world. When we are in a state of grace, we are in love with ourselves, others, life and God. There are no barriers to our loving—our love is expansive, encompassing everything, and it comes flowing out of us as joy.

Grace is a gift from God that enters our being when our hearts are completely open and free of fear. Grace is a natural outcome of growth. Likewise true growth, which is the healing of our fears and false beliefs and moving into faith, love and truth, is the result of grace. Grace through growth—and growth through grace.

As I said earlier, grace, peace and joy, like love, truth, creativity and beauty, are gifts of God. We cannot generate grace, peace and joy within our own being. These feelings enter our hearts when our hearts are open to receiving the fullness of God. We know God is with us when we feel peace and joy in our hearts. It is these feelings that let us know that we are taking loving care of ourselves.

God is the *experience* of love, peace and joy that fills our beings when we open our hearts. The Spirit that is God is always waiting to enter our hearts. We don't even have to reach out to God, for God is always reaching out to us. We only have to open. Healing our spiritual abuse leads us to the grace of God, offering us an ever-expanding, joyful and creative experience of life. When we embrace the sacred privilege of taking loving action to express and evolve our souls, we will feel the sense of oneness we long for. We will experience grace.

Freedom

Freedom—to be all that we are, to manifest our dreams and follow our bliss, to live with peace in our hearts—is another one of the sweet rewards of embracing the sacred journey. The more deeply we surrender to the love and guidance that is God, the more freedom we experience. Just as loving parents support their children's freedom to explore and learn and evolve into the fullness of their being, so God provides the loving support for us to do the same. That's why we never need to give ourselves up to be loved by God. Just as a young child reaches out to and receives love and guidance from his or her loving parents, so God is here to love and guide us when we reach out to that love.

As we heal the wounds that keep us enslaved, we come to know directly that it is never God who enslaves us. It is our fears and our false beliefs that fetter us, and as we heal them, we are released from the prison of our addictions. The more we fill our hearts with the love that is God, the more freedom we have to share that love with others.

We find that we no longer seek out others in order to *get* from them—we are free from desiring others' time, attention, approval, affirmation or validation. Now we seek out others to give to them, to share with them and to learn with them, and we experience great joy in the act of giving, learning and sharing. We find ourselves leaving behind controlling relationships based on taking and caretaking and moving into relationships where we are free to truly share love. Older friendships may fall away and new friends—friends who connect with us on a soul level, friends with whom we are free to be all that we can be—come into our lives.

Rather than losing our personal freedom by surrendering to God, we discover that we have acquired a freedom beyond price—the freedom to praise God in us every day, to love God in us and others, and to allow that love to spill out to everyone and everything.

Freedom, peace, joy, passion, wholeness, creativity, love, gratitude, forgiveness, faith, trust and grace—these are the rewards of the sacred journey, the narrow road, the intent to learn about loving. We reenter the paradise we lost when we decided we could find our way without God and plucked the apple from the tree of knowledge. We heal our "original sin" of separation from God. We heal our aloneness and discover our oneness.

Epilogue

A Prayer to Open the Heart

Sweet Spirit of Divine Love, we will to will thy will, to be thy will and do thy will and know thy will. We thank you for helping us to have the courage to look within, to heal all the dark places, all the shame and the anger and the guilt and the fear and the judgment. We thank you for the support and the love and the compassion that comes through us as we support ourselves and each other in this healing journey so that we may each become pure instruments of your love and your compassion, your peace and your patience, your truth and your wisdom, your joy and your freedom, your creativity and manifestation, and your healing and serenity. We thank you for helping us see and be open to what we need to heal, and for helping us remember the compassionate intention to learn, each and every moment. We thank you for helping us remember who we are in our souls and remember why we are here, which is to become love and share love. We thank you for helping us to remember that we have a Child within that needs our care each and every moment. We thank you for helping us to remember that when we are in pain, we can open to learning about what we are doing or thinking that's causing that pain and do the healing work that we need to do. We thank you for all opportunities that come our way to teach us, to help us to learn and to heal and to grow in love and compassion. We thank you for today, for the food, the flowers, for the clouds, and for all learning opportunities that come our way today, no matter how challenging. We thank you for each other, and the love that we can share. We send love and blessings for the highest good to those we love and to the planet, and we thank you for supporting our highest good and the highest good of all.

We are willing, sweet Spirit, to take full responsibility for our own feelings and needs. We invite you into our hearts to help us to learn about our fears and beliefs and about love and truth. And we open to learning now with our Inner Child and our Higher Guidance, asking what our Child and Higher Guidance would like to talk with us about today. We will then take loving action based upon this dialogue, and we will consciously and continually pay attention to how we are feeling throughout the day and how our own thoughts and actions are affecting us. We breathe in the light, bringing with us a state of openness and readiness to learn.

Afterword

Shortly after Margie and I had met many years ago, I was standing in her kitchen. "I can teach you to cook!" I offered as we eagerly explored our budding friendship. "And I'll teach you to throw pots!" Margie smiled. I thought to myself, "Gee, this woman really hates to cook!" A moment later I learned she was a master potter as well as a brilliant artist. We burst into screeching belly laughter and so began the first step in exploration that would last into the present.

We have spent all the days of our friendship in exploration. We talk endlessly and travel to each other's states to visit as often as possible. We have shared our families, our triumphs, our tragedies, our joy and frustrations and even summoned the courage to share our darkest natures. I have been Divinely blessed to have a kindred spirit to walk my journey with, step for step, and side by side. We have explored who we are and more importantly, the nature of being. We have confronted and comforted and challenged and healed.

While I have been blessed with clarity and depth, Margie has been gifted with vision and expression. The culmination of this process is, *Do I Have to Give Up Me to Be Loved by*

God? I believe Margie's exceptional work in this book is truly an inspiration and I am grateful for the part I have had in helping her to bring her thoughts to fruition.

Inner Bonding is not a panacea, but more like the graceful wings of a great sailplane that will allow you to soar as high and as far as you wish. Margie is a great designer. I hope your flight will be as exciting and freeing as ours.

Rev. Erika J. Chopich, Ph.D.
Santa Fe, New Mexico

References

Chapter 1

1. I John 4:8; 4:16.

Chapter 2

1. Anna Fynn, *Mister God, This Is Anna* (New York: Ballantine, 1974).

2. Ephesians 4:6.

Chapter 3

1. Matthew 7:13–14.

2. Marcus Borg, *Meeting Jesus Again for the First Time* (San Francisco: HarperCollins, 1996), 59.

3. Hope America Ministries Foundation: 310-391-3656.

4. The Serenity Prayer was written by Reinhold Niebuhr.

5. Carolyn Myss, *Anatomy of the Spirit* (New York: Crown, 1996), 132.

Chapter 4

1. Some clients wonder why I call explaining an attempt to control. Explaining is something we do from a defensive place. When you're explaining why someone should treat you differently, your intention is to get them to change their feelings and behavior toward you. The only time that explaining is not an attempt to control is when the other person has asked you to help them understand, thus signaling that they are open to learning. A healthy response when someone treats you in ways you don't like is to focus on what you need to do to take care of yourself in the face of their choice.

Chapter 5

1. Nearly all religions include the concept of God's messengers in their teachings, though they call them by different terms. The following information and citations of religious literature were prepared by Dr. Erika J. Chopich:

In the Koran, an angel appears repeatedly to Muhammad. There are angels, too, in the Torah; and the Kabbalah (the study of Jewish mysticism) includes the concept of Teachers: At the moment of *devekuth* (cleaving to God) a Kabbalist is said to experience his or her supernatural guide (the *maggid*).

In the New Testament I have counted 110 references to angels, and in the Old Testament 115. In the Bible, 1 Corinthians 12:7 states: "But the manifestation of the Spirit is given to every man to profit withal. For to one is given by the Spirit the word of wisdom; to another the word of knowledge . . . to another faith . . . to another discerning of spirits."

It is clear to me that the three major branches of Christianity; Roman Catholicism, Eastern Orthodoxy and Protestantism, all maintain a profound belief in spirits and angels.

Catholics do not necessarily expect supernatural experiences in this life. While they regularly celebrate prayers, hymns and feasts to the angels, the Church regards reported visions and the miracles associated with them with caution. The Catholic Church does not deny unequivocally that such events can occur; they permit the belief of the individual parishioner in this matter.

Orthodoxy has a foundational belief in mysticism. The Feast of the Archangels is celebrated in November and prayers are invoked not only to the angels, but also to one's particular guardian angel. A hymn is sung that the angels "fence us around with their intercessions and shelter us under their protecting wings of immortal glory."

Protestantism holds at its center the Bible, believing that it is literally "God's Word." With this doctrine one would assume that a belief in the angels and the Holy Spirit is essential, and it is to some degree. While vital life experiences are often believed to be the work of the Holy Spirit, however, a direct manifestation of spirit may also be regarded as evil. In 2 Corinthians 11:14, Paul states; "Satan himself transforms himself into an angel of light." This may engender suspicion among fundamentalists that an angel or a Teacher may not come from God but from Satan. To this I can only respond with the numerous other references that state that the angels were created by God (Colossians 1:16) to have charge over us (Psalms 91:11), to guide us (Genesis 24:40), to provide for us (1 Kings 19:5-8), to protect us

(Psalms 34:7), to direct us (Acts 8:26), to comfort us (Acts 27:23, 24) and to minister to us (Hebrews 1:14).

2. A process addiction is an addiction to an activity (as opposed to a substance). Process addictions include compulsive sex, gambling, working and shopping.

Chapter 6

1. The use of some form of hypnosis to take you into the past.

2. See Thomas Claire's *Bodywork: What Type of Massage to Get—and How to Make the Most of It* (Fresno, CA: Quill, 1996) to learn about the different types of bodywork and what each can do for you.

Chapter 7

1. If you need more suggestions, take a look at *Healing Your Aloneness, The Healing Your Aloneness Workbook,* and *Inner Bonding.*

2. For even more examples, see *Healing Your Aloneness* and *Inner Bonding.*

3. For information about energy release, contact Drs. David and Rebecca Grudermeyer at 800-915-3606. They teach Comprehensive Energy Psychotherapy, an extraordinarily powerful process for releasing old and present fear and anxiety.

Chapter 10

1. My favorite nutrition book is Jack Tips's *The Pro-Vita Plan* (Austin, TX: Apple-a-Day Press, 1993).

2. Kathleen DesMaisons, *Potatoes Not Prozac: A Natural 7-Step Dietary Plan* (New York: Simon & Schuster, 1998).

Chapter 11

1. Jean Liedloff, *The Continuum Concept* (Reading, MA: Addison-Wesley, 1977).

2. Marlo Morgan, *Mutant Message Down Under* (Lees Summit, MO: NM Co., 1991).

Chapter 12

1. This poem was first published in *Healing Your Aloneness*, 108.

Chapter 14

1. An incorrect version of this poem was included in a book I wrote with Jordan Paul, *Do I Have to Give Up Me to Be Loved by You? . . . The Workbook*. At that time we did not know the author. I have since learned that this poem was first published in Mr. Overton's book, *The Learning Tree* (The Bethany Press, 1975). He has since revised it and published it in *Rebuilding the Front Porch of America* (Columbia, MD: The Front Porch Institute, 1997), 129.

About the Author

Margaret Paul, Ph.D., is the co-creator of Inner Bonding, a transformational, Six-Step spiritual healing process. She is a bestselling author, noted public speaker, workshop leader, chaplain, educator, consultant and Inner Bonding facilitator. She has been leading groups, teaching classes and workshops, and working with individuals, couples, partnerships and businesses since 1973.

Dr. Paul is the coauthor of *Do I Have to Give Up Me to Be Loved by You?* (over 400,000 copies sold), *Do I Have to Give Up Me to Be Loved by My Kids?*, *Do I Have to Give Up Me to Be Loved by You? The Workbook, Healing Your Aloneness* and *The Healing Your Aloneness Workbook*, and the author of *Inner Bonding*. Her books have been translated into many languages.

She has three grown children. In her spare time she is an artist.

For information regarding Inner Bonding products, lectures, Inner Bonding workshops and five-day intensives, or if you would like copies of any of the charts, please contact Dr. Paul at:

Inner Bonding® Educational Technologies, Inc.
PMB #42
2531 Sawtelle Blvd.
Los Angeles, CA 90064-31124
phone: 310-390-5993
or toll-free: 888-6INNERBOND (888-646-6372)
fax: 310-390-1903

For further information about products, lectures, Inner Bonding workshops and five-day intensives, or to participate in the Inner Bonding community through a chat room and bulletin board, please see our Web site:

www.innerbonding.com.

Previous Books by Dr. Margaret Paul

Chopich, Erika J., and Margaret Paul, *Healing Your Aloneness*. San Francisco: HarperCollins, 1990.

Chopich, Erika J., and Margaret Paul, *The Healing Your Aloneness Workbook*. Los Angeles: Evolving Publications, 1993/1996.

Paul, Margaret and Jordan Paul, *Do I Have to Give Up Me to Be Loved by You?* Center City, MN: Hazelden, 1983/1994.

Paul, Margaret and Jordan Paul, *Do I Have to Give Up Me to Be Loved by You? The Workbook*. Center City, MN: Hazelden, 1987/1994.

Paul, Margaret and Jordan Paul, *Do I Have to Give Up Me to Be Loved by My Kids?* Los Angeles: Evolving Publications, 1985/1995.

Paul, Margaret and Jordan Paul, *Free to Love*. Los Angeles: J. P. Tarcher, 1975.

Paul, Margaret, *Inner Bonding*. San Francisco: HarperCollins, 1992.

A New Season of
Chicken Soup for the Soul

Chicken Soup for
the Golden Soul
Code #7257
$12.95

Chicken Soup for the
Unsinkable Soul
Code #6986 • $12.95

Chicken Soup for the
College Soul
Code #7028 • $12.95

Chicken Soup for the
Cat and Dog Lover's Soul
Code #7109 • $12.95

Each one of these new heartwarming titles will bring inspiration
both to you and the loved ones in your life.

Also available in hardcover, audiocassette and CD.
Prices do not include shipping and handling. Available in bookstores everywhere or call
1.800.441.5569 for Visa or MasterCard orders. Your response code is **BKS**.
Order online ***www.hci-online.com***